SILHOUETTES OF
MY CONTEMPORARIES

SILHOUETTES OF
MY CONTEMPORARIES

BY
LYMAN ABBOTT

*Who through faith subdued kingdoms,
wrought righteousness, quenched the
violence of fire, waxed valiant in fight,
turned to flight the armies of the aliens*

GARDEN CITY, N. Y., AND TORONTO
DOUBLEDAY, PAGE & COMPANY
1921

PREFACE

Mrs. Sanchez, in her Life of Mrs. Robert Louis Stevenson, describes her mother in Samoa, "making silhouettes of the different members of the strangely assorted company gathered from the four quarters of the globe. First she did the portrait of Ori by throwing the shadow of his head on the wall with the help of a lamp, then drawing the outline and filling it in with India ink. It turned out so good that Ori demanded likenesses of all the rest, and soon the house was turned into a veritable picture gallery." In this book I have attempted, by the help of a dim and flickering memory, to trace in outline the portraits of some of my contemporaries. The volume is a gallery of shadow pictures. When in 1876 I became associated with Henry Ward Beecher in the editorship of the *Christian Union*, I introduced into the paper a new department entitled "The Outlook." Its purpose was not merely to report current events, but to interpret them. Looking forward, I endeavoured to forecast their relation to the future and the probable effect of their lives upon it. The department was definitely intended to

v

be, as far as practicable, prophetic both of peril and of promise.

This, of course, involved a study of the men who were making history.

This volume contains some of the results of that study; they are shadow pictures of fellow-men whom I have known and whose careers I have studied, as looking back, they now appear to me. Leaders of their generations have usually some one characteristic which distinguishes them from their contemporaries. This distinctive characteristic I have sought to portray. To that extent these portraits are partial and imperfect, as all portraits, whether painted by the brush or the pen, are and must be. They are all portraits of men who I believe have contributed something toward the progress which is making out of this world a better world—one of justice, liberty, and peace.

Mr. Trollope, in his biography of Thackeray, attributes to him and phrases for him his defence against certain of his critics: "You will not sympathize with this young man of mine, this Pendennis, because he is neither angel nor imp. If it be so, let it be so. I will not paint for you angels or imps, because I do not see them. The young man of the day, whom I do see, and of whom I know the inside and the out thoroughly, him have I painted for you;

there he is, and whether you like the picture or not."

Perhaps I have been exceptionally fortunate, but I have sketched honestly and as well as I know how, the portraits of men as I have known them. All politicians are not like Presidents Hayes and Roosevelt, nor all reformers like Gough and Booker Washington, nor all preachers like Brooks and Beecher. But America is rich in such men as these. If he is greatest who serves his fellowmen the best, then I do not believe that any other country has produced in a century and a half as many great men as America has produced. Depressed and discouraged as we are apt to be by the flood of filth and falsehood, of corruption and crime, which the daily paper offers us for our daily food, it is well sometimes to stop, take a quieter and less partial view, and realize the right we have as Americans for pride in our past and for hope in our future.

LYMAN ABBOTT.

CONTENTS

ix

CONTENTS

SILHOUETTES OF
MY CONTEMPORARIES

SILHOUETTES OF MY CONTEMPORARIES

P. T. BARNUM, SHOWMAN

I HAVE a liking for the faith of the small boy who said to his mother: "God must have laughed when he made a monkey." Why not? If we argue from the beauty in the world that the Creator has an appreciation of beauty, why not from the humour in humanity that the Creator has a sense of humour? I have read the story of a dancer who, being converted, thereafter expressed his devotion to the Virgin Mary by daily dancing before her as the best possible method of bringing her honour. Dickens has rendered a good service by his sympathetic picture-stage life behind the curtain in his portrait of the Crummles family, and by his sympathetic picture of life in the sawdust ring by his portrait of Mr. Sleary. Let the reader of this article, then, understand the writer's point of view. There is a place in God's world for play, and the professional entertainer is doing God service if he carries into his profession the spirit

1

of honesty, generosity, and purity—that is, if he gives his audience their money's worth, treats his employees and associates with generosity, and rigorously excludes from his entertainments anything that panders to vice or tends to degradation.

In my collection of autographs, which number nearly if not quite a thousand, is the following characteristic letter from P. T. Barnum, written to me in answer to a request for some information concerning Tom Thumb:

Waldemere,
Bridgeport, Ct.,
Oct. 5, 1878.

REV. LYMAN ABBOTT:

DEAR SIR—Your letter is recd. and I with pleasure enclose an explanation of the T. T. matter.

By the way my big show opens at Gilmore's Garden on the 14th inst for a month & I hope you will take occasion to see a novel & interesting Exhibition.

Truly yours,
P. T. BARNUM.

I call this letter interesting not merely, not mainly, because it exhibits the born advertiser, but because it illustrates what I think was very characteristic of Mr. Barnum, his professional pride. He was a great showman, and he was proud of being a great showman; a great advertiser, and he had a naïve pride in his curiously ingenious advertising schemes. He made it clear in his autobiography that he considered himself called to be a showman; the business came to him, he did not seek it out. Looking back from the first success as the creator of "Barnum's Museum," he writes:

The business for which I was destined, and I believe made, had not yet come to me; or rather, I had not found that I was to cater for that insatiate want of human nature —the love of amusement; that I was to make a sensation on two continents; and that fame and fortune awaited me so soon as I should appear before the public in the character of a showman. These things I had not foreseen. I did not seek the position or the character. The business finally came in my way; I fell into the occupation, and far beyond any of my predecessors on this continent, I have succeeded.

He did not conduct his enterprises to elevate society. He was frankly an entertainer, and not a reformer. If I am right in defining a good-natured man as a man who desires to make other people happy, then the word good-natured would adequately describe him. He was desirous of making money, and he took at times what might be called a gambler's chance in making it. But he was much more than a mere money-maker. If from any entertainment that he provided the spectators had gone away disappointed, he would have regarded the entertainment as a failure, no matter what money it brought him. His ideals were not always of the highest, but he lived up to them. He never sacrificed his self-respect in order to get the money of the public into his own pocket. He writes: "As I always justly boasted, no one could visit my Museum and go away without feeling that he had received the full worth of his money." It was his ambition—and it was gratified—"to have men and women all over the country say: 'There is not another place in the United States where so much can be seen for twenty-five cents as in Barnum's American Museum.'"

When I came to New York City in 1849 to enter New York University, Barnum's American Museum was one of the best-known show places in the city. It was situated on the corner of Ann Street and Broadway, in what was then the centre of a city which now has grown so great that it has no centre, because it has many centres. Opposite it on Broadway was the best-known hotel in the city, the Astor House; three or four blocks to the north was the best-known restaurant, Delmonico's; between the two was "The Park," and in the Park the City Hall. The two most famous Episcopal churches of the city were Trinity and St. Paul's—Trinity five or six minutes' walk distant, St. Paul's on the corner opposite the Museum. St. George's

(Episcopal) and the Brick Church (Presbyterian) had a few years before moved farther up town. The *Tribune* and the *Times* newspapers were close at hand. In the afternoon a band of half a dozen pieces played on a balcony overhanging the street. At night a curious kaleidoscopic collection of highly coloured and illuminated glasses was kept by some contrivance boiling and bubbling on the walls of the Museum.

Within the Museum was a constantly increasing collection of all sorts of curiosities, real and spurious, natural and artificial. This was long before the days of the Metropolitan Museum of Art and the Natural History Museum, and before the days when those serious and instructive unadvertised collections would have drawn any such group of spectators as they now draw. It was a more credulous, perhaps a more curious, age. Periodically the newspapers took up for serious discussion the question: Is there a sea serpent? When, therefore, Mr. Barnum advertised a "Feejee Mermaid," the people thronged to see it. In truth, it was a curiosity, though an artificial one. A naturalist whose judgment on it he obtained replied that "he could not conceive how it could have been manufactured, for he never saw a monkey with such peculiar teeth, arms, hands, etc., and he never saw a fish with such peculiar fins; but he did not believe in mermaids." But it served Mr. Barnum's purpose: it advertised his museum. He subsequently concluded that it was a product of Japanese ingenuity.

He purchased for $200 a model of Niagara Falls in which the proportions of the falls, the hills, rocks, buildings, etc., in the vicinity were given with mathematical accuracy, "while the absurdity was in introducing 'real water' to represent the falls." When the Water Commissioners summoned him to pay an extra water tax, he showed them that the water flowed back into a reservoir, from which it was pumped up to repeat its service. "A single barrel of water, if my pump was in good order, would furnish my falls for a month."

The hazard and expense of new enterprises did not daunt him. He learned of the capture of a white whale at or near the mouth of the St. Lawrence; sent up an expedition; captured two of these whales; built a tank of salt water in the basement of the Museum; and while they lived they proved a paying feature.

These attractions served as advertisements, but he did not depend upon them. As an inventive advertiser he has had, I rather think, no equal in the history of American advertisers. A tramp applied to him for a job; would be glad to do anything for a dollar a day. Barnum gave

him a breakfast, then told him to lay a brick on
the corner of Broadway and Ann Street, another close by the Museum, a third on the corner
of Broadway and Vesey Street, and a fourth on
the sidewalk in front of St. Paul's Church; then
with a fifth brick in hand to "take up a rapid
march from one to the other, making the circuit,
exchanging your brick at every point and say
nothing to any one." At the end of an hour the
sidewalk was packed with curious people watching the inexplicable proceeding and enough of
the number followed the brick-layer at the end
of each cycle into the Museum to more than pay
for his hire. The profit to Mr. Barnum was in
the talk created and the consequent free advertising of the Museum.

He announced baby shows with prizes for the
finest baby, the fattest, the handsomest. Emu-
lous mothers crowded the Museum and the reports of the baby shows found their way into
the newspapers far and near. He set an elephant in charge of a keeper in oriental costume
ploughing on a six-acre lot close beside the track
of the New York and New Haven Railroad. The
keeper was furnished with a time-table, and did
his ploughing when trains were passing. A
friendly farmer criticized him for his folly.
"Your elephant," he said, "can't draw as much
as two pair of my oxen can." "You are mis-

taken, my friend," replied Mr. Barnum; "he can draw more than forty yoke of oxen; for he can draw the attention of twenty millions of American citizens to Barnum's Museum!"

One important feature of the Museum was its "Lecture Room." The theatre had a bad name, and thousands of people came every year to New York City who would not go to a theatre but who were delighted to go to Barnum's Lecture Room to be entertained by what in these days would be called a vaudeville performance. They included educated dogs, industrious fleas, automatons, jugglers, ventriloquists, living statuary, tableaux, gypsies, albinos, fat boys, giants, dwarfs, rope-dancers, and the like.

But from the first the Lecture Room differed from the average theatre—certainly the cheaper ones—in more than a name. Barnum forbade what was common at that time—the setting apart a certain section of the house, popularly known as the "third tier," where women of the town might ply their trade. He would allow no bar upon the premises, and, finding some of his patrons going out, as was the custom, for a drink between the acts, he ceased giving return checks to such as went out. My shadowy recollection of that time confirms his claim that he allowed on the stage no indelicacies of costume and no salacious dialogues. When the reputation of the Lecture Room was established he substituted for the educated dogs and industrious fleas "moral dramas" such as "Uncle Tom's Cabin" and "The Drunkard." In his Philadelphia Museum, where the prejudice against the theatre was greater than in New York, the Lecture Room was very popular. When "The Drunkard" was being played there was a temperance pledge at the box-office which thousands signed, and in his autobiography he tells us that "almost every hour during the day and evening women could be seen bringing their husbands to the Museum to sign the pledge."

Mr. Barnum had inherited from his father and his grandfather an irrepressible fondness for practical jokes, and he sometimes played them upon the public. But he always did it in such a fashion that the public enjoyed the joke with him. That his humbugging did not impair the public faith in his commercial honesty is sufficiently established by two incidents. When he wanted to buy Scudder's American Museum, which was financially a failure but which he believed he could make a financial success, he borrowed the necessary $15,000 on his personal credit, giving as security the purchased collection; and when eight years later, in order to carry out his contract with Jenny Lind, he had to deposit in the hands of her bankers in London the sum of $187,500, he borrowed a considerable portion of the sum largely on the confidence that American bankers had in his commercial ability and his financial honesty.

I have defined Mr. Barnum as a good-natured man and defined a good-natured man as one who desires to make other men happy. This is not the highest ambition of which man is capable, but it is a not unworthy ambition, and in Mr. Barnum it appeared not only in his resolve to send away contented all those who came to his entertainments, but also in his resolve to make his associates and his employees sharers in his happiness. The cynics may say that this is good business. I think it is. But not everyone has sufficient faith in this principle as good business to practise it. A slight illustration of Mr. Barnum's faith in it is furnished by his giving a dollar and a half a day to the brick-laying tramp who only asked for a dollar a day; a better illustration, by his steadily increasing Tom Thumb's share in the profits of their joint enterprise as its increasing profitableness became manifest. But the most striking illustration is that furnished by his proposal to Jenny Lind to change the contract between them after the first auction sale of tickets had taken place and before the first concert. This change I copy from Mr. Barnum's autobiography.

10

On the Tuesday after her arrival I informed Miss Lind that I wished to make a slight alteration in our agreement. "What is it?" she asked in surprise.

"I am convinced," I replied, "that our enterprise will be much more successful than either of us anticipated. I wish, therefore, to stipulate that you shall receive not only $1,000 for each concert besides all the expenses, as heretofore agreed on, but after taking $5,500 per night for expenses and my services, the balance shall be equally divided between us."

Jenny looked at me with astonishment. She could not comprehend my proposition. After I had repeated it and she fully understood its import, she cordially grasped me by the hand, and exclaimed, "Mr. Barnum, you are a gentleman of honour; you are generous; it is just as Mr. Bates told me; I will sing for you as long as you please; I will sing for you in America—in Europe—anywhere."

Mr. Barnum ends the narrative of his engagement with her by a financial statement of the "total receipts, excepting of concerts devoted to charity." They are given in detail. We report only the totals as reported by Mr. Barnum:

Jenny Lind's net avails of 95 concerts . . $176,675.09
P. T. Barnum's gross receipts after paying Miss Lind 535,486.25
_____
Total receipts of 95 concerts . . . $712,161.34

Mr. Barnum does not state what his net profits were; but as he paid all the expenses, including travelling expenses and hotel bills for Jenny Lind and the entire musical company, the amount

11

to be deducted from the gross receipts must have been considerable.

That Mr. Barnum recognized the human values as well as the commercial possibilities of his "natural curiosities" is evident from his relations with the famous dwarf, "General Tom Thumb," Mr. Barnum's own name for Charles Stratton, whom he discovered as a child of five and so trained that when the boy went some two years later to be exhibited in France, Mr. Barnum won a judgment from the authorities that the "General's" presentation of various characters in costume entitled him to be counted an actor, and therefore liable only for the 11-per-cent. "theatrical license", not for the 25-per-cent. license for "natural curiosities." From the European tour from which they returned in 1847, when the "little General" was ten years of age, Tom Thumb's father had acquired a fortune from which he settled a large sum upon his valuable son. Some ten years later, when Mr. Barnum "failed" as the result of an extensive real-estate development enterprise, among the letters of friendly offers that came to him was the following:

Jones's Hotel, Philadelphia,
May 12, 1856.

MY DEAR MR. BARNUM.—I understand your friends, and that means "all creation," intend to get up some benefits for your family. Now, my dear sir, just be good enough to remember that I belong to that mighty crowd, and I must have a finger (or at least a "thumb") in that pie. I am bound to appear on all such occasions in some shape, from "Jack the Giant Killer," upstairs, to the door-keeper down, whichever may serve you best; and there are some feats that I can perform as well as any other man of my inches. I have just started out on my western tour, and have my carriage, ponies, and assistants all here, but I am ready to go on to New York, bag and baggage, and remain at Mrs. Barnum's service as long as I, in my small way, can be useful. Put me into any "heavy" work, if you like. Perhaps I cannot lift as much as some other folks, but just take your pencil in hand and you will see I can draw a tremendous load. I drew two hundred tons at a single pull to-day, embracing two thousand persons, whom I hauled up safely and satisfactorily to all parties, at one exhibition. Hoping that you will be able to fix up a lot of magnets that will attract all New York, and volunteering to sit on any part of the loadstone, I am, as ever, your little but sympathizing friend,

GEN. TOM THUMB.

Although Mr. Barnum felt compelled to refuse this offer, he could hardly have forgotten it. When he had so far recovered himself that he was free to do so, he again went abroad, taking with him the "little General," repeating the former successes, and cancelling his indebtedness at the end of four years.

In 1862 the "General" had a country home in Bridgeport where he spent his "intervals of rest with his horses, and especially with his yacht, for his fondness for the water was his great passion." On one of his trips to New York, upon which occasions he always visited the Museum and Mr. Barnum, he met a recent acquisition of the showman—Lavinia Warren, a dwarf, a "most intelligent and refined young lady, well educated and an accomplished, beautiful, and perfectly developed woman in miniature." With the hearty sympathy of Mr. Barnum the young people shortly became engaged and Miss Warren was released from her contract to go abroad for exhibition. Moreover, although Mr. Barnum "did not hesitate to seek continued advantage from the notoriety of the prospective marriage," when his offer of fifteen thousand dollars if they would postpone the wedding for a month was declined, he did not lose his human interest with the momentary loss. "It was suggested to me," he writes, "that a small fortune in itself could be easily made out of the excitement. 'Let the ceremony take place in the Academy of Music, charge a big price for admission, and the citizens will come in crowds.' I have no manner of doubt that in this way twenty-five thousand dollars would easily have been obtained. But I had no such thought. I had promised to give the couple a genteel and graceful wedding, and I kept my word."

The ceremony took place in Grace Church, in the presence of an audience of ladies and gentlemen admitted only by cards of invitation, even to the exclusion of a highly irate pew owner, who afterward wrote the rector a sharp letter of protest and received from him a sharp though perfectly courteous and dignified reply. Numerous applications were made for tickets to witness the ceremony and as much as sixty dollars was offered for a single admission; but not a ticket was sold, and to the charge brought by disgruntled critics that the marriage was a money-making scheme, Mr. Barnum made the following characteristically good-natured reply:

"It was by no means an unnatural circumstance that I should be suspected of having instigated and brought about that marriage of Tom Thumb with Lavinia Warren. Had I done this, I should at this day have felt no regrets, for it has proved, in an eminent degree, one of the 'happy marriages'."

If this were a sketch of Mr. Barnum's life, it would be fatally defective, for I have said nothing of his temperance activities, his patriotic services during the Civil War, or his battle, when a member of the Connecticut Legislature, against political corruption of a formidable description. But I have deliberately confined myself to a sketch of his professional career as Showman, in which he did nothing to degrade, something to elevate, and much to entertain his generation.

EDWIN BOOTH, INTERPRETER

A FRIEND of mine, no longer living, conservative in his theology, consistent in his Calvinism, once said to me something like this: "If the actor is wholly evil, if there is no place in the kingdom of God for the actor's profession, why does God endow some of his children with the dramatic and mimetic instinct and seem to call them to the stage by an inward impulse as distinct as that by which he seems to call others of his children to the pulpit?"

The only answer I can give to that question is that the theatre is not wholly evil and that there is a place in the kingdom of God for the profession of the actor. No doubt there are in every one of the great cities some theatres that we could well spare and some actors we could see banished from the stage without regret. But if it were possible by edict to close all theatres and banish all actors from American life the loss to the community would amount to an irreparable moral disaster.

The theatre has a threefold service to render: it has to furnish amusement, rest, and inspiration.

We need amusement. It is an old saying that "All work and no play makes Jack a dull boy." The fathers and the mothers need it as well as their children. "A merry heart," says the proverb, "doeth good like a medicine." A hearty laugh is medicinal. A coöperative laugh, a laugh all together, promotes good fellowship. Sympathy in fun may be as valuable as sympathy in sorrow. A good play inspires us to comply with Paul's injunction: We weep with those that weep and rejoice with those that rejoice.

We need rest. America would easily turn into a great factory and Americans into machine-like drudges, if there were not literature to take us out of ourselves; and the theatre is enacted literature. The monotony of the kitchen, the more monotonous monotony of the shop, would become deadening if there were no provision for occasional forgetfulness. To many Americans the theatre is an oasis of restful enjoyment set in the midst of a desert of unvarying toil. I suspect that my experience is not uncommon. Reading stimulates; a concert inspires; a play rests. For two hours I am passive, played upon by a story which drives all cares and perplexities out of my mind; and I come away from a clean and healthful play refreshed in spirit as, from a swim in the ocean, refreshed in body.

17

But the highest service of the theatre is its inspirational power. Great literature is an interpreter of life; a great actor is an interpreter of great literature. If it was worth while for Shakespeare to write "The Merchant of Venice," it was worth while for Edwin Booth and Madame Modjeska to interpret it. Let me explain by an illustration what I mean by interpretation of literature.

Henry Ward Beecher was a remarkable elocutionist. He had to a very unusual degree the power to put himself into any mood of feeling that he wished to illustrate and to employ in its illustration the appropriate tones of voice and, if need be, the appropriate attitude of body. He was preaching once upon his favourite theme, the infinite pity of Jesus to sinners, when he stopped abruptly and said: Someone will ask me, did not Jesus also condemn sinners with wrathful indignation? That depends, he replied, upon how you interpret him. Then he took up his pocket Bible, which was his constant companion, and read a few verses from the denunciation of the Pharisees in the twenty-third chapter of Matthew, putting into his voice, and doubtless for the moment into his spirit, the wrathful indignation of a just judge: "Woe unto you, scribes and Pharisees, hypocrites! for ye are like unto whited sepulchres, which outwardly appear beautiful, but inwardly are full of dead men's bones, and of all uncleanness." Then, after a moment's pause, he read the same words again, but now as a lament, with tears in his voice, as of a mother weeping over her child. Then, without further comment, he went on with his sermon. He had in less than three minutes and by the actor's art given two interpretations to that passage; and since then it has had for me a new meaning.

This is what I mean by saying that the great actor is an interpreter of great literature. It is narrated in the book of Nehemiah that, at a camp-meeting there described, the Levites "read in the book, in the law of God, distinctly; and they gave the sense, so that they understood the reading." If ministers could cultivate the actor's art sufficiently to enable them to feel the mood of the sacred writers and interpret that mood by their voice, the Bible reading in church services would not be, as it now often is, an act of almost unmeaning formalism.

Edwin Booth's character and career illustrated these principles.

His father, Junius Brutus Booth, was a famous actor. Nature's equipment impelled the son to follow the father on the stage. "I had rather," he wrote his daughter, "be an obscure farmer, a hayseed from Wayback, or a cabinetmaker, as my father advised, than the most distinguished man on earth. But Nature cast me for the part she found me best fitted for, and I have had to play it, and must play it till the curtain falls."

At first he took such parts as were assigned him, generally comic parts in farces and burlesques. But he was not long in graduating, and his wonderful success as Richard III, acted for the benefit of a comrade, in which he showed the advantage of studies quietly pursued, introduced him at once to a first rank among the actors of his day. This early success was partly due doubtless to an inherited dramatic talent and to his early companionship with his father, but there are abundant indications in his daughter's charming biographical sketch and in the letters she has published that from the first a religious impulse inspired him; that the following sentences penned to a friend expressed, not the fleeting impulse of the moment, but the dominating principle of his life: "I cannot help but believe that there is sufficient importance in my art to interest them still; that to a higher influence than the world believes I am moved by I owe the success I have achieved."

This spiritual faith carried him through experiences of great personal sorrow and professional disappointment. His wife, to whom he was devotedly attached, died, leaving him to be both father and mother to the daughter two years old. Writing to the clergyman who had performed the marriage ceremony and had written him a letter of sympathy, Mr. Booth said: "You have been pleased to mention my art and to express the hope that I may be spared to serve it long and faithfully; if it be His will, I bow before it meekly as I now bear the terrible affliction He has seen fit to lay upon me; but I cannot repress an inward hope that I may soon rejoin her who, next to God, was the object of my devotion." Two years later the sorrow still remained, but his faith in immortality and in his art as a divinely inspired service had grown clearer and stronger: "Two years ago to-day," he writes to a friend, "I last saw May alive! But, my dear friend, a light from heaven has settled fairly and fully in my soul, and I regard death, as God intended we should understand it, as the breaking of eternal daylight and a birthday of the soul. I feel that all my actions have been and are influenced by her whose love is to me the strength and wisdom of my spirit. Whatever I may do of serious import, I regard it as a performance of a sacred duty I owe to all that is pure and honest in my nature—a duty to the very religion of my heart."

Nine years later the theatre that he had built

and in and by which he had helped to raise the dramatic standards in New York City to something which should at least approximate his ideals, had failed and he was bankrupt. "My disappointment is great, to be sure," he wrote to a friend, "but I have the consciousness of having *tried* to do what I deemed to be my duty. Since the talent God has given me can be made available for no other purpose, I believe the object to which I devote it to be worthy of self-sacrifice."

This spirit of consecration of what he believed was a divinely given power to a divinely ordained purpose inspired and guided him through the ordinary experiences of his life. A clergyman once wrote him asking if he could not be admitted to his theatre by a side or rear door, as he preferred to run no risk of being seen by any of his parishioners; to whom Mr. Booth replied, "There is no door in my theatre through which God cannot see." The theatre while it continued under Booth's control was maintained as one should be which lay open to God's sight. Mr. William Winter, whose dramatic ideals were unquestionably high, says of it that its affairs "were conducted in a steadfast spirit of sympathy with what is pure and good in dramatic art." And he quotes two testimonies in support of this statement: one from Joseph Jefferson:

"Booth's Theatre is conducted as a theatre should be—like a church behind the curtain and like a counting-house in front of it," and one from Dion Boucicault: "I have been in every theatre, I think, in civilized Christendom, and Booth's is the only theatre that I have ever seen properly managed."

The prevailing attitude of the Church toward the theatre and the acting profession was one of bitter hostility in 1877, much modified since; but it elicited from Mr. Booth no word of ill temper or counter-hostility. The only response to that hostility which I have been able to find in his correspondence is in a letter to a clerical friend, who was an exception to the general rule among the clergy and to whom he wrote: "I am glad that I have been the cause of so much pleasure to you and rejoice in your strong charity against prejudice. If the Church would teach discrimination between the true and the false in my profession, instead of condemning both as worthless, to say the least, the stage would serve the pulpit as a loyal subject, and both go shoulder to shoulder not with 'frowning brow to brow' through the fight."

His life was in some respects a lonely one. How lonely is indicated by the one incident in which his life and mine came together. Heartily sympathizing with his endeavour to secure an elevating and inspiring drama in New York, I wrote to ask of him an article on the subject, and received in reply the following letter, which was published with his consent in the then *"Christian Union"*:

Baltimore, April 18, 1878.

Lyman Abbott, Esq.

Dear Sir—

On my arrival here I found your favour of 1st inst. but have been prevented from answering it until to-day.

Having no literary ability whatever I must decline your flattering invitation; nor do I know how to aid the worthy cause you advocate; could I do so, be assured it should be *freely* done.

My knowledge of the modern drama is so very meagre that I never permit my wife or daughter to witness a play without previously ascertaining its character. This is the method I pursue; I can suggest no other—unless it might be by means of a "dramatic censor" whose taste or judgment might, however, be frequently at fault.

If the management of theatres could be denied to speculators and placed in the hands of actors who value their reputations and respect their calling, the stage would at least afford healthy recreation, if not, indeed, a wholesome stimulus to the exercise of noble sentiments. But while the theatre is permitted to be a mere shop for gain— open to every huckster of immoral gimcracks, there is no other way to discriminate between the pure and base than through the experience of others.

Truly yours.

Edwin Booth.

There were a few actors who shared Mr. Booth's spirit and to whom acting was truly an art. But the stage was passing under the control of money-making managers, and money-making and artistic ambitions never go well together. Mr. Booth was not a good business man, and lack of good business management, not of good dramatic management, caused the failure of his theatre. "Had I given proper attention to my dollar-and-cent dealings with men," he writes to his daughter, "I would now be at least a millionaire, perhaps doubly so; but I never considered that side of the question, taking from managers just what they offered." He defines in his letters his ambition, nowhere perhaps more clearly than in this pregnant sentence: "He [Betterton] is my ideal of an actor, both on and off the stage. He aimed at truth in his art and lived it at home." Successes always stimulated Booth to new effort. "Life," he wrote to his daughter, "is a great big spelling book, and on every page we turn, the words grow harder to understand the meaning of. But there *is* a meaning, and when the last leaf flops over we'll know the whole lesson by heart." He kept up his studies, professional and other, to the very end of his life, and this included a study of himself as impersonator. "When I am enwrapt in a character I am impersonating," he wrote, "there seems to be another and a distinct individuality, another *me* sitting in judgment on myself." This judgment was not always encouraging. Mr. Bispham in his autobiography tells us that one night when Booth seemed to have attained the very pinnacle of his powers a friend went round to congratulate him on his great success and "found Booth with his head upon his hands in the deepest dejection from which not even the praise of his old friend could arouse him, disgusted at having given so miserable a performance."

From this double consciousness Booth seems never to have escaped. "I believe," he writes, "you understand how completely I 'ain't here' most of the time. It's an awful thing to be somebody else all the while." Reserved he was, self-restrained, but not internally placid, and never self-conceited. Self-control to such a man is not the easy virtue it is to simple natures. He had inherited the drink appetite from his father; conquered it completely, but not without a hard battle. Nor was that his only struggle. The very ability to interpret different human passions was the mark of a composite character. "Much of my life's struggle," he wrote his daughter, "has been with myself, and the pain I have endured in overcoming and correcting the evils of my untrained disposition has been very great."

I must stop. This sketch has already overrun the limits I had set myself. Readers who wish an analysis of Mr. Booth's art upon the stage will find it in William Winter's "Life of Edwin Booth." I have wished in this sketch to introduce the man to readers to whom he is known only as an actor. For the re-reading of Mr. Booth's letters has not only reawakened my admiration for this great interpreter of the greatest literature, but also a new sense of indignation that so pure and brave a man should have been left to fight his battle for a purer theatre with so little sympathy and help from the Christian Church and the Christian ministry.

THE SMILEY BROTHERS, LOVERS OF HOSPITALITY

IN THE State of New York, running approximately parallel to the Catskill range of mountains, is a long and narrow range with elevations varying from six hundred feet to twelve or fifteen hundred feet above the valleys on either side. This is known as the Shawangunk Mountain, locally pronounced Shongurn. At a point in this range, about fifteen miles from the Hudson River at Poughkeepsie, is a spot of peculiar romantic beauty. A cliff here rises about one hundred feet above the mountain edge and at the foot of this cliff is a small lake perhaps half a mile long and an eighth of a mile wide, which bears the Indian name of Mohonk (Lake of the Sky). At this point the mountain is composed of enormous rocks piled on each other in great confusion, as though some grotesque Thor had thrown them up in sheer joyous exhibition of his strength, leaving them to lie there as they had fallen. It is reported that adventurous boys, in times past, have made their way down through the crevices of these rocks from the summit to the valley below. A geological friend of mine said to a local resident, acting as his guide: "I wonder by what great upheaval Nature produced this wonderful rock pile." The guide rebuked his ignorance: "What!" said he, "have you never read how at the crucifixion the earth did quake and the rocks were rent?" He regarded the earthquake at the crucifixion as a world-wide phenomenon as some scholars in past times regarded the deluge as a world-enveloping flood.

In 1869 there stood on the shore of this lake and under the shadow of this cliff a cabaret with a bar-room, a dance hall, and ten bedrooms with bunks for beds, and straw mattresses and one quilt each for bedding. When a visitor demanded dinner, the Irish boy would catch a chicken, kill it in front of the house, and pass it over to the woman to cook." There were some fish in the lake and some small game in the woods. How far the fish and the game, how far the bar-room and its contents were the attraction for the picnic parties that patronized the place, the reader must be left to judge.

One day in 1869 Mr. Alfred Smiley, who was then living near Poughkeepsie, took a day for an excursion to the top of the mountain to see the lake, which had already acquired a considerable local reputation. The natural beauty of the scene captivated him; he persuaded his twin brother Albert, then conducting a very successful school at Providence, Rhode Island, to come to Poughkeepsie and share with him the joy of his discovery. As a result of that visit, Mr. Albert Smiley put all the money he had, with a considerable sum that he borrowed, into a purchase of the place with approximately three hundred acres of wild mountain and forest land. The original proprietor doubtless considered himself lucky to find a purchaser fool enough to take this unpromising place off his hands. He is quoted as saying: "I suppose that the Creator made everything for some use; but what in the world he ever made this pizen laurel for I can't see. It never grows big enough for firewood and the cattle won't eat it."

From the beginning the brothers Smiley believed that there were people in America who wanted to get away from the excitements of society, as well as from the entanglements of business. From the first, therefore, the new hotel was administered on Quaker principles and pervaded by a Quaker spirit. When I visited it in 1872, Mr. Albert Smiley was still carrying on the school at Providence; the hotel was in charge of his brother Alfred. The bar-room and the dance hall had been abolished; beds had taken the place of bunks; a reading room had been substituted for the bar-room; and entertainments provided by the guests themselves had been substituted for the dance hall. The house had been enlarged to accommodate about forty guests; the atmosphere of the house was that of a home, not that of a cabaret; there was a service of worship in the parlour on Sundays and morning prayers for such as cared to attend them during the week. It was understood that cards, dancing, and drinking were prohibited; but there were not then, and there never have been, printed rules or regulations; the prohibition is enforced by common consent, and it is very rarely the case that even to-day, in a hotel with accommodations for upward of four hundred, any other enforcement is required.

The beauty of the place and the home atmosphere of the hotel so impressed me that the following year I returned with an artist to obtain sketches for an illustrated article which was published in the *Illustrated Christian Weekly*, of which I was then editor.

When I next visited Lake Mohonk, in 1884, Mr. Albert Smiley had left his school and had come to make Lake Mohonk his home. The boarding house had become a hotel capable of accommodating some three hundred guests; the estate had been increased by successive purchases to one of over a thousand acres; miles of roads had been built within the estate and innumerable footpaths had been opened through the woods and among the rocks; Mr. Alfred Smiley had finally left Providence and changed the profession of teacher for that of hotel keeper. Mr. Albert Smiley had purchased a similar estate seven miles distant upon the same range and erected a hotel upon the shore of a lake which gave its name of Minnewaska to the twin enterprise.

Who that has ever read "Nicholas Nickleby" did not regard the Cheeryble Brothers as a pretty fancy of an often extravagantly fanciful novelist? "What was the amazement of Nicholas when his conductor advanced and exchanged his warm greeting with another old gentleman, the very type and model of himself—the same face, the same figure, the same coat, waistcoat, and neckcloth, the same breeches and gaiters—nay, there was the very same white hat hanging against the wall!" But it is an old saying that fact is stranger than fiction; which is only another way of saying, cynics to the contrary notwithstanding, that life furnishes illustrations of ideas which surpass those of the novelist. The portrait of the Smiley brothers is best given in the words of Mr. Albert Smiley:

When my brother Alfred and I were born we were so much alike that our mother tied ribbons on either our arms or legs, I do not remember which, to distinguish us.

THE SMILEY BROTHERS

None of our neighbours or teachers knew us apart; we always worked together, walked together, slept together, had measles, mumps, and whooping cough together; never had a single article of clothing or money or anything else separate for twenty-seven years. In the morning we jumped into the first suit of clothes that came in our way, no matter who wore it the day before. All our studies and reading were from one set of books, reading and studying simultaneously. Until we were twenty-seven years old, when my brother married, we had never had anything to be called "mine," but always "ours." At my brother's marriage we had to divide clothing and some other things, but till his death, four years since, we had many of our interests in common.

In 1884 this identity of appearance still continued. Strangers could not easily distinguish between the brothers when they were together, and when they were not together never could tell which was Albert and which was Alfred. Even the brothers could not always tell. They once made an appointment to meet in a hotel in New York. Albert arrived first; walking down a corridor he saw his brother approaching; he reached out his hand to grasp the outstretched hand of his brother, with the greeting, "Are you here already?" and found that he was addressing his own image in a mirror.

They were as much alike in spirit and temperament as in appearance. The same simplicity that had characterized the boarding house with forty guests characterized the twin hotels. The same piety characterized both men, the same liberty under law characterized both hotels. If I write here only of Mr. Albert Smiley it is because he is the only one I at all intimately knew.

Some men are distinguished from their fellows by the possession of one characteristic in an abnormal degree. I was told a few years ago of a little girl, not yet in her teens, who came into the laboratory of her scientific grandfather with an insect for his inspection. "He is a very naughty fly," she said, "he keeps biting me." When she opened her fist she disclosed a wasp. She was a born scientist. Investigation was to her a passion. But some men are made great by the possession of seemingly contradictory qualities harmoniously working in a well-balanced character. Such was the greatness of Mr. Albert Smiley. He was a man of vision. At the first sight of Lake Mohonk he perceived the possibilities of a great estate; but he was also a man of practical judgment and did not retire from his successful school until he had laid up enough money to take with safety the hazard of abandoning a profession with which he was familiar for one of which he knew nothing. He was cautious, always looked before he leaped; but when he had looked he did not hesitate to leap. When he had once definitely formed his purpose to provide for persons like-minded with himself a true summer rest, he gave himself without reserve to the achievement of that ideal. Whatever interfered with it he regarded as an obstacle to be, if possible, overcome. When a railway proposed to build a branch to the foot of the mountain he discouraged the proposal; it might bring him customers, but it would hazard the repose that he wished to provide. When an inn just beyond the bounds of his estate threatened that repose, he bought the inn. He was a lover of liberty; and ordered liberty is a condition of repose of the spirit. Therefore, he put up few signs that indicated restraints on liberty. The only such signs to be seen are some scattered through the woods to protect the trees and flowers and one at every entrance of his grounds forbidding the use of automobiles.

But when enforcement of the common law of his estate was required he did not lack the courage to enforce it. A wealthy guest came with a large party prepared to spend a considerable time and a great deal of money, and assumed that, because of his patronage, the hotel would not enforce against him the rule prohibiting the use of liquor, and he brought down his bottle with him to the dinner table. Mr.

Smiley said nothing until the dinner was over and then notified his would-be guest that the rooms assigned to him were no longer to be at his service; that he was, in short, an "undesirable citizen." Another man of the same type, disregarding a sign at the gateway that automobiles were not allowed, drove up in his touring car to the door. Mr. Smiley ordered the automobile to be driven by a special road to the nearest entrance. After dinner, he provided a carriage to carry the unwelcome guest and his family to the same entrance and refused to take any pay for the dinner that the guests had received.

Such incidents get promptly into wide circulation and serve quite adequately as law enforcements. When depredations were committed by barbarians, possessing the appearance but not the reality of civilization, he neither submitted to the destruction of his property nor issued new prohibitions to protect it, nor called on the officers of the law for protection. He appealed, and not unsuccessfully, to the conscience of the community and to the depredators themselves. He provided a Picnic Lodge with grounds surrounding it for the free use of picnic parties, and then sent a courteous letter to the newspaper press in which he narrated some of the abuses that had been perpetrated, and

prescribed certain rules which all picnic parties
should observe. The letter was very widely
published and editorially commended. "I must
ask," he said, "my friends and neighbours and all
who bring or send parties here to see that no
damage is done to property of any kind," and
he added, "unless the few can be prevented from
damaging property it will become positively
necessary to exclude all picnic parties from
the estate." This appeal to the public and the
picnickers themselves was sufficient; at least in
my riding and walking about the grounds to-day
[June, 1921] I see no signs of depredations
against which in 1906 Mr. Smiley very justly
protested.

Since the financial success of Mr. Smiley's experience has proved that he correctly interpreted a before unrecognized demand, other hotels formed as his plan and inspired by his spirit
have been successfully established, and many
hotels which have neither vanished card playing and dancing from their parlour nor provided
libraries for their guests during the week nor
religious services on the Sabbath, have become
less noisily gay and more quietly comfortable.
At the same time summer camps in increasing
numbers furnish rural recreations and the simple life to an increasing number of toilers from
the towns and cities who want something bet-

ter for summer recreation than a mere change of place in which to continue their city amusements. But that Mr. Smiley's experiment in 1871 was a surprising invocation is indicated by the following incident for which I am indebted to a western correspondent.

A Kentucky tourist travelling in California came upon Mr. Smiley's beautiful winter home in Riverside, created by his genius out of a desert land, and the following conversation ensued between the Kentuckian and the driver of his carriage:

Tourist. That's a beautiful place. Whom does it belong to?

Driver. A Mr. Smiley.

Tourist. It must have cost a lot. How did he make his money?

Driver. By a queer kind of hotel in New York.

Tourist. What kind of a hotel?

Driver. Well, he didn't have any bar, or allow any wine to be served on the table; they didn't allow card playing, or dancing in the parlour; guests were not received nor taken away on Sunday; they have family prayers in the parlour every morning and church services every Sunday.

Tourist. Where in hell can they get patrons for such a hotel?

Driver. They do not get their patrons from that region.

Under the administration of Mr. Albert Smiley and his younger brother Daniel—who with his wife have been active partners with Mr. Albert Smiley since 1890 and are with their sons carrying on the enterprise in the same spirit since the death of Mr. and Mrs. Albert Smiley—the Lake Mohonk House has been more than a home of rest for the overworked and the brain-weary; it has been a nesting place for reform movements.

Miss M. P. Follet, a few years ago, published a notable book entitled "The New State." It might better have been entitled "The New Democracy." The cardinal doctrine of this book may be concisely stated thus: Democracy is not merely government by the majority. It is creative. By an interchange of conflicting views in a spirit of mutual respect a new view is created which embodies some elements of these conflicting opinions, but not all the elements of any one of them. The Indian Conference initiated by Mr. Albert Smiley in 1884 at Lake Mohonk affords the best illustration of "The New Democracy" I have ever seen.

The success of the earlier meetings was such that when the Spanish-American War brought under the protectorate of the United States Porto Rico and the Philippines, the Indian conferences were broadened so as to include "all Dependent Peoples" Later a second series of conferences were called to consider what means, if any, were practicable to substitute an appeal to reason for the appeal to force as a means of settling international differences. The Conference possessed no formal organization. The attendants were not delegates but invited guests of Mr. Smiley. From twelve at the first conference in 1884 they grew by natural accretion to three hundred before 1913. They included men and women of every variety of temperament and opinion. Roman Catholics, Protestants, and Jews, High Churchmen and Friends, Republicans and Democrats, government officials and newspaper critics, Radicals and Conservatives met to engage in a perfectly free Forum, not to win a victory over each other, but to comprehend each other. Factions were difficult and factional victories were impossible. For from the first it was agreed that no opinion should ever be affirmed to be the opinion of the Conference except by unanimity. A platform committee was appointed at the opening of the Conference; it watched the debate, framed a platform intended to express a conclusion to which all could agree, and reserved all disputed questions for subsequent consideration. When, therefore, a committee from this conference went to Washington with its well-thought-out policy, it had a real political power, because its platform was the expressed opinion of Roman Catholics and Protestants, Reformers in the East and dwellers on the Western Border, Idealists from the library, and practical experts from the field. I remember one visit we, as a committee, made to Washington just after Mr. Cleveland's election and his saying to me afterward: "I had the idea when I took the Presidency that we ought to put all the Indians in one reservation under one control, but the friends of the Indians sat down on that proposition with such determination that I gave it up."

I do not believe that any one influence has had so much to do with producing the revolution wrought in our Indian policy in the last quarter of a century as the influence exercised by the late Indian Conference at Mohonk, and I am sure that the proposal to establish an International Supreme Court, somewhat analogous in its nature and functions to the United States Supreme Court, first came from the Lake Mohonk Conference on International Arbitration in 1895. It would probably have been adopted nearly ten years ago by the civilized powers if it had not been for the jealousy of some of the South American republics and the bitter hostility of Germany. It is not improbable that

41

the apparently approaching era of international peace incited the German military party to undertake the subjugation of Europe under a universal German Empire before it was fully prepared for so insane an attempt.

Mr. Albert Smiley selected with care the guests who attended these conferences. He appointed the chairman and, in consultation with others called together for that purpose, selected the Business Committee, and he always attended the morning and evening meetings of the Conference. The afternoons were set apart for drives and walks and other forms of recreation. On both the Indian and the Arbitration Conferences there were radical differences of opinion, perfect freedom of expression, often warm, and sometimes hot, debates; but I do not think that parliamentary courtesy was ever violated or that any speaker was ever called to order, except occasionally for over-running his allotted time. The combination of freedom and courtesy in the speeches at these conferences must have struck any one accustomed to attend meetings for public debate whether held by politicians, ecclesiastics, or reformers. That this was largely due to the personal influence of our host I am sure we all felt, though he rarely took any active part in the debates. From some men an indescribable influence exudes; other men as virtuous and as able are without that peculiar influence. I can no more understand it than I can understand why some flowers are fragrant and others are not. Mr. Smiley was a born peacemaker, making peace not so much by what he said as by what he was.

I attended nearly all the Indian Conferences at Lake Mohonk and most of the Arbitration Conferences, and, as a journalistic historian of current events, have traced their subsequent influence on public opinion and on national and international action. In my judgment, the world owes much more than it knows to the Smiley Brothers, and especially to Mr. Albert Smiley's skill in inspiring and directing team work. Before Mr. Smiley died in 1912, a large proportion of the Boards of Commerce throughout the United States had sent representatives to the International Arbitration Conference and had carried back to their various communities the plan for an international tribunal proposed by Mr. Everett Edward Hale* at the first of those conferences and adopted by the Conference without a dissenting voice. The growing recognition in this country of the duty of service which advanced races owe to dependent races, and the growing determination in this country to find

---

*In the silhouette entitled "Everett Edward Hale, an American Abou Ben Adhem," the reader will find further information respecting his proposal and advocacy for a Supreme Court of the Nations.

in law, interpreted by an international tribunal, a better method for securing international justice than can be found in an army equipped with warlike instruments, found at Lake Mohonk their first formal and forcible expression and there received their first equipment of power.

JOHN B. GOUGH, APOSTLE OF TEMPERANCE

IN APRIL, 1840, the Rev. Matthew Hale Smith delivered a temperance lecture in Baltimore. Two members of a drinking club which was accustomed to meet in a tavern in that city were appointed, probably in jest, to attend and bring back a report to their comrades. On their report a hot debate ensued. The interference of the landlord added fuel to the flames. As a result, six of the members formed a temperance society on the spot, which they entitled the Washington Total Abstinence Society. A year or two later John B. Gough, then apparently a confirmed inebriate, was by this total-abstinence movement rescued from self-destruction, and at once gave himself to the rescue of others.

He was born in 1827 in England, of humble parentage; was apprenticed at twelve years of age to a family migrating to America; entered the bookbinder's trade; took to the stage as a vaudeville performer; fell into bad habits, increased by despair on the death of his wife and infant child; had two attacks of delirium tremens; by a kind word from a stranger was interested in temperance reform, signed the pledge, and began his real life—the life of an apostle of temperance. He brought into his new life the arts of the actor acquired in the theatre, and was at once a favourite speaker in the temperance meetings held in district schoolhouses, public halls, and sometimes, although at first rarely, in churches.

He married again. His wife brought him those staying and steadying qualities which this impulsive, ardent, sensitive orator sorely needed. His newly acquired moral earnestness gave to him the artistic quality of sincerity and reality which the vaudeville performer had not possessed. He united with the Church and brought into the total-abstinence movement a Christian spirit which at first it had lacked. He early made enthusiastic friends; but he had also to encounter bitter, unscrupulous, and astute enemies. They concealed their enmity under a guise of hospitality. Twice he fell under his old temptations—once a physician's prescription awoke the old appetite, once he was drugged. From both falls he recovered, and by both falls his hatred of drink was intensified, his power to combat it was strengthened.

When I first knew him, this period of conflict was wholly in the past; but it was a past that he never forgot, and never could forget. He told me once that he never came into a roomful of company that he did not think, "These people are saying to themselves, Here comes the man who has twice had delirium tremens," and that he never dared take communion when alcoholic wine was used lest the fragrance of the wine should be too much for him.

But he carried with him none of the marks of his upbringing; no vulgarities and no coarseness of speech, no lack of courtesy in behaviour. He was a cultivated gentleman, able to grace any social circle, and the best social circles in England and America were opened to him. He was one of the very few absolute total abstainers I have ever known. He never touched wine or pretended to touch it at weddings or receptions; never tasted it at the sacrament; never used it as a medicine. He was the best story-teller I have ever known and told stories with the same dramatic impersonation at the dinner table as on the platform. Of them he had an inexhaustible supply, because, although he was always drawing from his reservoir, he was also always replenishing it. The Lecture Lyceum was in a decline; Chautauqua had not yet been born; the Y. M. C. A. was still in its youth. But John B. Gough never failed to draw. He no longer confined himself to temperance, but I doubt whether he ever lectured on any theme that he did not introduce some reference to temperance into the lecture. On one of my visits to him at his country home a few miles out from Worcester he took me over his farm and showed me half a score or more of cattle of a special breed. "Can you make this farm pay?" I asked him. "Pay!" he exclaimed. "Pay! It takes eight months of lecturing as hard as I can lecture to earn the money which my wife has to have in order to run this farm."

He was a consistent Puritan. If I did not fear being misunderstood, I would say he was an Old Testament Christian. He was *for himself* a very strict constructionist of the Old Testament laws. He spent eight months of the year on an itinerant lecture tour, but he would never travel on Sunday. I believe he would never ride in a horse car on Sunday. Does not the Fourth Commandment say: "Thou shalt not do any work, thou, nor thy son, nor thy daughter, thy manservant, nor thy maidservant, nor thy cattle"? To ride in a horse car is to make a servant and a horse work; therefore he would not ride. But, unlike some Puritans, he never attempted to impose his conscience on another. He was strict with himself, liberal with others. In this regard he was unlike many of us who are more inclined to be liberal in

48

judging for ourselves and strict in judging for others.

He was in Edinburgh one Sunday (he himself told me this anecdote, and I do not think it has been before in print) and heard Doctor Finney preach on the seventh of Romans: "For that which I do I allow not; for what I would, that do I not; but what I hate, that do I." The sermon produced a profound impression on Mr. Gough's sensitive nature. The next morning he called on Doctor Finney at his hotel, was shown to his room, and, with characteristic directness, went straight to his point.

"Doctor Finney," said he, "I am Mr. Gough. I heard you preach yesterday morning; and I am afraid that I am living in the seventh of Romans."

With equally characteristic directness Doctor Finney met his visitor.

"Let us pray," said he; and knelt down at his chair. Mr. Gough knelt also. After a fervent prayer for his visitor's emancipation from the law Doctor Finney called on Mr. Gough to pray.

Mr. Gough.   I can't, Doctor Finney.

Dr. Finney.   *Pray*, Mr. Gough.

Mr. Gough.   I can't, Doctor Finney.

Dr. Finney (with renewed emphasis).   *Pray*, Mr. Gough.

Mr. Gough. I can't, Doctor Finney; and, what is more, I won't.

Dr. Finney. O Lord, have mercy on this wiry little sinner.

What was said in the conversation that followed I do not know. The incident is worth recording because it illustrates one distinguishing feature in Mr. Gough's character—his absolute sincerity. When he said, "I cannot pray," he spoke the literal truth. A sincerer man than he I have never known. He was incapable of pretense. The emotion that he did not feel he could not utter. This was one element, perhaps the most important element of his power as an orator. Because what he said he always himself felt, he compelled his audience to feel it with him. He was always real. Even in his impersonations he was for the moment the individual he impersonated.

At the time of which I am writing the temperance army existed in two wings—the legal and the moral suasion. The leaders of the one sought by law to prohibit the sale of liquor; the leaders of the other sought to dissuade the drinker from continuing to use it. Mr. Gough belonged to the latter wing. He was essentially a Christian evangelist. He characterized the temperance movement as a "Christian enterprise"; he sought, and not in vain, the coöperation of the Christian clergy and the Christian churches; he appealed to the sleeping pride in man, which the most degraded rarely entirely lose, and he often roused it to self-assertion. At the close of one of his meetings the most notorious drunkard in the town arose and, pulling a bottle out of his pocket, said: "Mr. Gough, those young men in the gallery gave me this bottle and offered me half a dollar to drink your very good health at the close of your lecture. But you have told me that I am a man, and I believe I am"; and he broke the bottle in pieces then and there, signed the pledge —and kept it.

If Mr. Gough treated the "drunken Jakes" in every community as men, he also treated genteel and reputable drunkenness as a sin. He condemned it, not because it always leads to poverty, disease, and crime, for it does not; but because it always does lead to a loss of self-control; and if self-control is not the foundation of all the virtues, no virtue can be exercised without it. I wrote to him once inviting him to deliver an address at a Congregational Club in New York City, and received the following reply:

I am glad that the subject of Temperance is to be the topic of discussion and I would have gladly occupied a few minutes in the expression of some thoughts on the subject before such an audience. I fear we do not sufficiently recognize the importance of a more strict definition of the meaning of the term drunkenness or intemperance. We are apt to decide that drunkards are those only who beat their wives, neglect their children, and outrage the decencies of life; who love filth and are wedded to all abominations, moral and physical. Are there not men and women who are able to maintain a decent or respectable appearance, who are really drunkards as essentially as the poor victim who rolls in the gutter? Only differing in degree. A man who prays louder or with more apparent unction under the influence of intoxicating stimulants is as drunk as the man who blasphemes under the same influence, or he who slobbers in his silly maudlin affection as he who beats his wife, &c.

These two incidents illustrate the spirit that always animated Mr. Gough. His primary object was the redemption of the individual; the social betterment of the community took a second place in his customary thinking. But though he rarely spoke in advocacy of legal measures of any kind—high license, local option, or prohibition—he was too good a strategist to criticize his co-workers in a common enterprise. The prohibitionists were not always as wise. With that intolerance that has too often characterized radical reformers from the days of the ancient Pharisees, some of them sneered and a few of them bitterly condemned the moral-suasionists. This led to one of the most dramatic incidents in Mr. Gough's dramatic career.

JOHN B. GOUGH

In 1857—I believe I have the date right—Neal Dow, the author of the Maine Law, was about visiting England to take part in a prohibition campaign in that country. At that time the prohibition movement in the United States was suffering a relapse. Mr. Gough in a private letter to a friend stated the facts. "The cause in this country," he wrote, "is in a depressed state. The Maine Law is a dead letter everywhere—more liquor sold than I ever knew before in Massachusetts—and in the other states it is about as bad." At the same time he commended Neal Dow and referred to him for further information. "I see," he said, "that Neal Dow is to be in England. I am glad. You will all like him; he is a noble man, a faithful worker. He can tell better than any other man the state of the Maine Law movement here."

There is no doubt that Mr. Gough's statement was true. But the radical reformer does not wish the truth told if it will hurt his cause. He is generally quite sure that nothing can be true which will hurt his cause. When a little later Mr. Gough landed in Liverpool, he found the prohibition circles in England in a fever of excitement which the publication of this private letter had caused. That he was a liar was the least of the charges preferred against him. Mr. Gough met the charges of falsehood by letters from distinguished advocates of temperance in the United States testifying to the facts as he had portrayed them. Resolutions by his friends which fully and heartily vindicated him had no effect to still the abuse. The reverse was the effect. Slanders, at first whispered from circle to circle, were at length openly published. One prohibition leader, bolder or more unscrupulous than his colleagues, printed a letter in which he declared that Mr. Gough had been often intoxicated with drugs—once insensibly so—in the streets of London, many times helplessly so in the streets of Glasgow; that there were many witnesses to the facts; that two of these occasions were within the writer's personal knowledge; and he challenged Mr. Gough to bring the matter before a jury of twelve Englishmen and pledged himself "on the honour of a gentleman and the faith of a Christian to furnish names and adduce further evidence of what I have now asserted."

Mr. Gough accepted the challenge of Doctor Lees, sued him for libel, and brought him before the court to make good his charge.

I should not venture thus to report this incident in the life of Mr. Gough if I depended solely on my memory of events occurring more than sixty years ago. But I wrote in 1884 a brief sketch of Mr. Gough's life which is now out of print. A copy of that sketch lies before me now, and from it I quote the following brief report of this extraordinary trial:

Mr. Gough's counsel opened the case, stated the facts, and called Mr. Gough to go into the witness-box. Mr. Gough thus at the outset offered himself to the opposing counsel for a searching cross-examination into his whole life. It was a simple thing to do if the charges were wholly false; it would have been a disastrous thing to do if there had been any colour of truth in them, any ground even for a reasonable suspicion of their truth. Mr. Gough carried with him into the witness-box a little handbag. He swore positively that since 1845 never had wine, spirits, or any fermented liquor touched his lips; that he had never eaten opium, bought opium, possessed opium; that he had never touched or owned laudanum except on that one occasion before his reformation, when he stopped on the edge of suicide; that the whole story in all its parts was an absolute fabrication. . . . Then, in answer to a question from his counsel, he opened his hand-bag and took out a little memorandum book. It was one of several. It then appeared that ever since the commencement of his lecturing experiences he had kept a diary. In this diary he entered upon every day the place where he spent it, the persons with whom he spent it, his occupation, and, if he had lectured, the price received for his lecture. He was thus able to fix with certainty his exact place and the witnesses who could testify to his condition on every day. Slander was dumb. It dared not face that diary. A hurried consultation took place between Doctor Lees and his counsel. Then, in Doctor Lees's name, and in his presence, his counsel retracted the charges. He retracted the statement that his client knew of his own certain knowledge of Mr. Gough's intoxication. Everything was withdrawn. Mr. Gough left the witness-stand without even being cross-examined. By consent a verdict was given to him of five guineas, a sum sufficient to carry costs.

The subsequent endeavours of Doctor Lees to retract his retraction had no effect upon public opinion. The verdict of the English people unanimously sustained the unanimous verdict of the English jury. What I wrote in 1884 is still true: "From that day to this slander against his [Mr. Gough's] good name has never been repeated. Neither envy, nor malice, nor even partisanship, dares face that diary."

No influence is so difficult to retain as that of the popular orator. Curiosity listens to him at first with enthusiasm: but repeated hearings satisfy curiosity, and enthusiasm gives place to a languid interest. This makes the position of the preacher so difficult, and the tenure of the pastorate so brief; this makes the blunder so serious of any preacher who allows himself to depend on his oratory for his permanent power over his people. If the popular orator defies public sentiment, it either overwhelms him or flows away and leaves him without an auditor. If he flatters the public, every new flattery must surpass its predecessor, till by and by flattery dies of its own extravagance. Mr. Gough not only achieved a preëminence among the orators of America and England, and this without advantages of either birth or culture, but he retained that position during nearly half a century, in spite of changes of public thought and feeling respecting his chosen theme which would have rendered the speech-making of any ordinary man upon the platform in 1840 an anachronism before 1886.

The closing years of Mr. Gough's life were spent in his rural home a few miles from Worcester, Massachusetts. Without education he became a master of the English language; without advantages of birth or early training he became a refined and cultivated gentleman; rescued from the depths of degradation by a kind word fitly spoken, he became a devout Christian. He was a great orator because he was in the best sense of that often-abused term, a great man. Endowed with a musical voice, a mobile face, a vivid imagination, a human sympathy equally capable of irresistible pathos and of an almost rollicking humour, all controlled and directed to a noble end by common sense and a masterful conscience, Mr. Gough rendered to his native land and to the land of his adoption a service the effects of which surpass all calculation.

And when he died men came from various parts of this country, and messages from all parts of the civilized world, to do honour to his memory at the simple funeral services held in his country home near Worcester, Massachusetts.

HENRY F. DURANT, a successful lawyer in Massachusetts, was converted under the preaching of Dwight L. Moody in 1864, became himself a lay preacher, eleven years later set apart a large portion of his very considerable fortune to the foundation of a college for girls at Wellesley, a suburb of Boston, and thereafter devoted to the organization and management of the college most of his time and his thought until his death in 1881. The college building was erected on an eminence above a lake, on the opposite shore of which was Mr. Durant's home. The ample college grounds, beautifully diversified, included three hundred acres—one, he once told me, for each pupil. When I first visited Wellesley College, probably in 1879, Mr. Durant was spending much of his time in the college, exercising a controlling influence in the conduct of its affairs, and Miss Alice Freeman was teaching history and, if my memory does not mislead me, was also busy creating a library out of a growing collection of books.

From the first she fascinated me. Whether a

sculptor would consider her features beautiful
I do not know. Beauty of features has never
much appealed to me. But through her always-
expressive face shone a beautiful spirit. Native
refinement, scholarly culture, intuitive imagination, unhesitating courage, womanly grace
and spontaneity of life combined to make that
beauty. Profoundly interested in the movement to widen the intellectual horizon of woman
and open to her the long-locked doors of opportunity to public service, she was then and
always feminine. This, my first impression, I
want to impress upon my reader, because, if I
fail to do so, I shall lamentably fail to interpret
the subject of this portrait. If I am asked what
I mean by "feminine," I reply frankly that I do
not know. No man can define "feminine." For
to man the charm of woman is that she keeps him
guessing. For this reason novelists fail in their
heroines. The masculine reader of "David Cop-
perfield" approves of Agnes, though she rather
bores him, but delights in Dora, though he dis-
approves her. On the other hand, Portia in "The
Merchant of Venice" is a delightful heroine to
the masculine mind because the Portia of the
casket scene is so different from the Portia of
the judgment scene. Alice Freeman Palmer
seemed to me, I think from that first introduction to her, like an opal; you can always be

sure to find a wonderful light in it, but with what changing colours it will glow when you next look at it you cannot tell; no one can tell.

I think it was because she was so feminine that she exercised over Mr. Durant an influence which no one else exercised and no one else could quite comprehend. This influence inspired him to select her, at the age of twenty-six, to be president of the college. He was a Puritan Christian. Prompt obedience to law was to him the sum of all virtues. One day as he and Miss Freeman were consulting together on some college business, a college girl passed by the open door. The following colloquy took place.

Mr. Durant. Miss Freeman, I wish you would speak to that girl about her soul's salvation. She is in need of such counsel as you could give her.

Miss Freeman. I will make it my business to get acquainted with her. What is her name?

Mr. Durant. No! No! I want you to speak to her now. She has just passed by.

Miss Freeman. I can't do that. I can't talk on this most sacred of subjects with a girl I have never known.

Mr. Durant. Yes! Now! Now is the accepted time, now is the day of salvation.

Miss Freeman (after a little longer parley).

61

Why, Mr Durant, it is impossible. You don't know anything about girls.

Mr. Durant. I don't know anything about girls! Why, I have founded this college for girls; and I have been meeting them every week, almost every day, for the last three years. Why don't I know anything about girls?

Miss Freeman. Because you have never had a daughter; your wife is not like any other woman that ever lived; and you've never been a girl yourself.

Mrs. Palmer, who told me this incident, which I have here for brevity's sake put in dramatic form, added that often afterward when in their conferences she could not agree with him, he would bring the conference to a close by saying: "Well, I suppose I don't understand girls; I've never been a girl myself."

This combination of courage, grace, and tact is strikingly illustrated by a subsequent incident when she had become the president of the college.

Monday was the college holiday. Every Monday morning some seventy or eighty college girls went to Boston on the Boston and Albany Railroad. As no extra provision on the railroad was made for this weekly exodus, the girls generally had to stand. Miss Freeman first called the attention of the station-master to the need of better accommodations; then she wrote to headquarters; then, getting no improvement, she wrote again; and then the impatient girls took the matter into their own hands. One Monday morning the usual eighty girls were at the station to take the train. One of their number, more courageous than her companions, collected all their tickets from them; they all poured into one car and took their customary places in the aisle. The car door opened. "Tickets, please!" said the conductor. The leader at the head of the long line of swaying girls replied, "I have the tickets for our whole party, and will give them up as soon as you provide us with seats." The conductor took in the situation at a glance. He could not stop the train and bundle eighty girls out on the side of the track. "Give me your name, please, miss," said he. "Certainly," she replied, and handed him her card. But when she got back to the college she began to fear the consequences of her act and went directly to the president for counsel. "Then I knew," said Miss Freeman, in telling the story to me, "that my time had come." "If you hear from the railway," she said to the girl, "report to me." The next day the girl brought her a letter from the superintendent calling upon her to deliver the railway tickets. This she reported at once to the president, who took the letter. The next day a second letter was received; it was severer than the first and threatened to report her to the president. That also she reported to the president. The president reassured her. "Don't worry," she said. "You have already reported the case to the president; give me the letter." The third day Miss Freeman, going in to Boston, called on the superintendent; but not to apologize—to complain. "Wellesley College," she said, "asks no favours of the railway. But you have been twice informed that every Monday some seventy or eighty girls go in to Boston from Wellesley; they pay for seats and are entitled to seats, and no seats are provided for them." The superintendent apologized, and promised that in the future the seats should be provided. She rose to go. The superintendent begged to detain her a moment. Somewhat shamefacedly he narrated the incident and said he had no doubt that if she would ask the girls for the tickets which they possessed the girls would deliver them. Miss Freeman replied that the president of Wellesley College was not acting as collecting agent for the Boston and Albany Railroad and referred him for his claim against the college or its students to the legal adviser of the college whose address she gave him. Thereafter there was always accommodation on Monday's train. The girls got their seats: the railroad never got the tickets. What sort of standing this incident gave to the president with the students the reader can better imagine than I can describe.

Another incident, not less significant of the power of her personality, can be told in a few sentences. There had been some stealing in the college. Circumstances convinced the president that some one of the students was guilty, but did not point to any one. Her indignation, hot but controlled, coupled with the fellowship with the students which made them all recognize her as their best friend, enabled her so to speak in chapel one morning—how I wish I could have heard that chapel talk!—that the culprit came straight to her with a full confession. I do not recall that I ever heard of another sermon so immediately and personally effective.

I do not think that I am mistaken in the opinion that Mr. Durant was more eager to make missionary Christians than to make ripe scholars. The incident already narrated illustrates his spiritual eagerness. Miss Freeman (I use the name she bore during those college days) was not less spiritually eager. But she did not think that Christian character and ripe scholarship were separate goals to be reached by separate roads, or that either was to be used merely as a means to attain the other. She habitually thought of the Christian religion in New-Testament terms as "life"; to inspire her pupils with life was always her inspiring purpose. Professor Palmer in his delightful biography of his wife brings out this characteristic very clearly:

"Why will you," I said, "give all this time to speaking before uninstructed audiences, to discussions in endless committees with people too dull to know whether they are talking to the point, and to anxious interviews with tired and tiresome women? You would exhaust yourself less in writing books of lasting consequence. At present, you are building no monument. When you are gone people will ask who you were, and nobody will be able to say." But I always received the same indifferent answer: "Well, why should they say? I am trying to make girls wiser and happier. Books don't help much toward that. They are entertaining enough, but really dead things. Why should I make more of them? It is people that count. You want to put yourself into people; they touch other people; these, others still; and so you go on working forever."

"It is people that count." That I think is one of the keys to Alice Freeman Palmer's character. She was not especially interested in themes or theories; but she was tremendously interested in people. I was once told by a friend of a young graduate who had just taken up teaching, and who, asked by a companion, what she was teaching, replied, "Twenty children."

66

ALICE FREEMAN PALMER

When I first knew her, Miss Freeman was teaching three hundred college girls. They absorbed all her attention. She had especially prepared herself to teach history. But my guess is that she could have given points to any teacher in her faculty. She probably did not know mathematics as well as the professor of mathematics, or philosophy as well as the professor of philosophy, or Greek as well as the professor of Greek, but she knew girls, and she could have shown any specialist in her faculty how to get the girl's mind open to any truth the specialist wanted to get into that mind.

There lies before me an address of hers entitled "Why Go to College?"* There is nothing in the publication to indicate when and where it was published, but it furnishes a singularly lucid interpretation of the ideal of education which, though possibly unformulated, directed and controlled all her educational work from my first acquaintance with her. Something of that ideal the reader may perhaps catch from a paragraphal abstract.

Preeminently the college is a place of education, and a good education emancipates the mind and makes us citizens of the world. No student who fails to get a little knowledge on

---

*"The Teacher: Essays and Addresses on Education," by George Herbert Palmer and Alice Freeman Palmer.

many subjects and much knowledge on some can be said to have succeeded. The college is a place of happiness. "Merely for good times, for romance, for society, college life offers unequalled opportunities." She quotes Wordsworth, "We live by admiration, hope, and love," and adds "The college abounds in all three. . . . Books, pictures, collections, appliances in every field, learned teachers, mirthful friends, athletics for holidays, the best words of the best men for holy days—all are here." The college is a place for gain in health. "The steady, long-continued routine of mental work, physical exercise, recreation, and sleep, the simple and healthful food in place of irregular and unstudied diet, work out salvation for her." The college is a place of broadening influence. The girl "goes to college with the entire conviction, half unknown to herself, that her father's political party contains all the honest men, her mother's social circle all the true ladies, her church all the real saints of the community. . . . Before her diploma is won she realizes how much wider a world she lives in than she ever dreamed of at home. The wealth that lies in differences has dawned upon her vision." In college we make broadening and inspiring friendships, and through them obtain new and more catholic, more generous ideals. "The greatest thing any friend or teacher either in school or college can do for a student is to furnish him with a personal ideal."

This Miss Freeman was doing during the six years of her college presidency. I was startled to read in her husband's biography of her that only for six years did she fill that position; and now looking back upon that period I am still filled with wonder that her never-failing fountain of life could have accomplished so much in so brief a time. For it is not only Wellesley College that still feels her influence. What she said to her husband still proves true: "You put yourself into people; they touch other people; these, others still; and so you go on working forever."

My first college sermon was preached at Vassar College probably about 1878. Arriving there Friday night or Saturday morning I had an opportunity for a conference with one or more of the teachers and learned that there was in the student body a great deal of religious questioning: their traditional faith had been shaken, a new faith had not come to take its place. So I took for my theme: "The foundations of faith" which I found to be in man's spiritual nature: the Bible and the Christ were authoritative because they interpreted man to himself. From Vassar I went to Wellesley. Mr. Durant was, if not

its president, its controlling spirit. The teachers
I talked with thought there was little or no
skepticism in the student body, that the college
was Evangelical from centre to circumference.
The college was making much of a daily course
of Bible study. So I took for my theme: "What
is the Bible and how shall we study it?" In the
evening, with the cordial approval of the college
authorities, I held a "Question Drawer." The
girls were invited to send to my room any religious questions on which they desired light for
themselves or for a comrade. They were not to
sign their name, and as no one but myself would
see the questions and the handwriting would
mean nothing to me, the secrecy of the con-
fessional would characterize the meeting. The
questions surprised the teachers as much as they
surprised me: they covered the whole field of
lay thinking from "What are the six days of
creation?" to "Why should we believe in God?"

In 1881 Mr. Durant died and Miss Alice Freeman became the president of the college. By
the end of the first year of her administration she
had cleared its atmosphere. Doubtings were no
longer discouraged. Spring had followed winter.
The eager quest for truth had taken the place of
an acceptance of authority more apparent than
real. In 1883 or 1884 I spent a week or ten days
in the college preaching on the two Sundays,

lecturing nearly every day during the intervening week, and giving daily "office hours" to girls coming with questions, sometimes in twos or threes, sometimes in larger groups, oftenest alone. There was no limit to their coming; the only limit was set by my strength to receive and answer them. I took for the basis of my lectures the theme of the Vassar College sermon, "The foundations of faith," and out of them subsequently made a book entitled "In Aid of Faith" which is still in circulation. This gave me an opportunity to study the effect of the "higher education" on the religious life of girls, and incidentally to study the president of Wellesley College.

Walking through the college corridors with her almost daily, her personal familiarity with her three hundred pupils filled me with ever-increasing amazement. She not only seemed to know them all by name: she knew their families and their interests. She asked one about her sick mother, another whether her father had yet returned from Europe, another whether her younger sister was getting ready to come to college. "How ever do you do it?" I asked her. "I never could." "Oh, yes!" she replied; "you could if you had to. It is simply that you never had to. Whatever we have to do, we can always do." In narrating after her death this conversation to her husband, I added, what I venture to quote here, "This quiet confidence in the ability to do what needs to be done seems to me one of the secrets of her power. She leaned on her necessities, instead of letting herself be broken by them; and that simple disclosure of her method greatly added to the power of my life."

No doubt this power to carry in her busy mind these details of the lives of others was in part a native gift; but it was one which she had assiduously cultivated, and she told me once what she did to cultivate it. She kept a memorandum book in her bedroom in which were the names of all the freshman class. Under each name she wrote whatever information she from time to time acquired. These notes of her pupils' characters and experiences she studied as they studied their notes of the lectures of their instructors. Thus while her students studied their lessons she studied her students, and she put no less painstaking into her studies than the most studious of them put into theirs. This was no compulsory or professional study. She delighted in it. She wished to know every pupil that she might better befriend every pupil. It was true for her then, as it was true for her always: "It is people that count."

She had not merely interest in her pupils and

affection for them. She had faith in them, believed in them, and by her faith inspired them to have faith in themselves. Little beginnings of desire, mere seeds of purpose sprouted in the sunshine of her appreciative faith. It often happens that our deeper desires are hidden even from ourselves by some superficial wishes, our enduring purposes by some temporary inclinations. Miss Freeman saw these subconscious forces and gave them power. She could control by authority when necessary; but she much preferred to call into life the power of self-control. Her life was full of such incidents as the following narrated by her husband:

Amusing stories are reported of girls who came to ask for something, and went away delighted to have obtained the opposite. One of them says: "In the spring of my senior year I had an invitation to spend the holidays in Washington, and my family strongly urged me to arrange the visit. Overjoyed, I went to Miss Freeman to obtain permission to leave college several days before the vacation. She was very warm, envying me the prospect of seeing the Capitol for the first time. She promised to ask the Faculty for permission and to state to them how great the opportunity for me was. But she inquired how many examinations and written exercises I should miss, incidentally calling attention to the fact that the professors would have to give me special ones in the following term. Gradually I felt the disadvantage of this irregularity. Still, there was Washington! And I asked if she herself would not be tempted to go. Indeed she would, she said, but college work was nearest, the first business. A Washington invitation might come again, a senior year in college, never. So, quite as if my own judgment had been my guide, I decided that I did not want to go to Washington. A little later, when the office door had closed, I stopped on the stairs and asked myself if this was the same person who had passed there half an hour before, and what had induced me to give up the coveted journey when there was no hint on Miss Freeman's part of compulsion, much less of refusal."

In laying emphasis, as throughout this paper I am doing, on Miss Freeman's power to awaken the spirit of life in her pupils and direct it in healthful channels, I must not leave the impression that she shared the extraordinary opinion of some skeptics of our time that it is possible to cultivate in any community the spirit of religion without its institutions. As well expect to cultivate the spirit of music in a community without concerts, of art in a community without picture galleries, of education in a community without schools. She conducted the daily chapel exercises herself and they were never perfunctory. The Scripture readings and the hymns were selected with care, and the services, varying with the varying need of the college or the varying mood of the president, were always characterized by a sincere and simple spiritual beauty. She herself se-

74

lected with care the preachers for the Sunday
services; what she expected from them and
how much she herself, by her phrasing of her
invitations put into them, the following much-
prized letter may here indicate:

Wellesley College,
January 18th, 1886.

MY DEAR DR. ABBOTT:

Is it not time that we should hear your voice in the
chapel again? It seems so to us, and that *the* time of times
is approaching when you can help and strengthen us here.
The last Thursday of this month, the 28th, is the Day of
Prayer for colleges. It has always been a great day in
Wellesley, a day full of seed-sowing, and often of decisions
at which we have long rejoiced. All college exercises are
suspended for the day. We have a sermon in the morning,
and such other services for prayer and conference as seem
to be useful at the time; but the day and evening are given
up to thought and prayer for all colleges and schools,
especially for our own, and for all here who are not Christians. We want you and Mrs. Abbott with us on this
day very much. The work you did with the students
last year makes it possible for you to do more for them now
than any one else, and I long to have this serious and
prayerful spirit which now prevails in the College, guided
and deepened until we shall be *one* in Him. If you can
come on for Thursday and follow the work of that day,
by speaking to the students Friday following at their
Bible hour in the afternoon, it would just meet our desire.
You see, dear Dr. Abbott, what we need. We have had
very good daily meetings during the week of prayer, growing in interest, so that we have continued to have meetings

in the chapel Tuesday as well as Thursday evenings, and each one is more hopeful than the last. Yet there are nearly a hundred here whose names are not on the Christian Association roll and whose lives are not devoted to our Master; and so many more who need clearer ideas of duty and larger faith in Him. I know you need no assurance of our desire and no urging to come to our help. If you can find it possible and wise for yourself, you will make us a visit now and stay as long as you can and bring "the family." The Cottage is not yet finished, but we can make you comfortable *in the midst of things*, and you shall have so many chances to do good! There is nothing I can offer beyond that, is there? And there is much to tell and hear and many bits of advice you two people can give us.

I should have written this to Mrs. Abbott, but I have no doubt she is reading it to spare you the trouble, like the wife she is. Otherwise I would assure you that she needs a vacation and that we will be better to her this time if she will come and bring you. As it is I leave it all to you both, with Wellesley's love always.

Yours faithfully
ALICE E. FREEMAN.

Once and only once did I see Miss Freeman angry, and then it was her religion that made her so. An unselfish anger is not a brief madness and her anger did not disturb her quiet and wise judgment or lead her even for a moment to lose her perfect self-control. The committee of the American Board (Congregational) for Foreign Missions, acting under the leadership of one of its secretaries, who subsequently resigned his office, adopted the policy of refusing volunteers for foreign missionary service unless they could subscribe to the secretary's affirmation that all the heathen who had never heard of Christ were foredoomed and irreparably lost. Her indignation, in which I fully shared, was as much because of the wrong it did the Christian Church as because of the wrong it did two of her pupils, devoted followers of Christ, fully equipped for a Christian service to which they had dedicated themselves and for which they had for some years been preparing. During the controversy in the Congregational churches which that refusal created, and which lasted for two or three years, I was in frequent consultation with Miss Freeman and admired alike her indignation and the strong will that controlled and the wise judgment that directed it to beneficent ends. Emotion, like fire, is a good servant. Alice Freeman Palmer was a woman of strong emotions but they were always under the control of a stronger will.

Another incident in her life indicated this self-control. For nothing perhaps better illustrates this habitual control over the emotions than the power to lay aside a fascinating work on occasions and give the overstrained nerves a rest. The ability to do this is the best preventive of nervous exhaustion. Miss Freeman, who followed her Master in daring to undertake

great things and in giving herself without reserve to their accomplishment, followed him also
in dropping her work from time to time for
periods of absolute repose.   Occasionally, leaving
word with one companion whither she was going,
she would disappear, no one else knew where or
why.   In fact, she engaged a room in a hotel in
Boston, stayed in retirement for one, two, or three
days, and then came back to take up her work
again with rested nerves and recuperated strength.

When in December, 1887, she married Professor George H. Palmer of Harvard College
she resigned the presidency of Wellesley College
and with it the professional vocation of teacher.
She continued to teach by pen and voice and to
take an active part by her counsels in the educational work of her state by her service on the
Massachusetts Board of Education.   But her
personal relation as teacher to pupil came to an
end.   And therefore with that change in her
life-activity this sketch comes to an end, for this
is not a Life but a portrait, and a portrait only
of the teacher.   All her friends did not congratulate her on her marriage.   Some thought she
might have married and still retained her office—
been both president and wife; some thought she
was giving up a position of great influence and
power for a minor position.   I shared neither
opinion.   A happy marriage, I believe, is always

a promotion, always adds not only to the happiness but to the largeness and richness of life. A warm personal friend of both, I congratulated both without any reserve. And I had no wish to see Alice Freeman become a divided president and a divided wife; and I had no apprehension that she would do so. I felt what in the following verse she has expressed with a beauty of diction which I could never emulate:

> Great love has triumphed. At a crisis hour
>   Of strength and struggle in the heights of life
> He came, and, bidding me abandon power,
>   Called me to take the quiet name of wife.

If any of my readers desire a better acquaintance with Alice Freeman Palmer, the material is available in her biography written by her husband with a simplicity that is more than eloquence and with a frankness that is the best possible reserve. From a little book of her verse, not written for the public but published by her husband after her death, I select here one verse, because it is a revelation of the deeper experience of her hidden life:

> I said to Pain, I will not have thee here!
> The nights are weary and the days are drear
>   In thy hard company!
> He clasped me close and held me still so long
> I learned how deep his voice, how sweet his song,
>   How far his eyes can see.

SILHOUETTES OF MY CONTEMPORARIES

It was customary in the 'eighties for Wellesley College girls to elect honorary members to their classes. That honour was conferred upon me. Thus enrolled among the pupils of Alice Freeman Palmer I venture to represent them as well as myself by writing beneath this simple pen-picture of our honoured teacher:

Thy gentleness hath made me great.

JOHN FISKE, EVOLUTIONIST

A YOUNG man once called to see me with the following account of his experience: "I was brought up to believe that the Bible is inspired and infallible in all its statements; that the world was made out of nothing in six days of twenty-four hours each; that God made a perfect man six thousand years ago; that he fell; and that because of his fall sin, misery, and death have entered into the world. In that faith I joined the Church when I was a boy. I have since learned that the world was not made in six days; that man has lived on the earth a great deal longer than six thousand years; that he was gradually developed out of a lower animal form; and that the only fall has been a fall upward. The Bible is gone; my faith is gone with it; and now I do not know whether there is a God in the universe or a soul in the body."

This interprets the overthrow of the faith of thousands which characterized the latter half of the nineteenth century. It was a faith founded on a book and on a false interpretation of that book; and when science undermined the foundation the superstructure fell.

SILHOUETTES OF MY CONTEMPORARIES

It was in this period that John Fiske lived. He was born in 1842, died in 1901. His father died, his mother married again; and his boyhood was spent in Middletown, Connecticut, with his grandmother, whose name he took. His mother and his grandmother were devout souls whose genuine piety was mated with a mechanical though harmonious philosophy. Mr. Clark in his biography of Mr. Fiske* gives in twelve propositions a fairly accurate skeleton of Calvinism, but as a portrait of living Calvinism it is about as accurate as was Yorick's skull of Hamlet's friend. The reverence for God, the obedience to law, the sense of human dignity and worth lost in the fall, but to be regained in redemption, are all left out. Happily they were not left out from the experience of Mrs. Stoughton and Mrs. Fiske. The boy was not only instructed in the theology of his mother and his grandmother, but he imbibed something of their spirit. When he threw away their dogmas, he retained the inspiration of their lives and reconciled in himself science and religion. His broad scholarship and his literary skill enabled him later to illustrate by his pen what he experienced in his life—both the overthrow of faith and its reëstablishment on a firmer foundation than before.

* "The Life and Letters of John Fiske." By John Spencer Clark. Illustrated. 2 vols. Houghton Mifflin Company, Boston. $7.50.

JOHN FISKE

In boyhood he was an omnivorous reader. Everything interested him in the world of things and the world of ideas. He had an extraordinarily open mind and an eager curiosity. The story of his boyhood makes the reader wonder whether our present system of education is not lamentably inefficient and wasteful, whether a better system could not accomplish for ordinary boys what this extraordinary boy accomplished for himself. At eleven years of age he wrote to his mother: "We had an examination Thursday. I was examined in Greenleaf's Arithmetic; Perkins and Loomis' Algebra; through four books Euclid; through Hedge's Logic; through four books Cæsar; eight books Virgil; four Orat. Cicero and the Græca Majora; through the Latin and Greek grammars; and last, but not least dreaded, through Greek syntax. Mr. Brewer said I passed an admirable examination. I am reading Sallust, which is so easy that I have read forty-eight chapters without looking in the dictionary." A year later he earned the money with which to buy a good Greek-English dictionary. His grandmother thought five dollars a large sum for so unpractical a luxury; but when he had earned by hard work $3.60 she gave him the balance needed for the purchase. At thirteen years of age, in addition to his school studies, carried on to the satisfaction of his teachers, he was reading, among other authors, Grote, Emerson, Bayne, Shakespeare, Milton, Hugh Miller, and Humboldt's "Cosmos." He wrote his mother: "Do you not consider Humboldt the greatest man of the nineteenth century, and the most erudite that ever lived?" His leisure time he gave to music and religion: taught in the Sunday-school, assigned two evenings a week to revival meetings, led the singing, and took an active part in the speaking. He entered Harvard in preference to Yale because "the course at Harvard is very different and much harder. . . . It is a bad place for a careless scholar, but unequalled in facilities for an ambitious one."

By this time (1860) his scientific studies had led him, after much questioning, to reject what our author calls "dogmatic Christianity," but I should call dogmatic Calvinism. Unfortunately, the pastor of his church was wholly unable to understand the working of his mind. This pastor called upon the grandmother to get more light on the cause of John's backsliding. The grandmother stoutly maintained that John could not be an infidel.

"Why," said she, "he never did a bad thing in his life, and then, he is such a faithful student." "Yes," said Doctor Taylor, "that makes him all the worse. He does not believe in the inspiration of the Bible nor in the Divin-

84

ity of Christ, and he has given up the Church." Still she maintained he could not be an infidel, and in the innocence of her heart she took Doctor Taylor into John's library to see the fine collection of books he had got together, all of which she knew he had read. Alas, to the heresy-hunter the exhibit was too conclusive! There side by side with books of sound orthodoxy were many ancient classics, and the works of Humboldt, Voltaire, Lewes, Fichte, Schlegel, Buckle, Cuvier, Laplace, Milne-Edwards, De Quincey, Theodore Parker, Strauss, Comte, Grote, Gibbon, and John Stuart Mill. Doctor Taylor had no praise to bestow upon such a collection of books in the hands of his young parishioner, and in response to the inquiry as to what he thought of them, he could only shake his head.

The Harvard of 1860 was very different from the Harvard of to-day. It had its theological standard, which its students were expected to accept on the authority of their teachers. It was as dogmatic as Princeton, though the standard was different. "The College," says Senator Hoar in his autobiography, "had rejected the old Calvinistic creed of New England and substituted in its stead the strict Unitarianism of Doctor Ware and Andrews Norton, a creed in its substance hardly more tolerant or liberal than that which it supplanted." No New England college had yet learned that the object of education is to enable the pupils to do their own thinking.

But young Fiske was already on his way to the

definition of education which seven years later he expressed in a characteristic sentence. The object of education, he said, is the teaching "of the student to think for himself and then to give him the material to exercise his thought upon."

When at eighteen years of age he entered Harvard he had already become a convinced and enthusiastic though imperfectly educated evolutionist. So enthusiastic was he that when he found in a Boston book store the original prospectus of Herbert Spencer's system of philosophy to be published in quarterly numbers and sold by subscription if a sufficient number of subscribers could be found, he put his name down for $2.50 a year and wrote to his mother that if he had two thousand dollars he would lay one thousand at Mr. Spencer's feet to help him execute his great work.

But in Cambridge he found as little sympathy for his new thought as in Middletown, and scarcely any more liberty for either thought or action. In one respect the difficulties he encountered were greater. In Middletown they were wholly religious; in Cambridge they were also academic. For not only was the philosophy taught hostile to the new doctrine, but Agassiz, at that time the most popular and famous teacher of natural science in America, was as strongly opposed to evolution as were the orthodox theologians.

John Fiske was summoned before the Faculty and charged with disseminating infidelity among the students, and escaped a sentence of suspension only after a hot battle between the accused and the defendants of intellectual liberty. The offence of reading in chapel, which was made the occasion of a charge against him, he admitted, apologized for, and never repeated.

The American hostility to the doctrine of evolution was not unnatural. For in England the leading evolutionists were frankly agnostic. They reluctantly discarded or were avowedly indifferent to the theological dogmas which were then generally regarded and still are often regarded, as essential parts of the Christian faith, and if they did not reject, they certainly did not uphold, beliefs which are essential to any rational recognition of the reality and trustworthiness of the spiritual belief in a personal God and in a conscious personal immortality. The evolutionists were indignant that they were charged with being materialists, but if we consider the poverty of language and the universal tendency among the mass of men to misunderstand any new philosophy, we cannot wonder at the charge.

The four most eminent evolutionists in England were Spencer, Huxley, Darwin, and Tyndall.

The clearest expression of faith in a personal God that I have been able to find in the writings of either one of these evolutional philosophers is contained in the famous "Belfast Address" of John Tyndall, who quotes Thomas Carlyle as saying, "Did I not believe that an Intelligence is at the heart of things, my life on earth would be intolerable." Tyndall neither criticises nor endorses this statement; he merely adds: "The utterance of these words is not, in my opinion, rendered less but more noble by the fact that it was the need of ethical harmony here, and not the thought of personal happiness hereafter, that prompted his observation."

Herbert Spencer could get no nearer Christian faith in God as a Father than the assurance that "amid the mysteries that the more they are thought about, the more mysterious they appear, there still remains the one absolute certainty that he is ever in the presence of an Infinite and Eternal Energy, from which all things proceed."

Charles Darwin never denied but never affirmed that there is any evidence of an intelligent purpose in nature. Reporting a conversation with Mr. Darwin during the last year of his life, the Duke of Argyll says: "I said to Mr. Darwin, with reference to some of his own remarkable works on the 'Fertilization of Orchards' and on 'The Earthworms,' 'it was impossible to look at these without seeing that they were the effect and expression of mind.' I shall never forget Mr. Darwin's answer. He looked at me hard and said: 'Well, that often comes over me with overwhelming force; but at other times,' and he shook his head vaguely, adding, 'it seems to go away.'"

Mr. Huxley, after reciting some of the controversies among philosophers respecting the nature of the Deity, contemptuously dismisses the whole subject with the words: "Truly on this topic silence is golden; while speech reaches not even the dignity of sounding brass or tinkling cymbal, and is but the weary clatter of an endless logomachy."

Though John Fiske definitely abandoned certain of the dogmas held as an essential part of the Christian faith by his ancestors, he never abandoned his faith in the reality of the spiritual life—involving faith in a personal God and in personal immortality. But when in 1869 Charles W. Eliot was elected president of Harvard College and introduced the new régime of intellectual liberty by inviting Ralph Waldo Emerson and John Fiske to lecture, Mr. Fiske became the target for bitter attacks in which honest misunderstanding and malicious misrepresentation united in an endeavour to down the young man who was then the foremost representative in America of the new philosophy.

89

The publication of his Lectures was characterized as part of a plan obtaining among free-thinkers to disseminate far and wide attacks upon the system of "revealed religion," and the new policy inaugurated by the new president was labelled "Harvard's Raid on Religion." When in 1870 Fiske was nominated as temporary Acting Professor of History, the nomination was confirmed, but only by a bare majority. "It was openly charged that Fiske was a pronounced atheist, and the more dangerous because of his learning and ability." The hostility was so great to his holding any permanent position in the Faculty that no attempt was made to secure for him a permanent appointment.

This hostility did not cause Mr. Fiske to modify his views nor did it embitter him against his assailants. He apparently never attacked them and rarely defended himself. He went on completing his preparations for the publication both in England and the United States of his exposition of evolution, entitled "Cosmic Philosophy," and he repeated his message in lectures to such audiences as wished to hear them. But if he neither attacked his enemies nor directly defended himself from them he showed ability, very rare in pioneers, to learn from them. A cartoon casting ridicule on evolution by depicting Spencer and Fiske endeavouring to fly a kite labelled "The doctrine of evolution" with a frog, a crocodile, two monkeys, and some other animals tied to it to constitute its tail, he had framed and hung in his study. His comment was: "I like to keep this design before me as a sort of theological barometer—objections to it show how rapidly the religious mind is moving toward the great truths of 'Cosmic Evolution.'" He studied the current criticisms both scientific and theological, not to conform his teaching to the current beliefs, but to understand how so to explain the new outlook upon the universe as to make it understandable even by those prejudiced against it. He wrote to his mother:

When my "Cosmic Philosophy" comes out, you will see how utterly impossible it is that Christianity should die out; but utterly *inevitable* it is that it should be metamorphosed even as it has been metamorphosed over and over again.

From the scholars, who are quite often the ones most prejudiced by tradition, he appealed to the reason and to the reasonable emotions of the people. The spirit in which these lectures were given and how they were received I can best indicate by an extract from a letter written to his mother from Boston in 1872:

My concluding lecture—on the "Critical Attitude of Philosophy toward Christianity," in which, as the consummation of my long course, I threw a blaze of new light

91

upon the complete harmony between Christianity and the deepest scientific philosophy, was given Friday noon, and was received with immense applause. You ought to have been there. I suppose there was some eloquence as well as logic in it, for many of the ladies in the audience were moved to tears. Many were the expressions almost of affection which I got afterward. The best effect of it will be to destroy the absurd theological prejudice which has hitherto worked against me, chiefly with those people who haven't had the remotest idea of what my views are.

I have long known that my views needed only to be known to be sympathized with by the most truly religious part of the community of whatever sect; that when thoroughly stated and understood, they disarm opposition, and leave no ground for dissension anywhere—and this winter's experiment has proved that I was right.

Twelve years later, invited to present his views before the Concord School of Philosophy at Concord, Massachusetts, he gave in two successive years two lectures subsequently published in small books entitled respectively: "The Destiny of Man" and "The Idea of God." The relation of modern scientific thought to the religious life has been more fully treated since then by different writers, but I do not know where the student can find, even now, presented with equal brevity and clearness, the new arguments which the evolutionary hypothesis furnishes in support of faith in personal immortality and a personal God. Here all I can do is to indicate very

92

briefly and therefore imperfectly the line of Mr. Fiske's thought in these volumes.

The Destiny of Man. It is true that life beyond the grave is incapable of scientific demonstration since it is a hope, and "hope that is seen is not hope: for what a man seeth why doeth he yet hope for it?" But it is also true that development must have a goal as well as a beginning, and the opinion that the human race is ascending from a purely animal ancestry and has not yet reached its goal gives a right to anticipate a further development in a future life. And Mr. Fiske found in the materialists' philosophy the same kind of assumption that the materialists treated with such scorn when they found it in the philosophy of the theologians.

The materialistic assumption that the life of the soul ends with the life of the body is perhaps the most colossal instance of baseless assumption that is known to the history of philosophy. No evidence for it can be alleged beyond the familiar fact that during the present life we know Soul only in its association with Body, and therefore cannot discover disembodied soul without dying ourselves. This fact must always prevent us from obtaining direct evidence for the belief in the soul's survival. But a negative presumption is not created by the absence of proof in cases where, in the nature of things, proof is inaccessible. With his illegitimate hypothesis of annihilation, the materialist transgresses the bounds of experience quite as widely as the poet who sings of the New Jerusalem with its river of life and its streets of gold. Scientifically speaking, there is not a particle of evidence for either view.

The Idea of God. The Darwinian biology by exhibiting Man as the terminal fact in that stupendous process of evolution whereby things have come to be what they are, makes a future continuation of that process a reasonable hope, and faith in a spiritual Power producing and directing it a reasonable and indeed a scientifically necessary faith. "The whole tendency of modern science is to impress upon us even more forcibly the truth that the entire modern universe is an immense unit, animated through all its parts by a single principle of life"; "there appears a reasonableness in the universe such as had not appeared before"; and it is seen that "the presence of God is the one all-pervading fact of life from which there is no escape." It is true that this God is indefinable, but he is not unknown.

Though we may not by searching find out God, though we may not compass infinitude or attain to absolute knowledge, we may at least know all that it concerns us to know, as intelligent and responsible beings. They who seek to know more than this, to transcend the conditions under which alone is knowledge possible, are, in Goethe's profound language, as wise as little children who, when they have looked into a mirror, turn it around to see what is behind it.

JOHN FISKE

This imperfect interpretation from Mr. Fiske's little books may, I hope, send some of my readers to the books themselves for their singularly lucid explanations of the spiritual significance of the doctrine of evolution. The conclusion to which Mr. Fiske brings his readers in the concluding paragraph of the second book may fairly be regarded as the confession of faith of the foremost American evolutionists of his time.

Of some things we may feel sure. Humanity is not a mere local incident in an endless and aimless series of cosmical changes. The events of the universe are not the work of change, neither are they the outcome of blind necessity. Practically there is a purpose in the world whereof it is our highest duty to learn the lesson, however well or ill we may fare in rendering a scientific account of it. When from the dawn of life we see all things working together toward the evolution of the highest spiritual attributes of Man, we know, however the words may stumble in which we try to say it, that God is in the deepest sense a moral Being. The everlasting source of phenomena is none other than the infinite Power that makes for righteousness. Thou canst not by searching find Him out; yet put thy trust in Him, and against thee the gates of hell shall not prevail; for there is neither wisdom nor understanding nor counsel against the Eternal.

The opposition to Mr. Fiske was for a time seemingly successful: it disappointed his ambition and President Eliot's desire, for it prevented his appointment to a professor's chair in Harvard University. But it can hardly be doubted that it added to his usefulness. It enabled him to understand the religious opposition to the doctrine of evolution and to give to that doctrine an exposition of its spiritual implications which none of the leaders of the new thought in England had ever attempted to do. The bitterness of the opposition was gradually mitigated and finally almost wholly disappeared. He began to be invited by ministers to preach in their pulpits; his biographer gives the title of three addresses that he prepared to meet these invitations: "The Mystery of Evil"; "The Cosmic Roots of Love and Self-Sacrifice"; "The Everlasting Reality of Religion." And in 1879 he was elected a member of the Board of Overseers of Harvard College, the body which with difficulty had been induced to allow him to occupy a professor's chair, even temporarily, less than ten years before. Of his subsequent service to his countrymen by his deservedly popular contributions to the history of his country I do not speak, for this essay is devoted solely to an estimate of John Fiske—Evolutionist.

Here, therefore, I must leave him, at forty-three years of age, the acknowledged leader of the evolution movement in the United States, and recognized as their colleague and peer by such leaders of evolutionary thought in England as Spencer, Huxley, Tyndall, Lewes, Lyell, and Darwin. Of his home life an indication is afforded by his charming dedication to his wife of the volume in which he brought his career as a teacher of evolutionary philosophy to its close:

TO

MY WIFE

IN REMEMBRANCE OF THE SWEET SUNDAY MORNING
UNDER THE APPLE-TREE ON THE HILLSIDE
WHEN WE TWO SAT LOOKING DOWN INTO FAIRY WOODLAND
PATHS AND TALKED OF THE THINGS
SINCE WRITTEN IN THIS LITTLE BOOK
I NOW DEDICATE IT

Something like a quarter of a century ago, preaching at Yale University, Sunday morning, I announced that in the evening I would speak to the students on evolution and religion. The lecture room of the Y.M.C.A. building was crowded and overflowed into an adjoining room and into the hallway; and when, after speaking nearly half an hour, I announced a recess in order that young men who were engaged or desirous to attend evening service in any of the churches might do so, not enough went out to leave room for outsiders waiting an opportunity to come in. To-day such an announcement would detract rather than attract. The student world is no longer perplexed by the supposed contradiction between science and religion; that is, between the recognized laws of the material world and the spiritual consciousness of men. This world neither rejects science as infidel nor religion as a superstition, though it has rejected much of the old theology and has reinterpreted and reëstimated the Bible.

This change has been accompanied by radical changes in religious thought, but not by a loss of faith. On the contrary, and any one who is familiar with college life knows that much more respect is paid to-day by our college students not only to ethical rules, not only to the spirit of Christianity, but also to its institutions. The work of the Y.M.C.A. is far more effective; the attendance at church service where attendance is voluntary is larger; where attendance is required the attention is better and more reverent. That this change in doctrinal views has been accomplished in this country with a gain, not a loss, in religious life is largely due to the influence of three men—James McCosh, Henry Ward Beecher, and John Fiske.

In England the churches met the evolutionists either with bitter hostility or with cold indifference. Doctor Martineau signified a qualified acceptance of evolution; but his qualifications involved a flat denial of an unbroken progress, and therefore of evolution, as John Fiske defines it, "God's way of doing things." The whole subject is conspicuous by its absence from the writings of such liberal theologians as Maurice, Stanley, and Robertson. In this country evolution was welcomed by Doctor McCosh, the president of its largest Presbyterian college, and by Henry Ward Beecher, the pastor of what was then its largest and most famous Puritan church. And Mr. Beecher was instrumental with others in procuring the republication in this country of the work of the leading evolutionary authors in England, preached and lectured extensively in favour of the theory and of its application to the problems of the religious life, and joined with Mr. Fiske in a testimonial dinner to Herbert Spencer on the occasion of Mr. Spencer's last visit to this country. Mr. Fiske, approaching the problem of evolution and religion from the scientific side, separated himself from his English contemporaries by his faith in "The Everlasting Reality of Religion," and in the immortality of the spirit of Christianity. To no one man more than to John Fiske do we owe the fact that in this country science and religion are not foes, and that in increasing numbers their respective advocates recognize in each other comrades, seeking by different paths to come to a knowledge of the truth.

EDWARD EVERETT HALE, AN AMERICAN ABOU BEN ADHEM

Abou Ben Adhem (may his tribe increase!)
Awoke one night from a deep dream of peace,
And saw, within the moonlight in his room,
Making it rich, and like a lily in bloom,
An angel writing in a book of gold:—
Exceeding peace had made Ben Adhem bold,
And to the Presence in the room he said,
"What writest thou?"—The vision raised its head,
And with a look made of all sweet accord,
Answer'd, "The names of those who love the Lord."
"And is mine one?" said Abou. "Nay, not so,"
Replied the angel. Abou spoke more low,
But cheerily still; and said, "I pray thee then,
Write me as one that loves his fellow men."
The angel wrote and vanished. The next night
It came again with a great wakening light,
And show'd the names whom love of God had bless'd
And lo! Ben Adhem's name led all the rest.

NO ONE who really knew Edward Everett Hale could have doubted that he loved God. As much as any man I ever knew he understood the saying of Christ: "I call you not servants, but I have called you friends."

100

He and I many years ago conducted together one Sunday morning a service in a Baptist church in the Adirondacks. I preached the sermon; he made what is infelicitously called the "long prayer." After he had prayed, it seemed to me quite unnecessary for me to preach. For by his prayer he had brought us into the immediate presence of God, and that is what we go to church for, is it not? I was specially impressed not with the literary beauty of his prayer as with the prayers of Robert Louis Stevenson, but with the spiritual beauty of his prayer, as with some of those in the Book of Common Prayer. I did not notice then, I do not recall now, the form of his prayer. But I was conscious of an invisible presence in the room, of One with whom he was talking "face to face." Nothing else counted.

There is a great difference between the Religion of Humanity and the Humanity of Religion. John Cotter Morison has interpreted the Religion of Humanity. In his volume entitled "The Service of Man" he contends that the service of God has been an injury to the human race and for it we need to substitute the service of our fellowmen. That was not Edward Everett Hale's faith. Nevertheless, I think if the Angel had come to him he would have hesitated to write himself down as one who loved the Lord and would have said with Abou Ben Adhem

> "I pray thee then,
> Write me as one that loves his fellow men."

Under the title "A New England Boyhood" Doctor Hale has written a charming account of his early home, his school and his college life, and of Boston in the second quarter of the nineteenth century. To that story and to the remarkable biography by his son Everett Hale, Jr., I am indebted for the little history in this article beyond my own personal recollections.

Edward Everett Hale was born in Boston, May 14, 1822. His father was the owner and editor of the Boston *Daily Advertiser* when that journal was the recognized organ of the intellectual aristocracy of eastern Massachusetts. The daily paper was less a gatherer of news than it is to-day, but its editorial pages exercised a greater influence on public opinion. His father was a cultivated scholar; had a fine literary sense; kept up his Latin; read French and German easily. His mother, the son tells us, "was the only woman in Boston who could read German when I was a boy," by which I understand that he simply means that she was the only woman in Boston within his acquaintance who read German. The boy was born into a literary atmosphere, and from early boyhood was used to books, newspapers, and magazines, and the machinery of producing them. "All of us," he says, "were born into a home crammed with newspapers, books, perfectly familiar with types and ink and paper and proof-sheets and manuscripts." The children wrote and printed books and newspapers. At one time "they wrote a whole library. It still exists—the Franklin Circulating Library—little booklets of perhaps three or four inches square, in which are printed by hand youthful tales in many volumes." Thus the boy was born, not with a silver spoon in his mouth, but with a pen in his hand, and acquired the kind of culture which can be acquired only during childhood and in a cultivated home.

He entered Harvard College at thirteen years of age, after four years at the Latin School. There are no advantages without some conpensating disadvantages. To an eager mind accustomed to living among books and getting knowledge by a process as natural as breathing the mechanical processes of the school were wearisome. "I may as well say," he says, "first as last, that school was always a bore to me. I did not so much hate it as dislike it as a necessary nuisance." Nevertheless, he proved himself a good scholar, both in school and college. He had parts in the sophomore, junior, and senior entertainments and exhibitions; won college prizes for two dissertations; was one of the first eight in the Phi Beta Kappa; and graduated second in his class.

The college in his time was scarcely less mechanical than the school. The students learned their lessons and recited them to the professors. Young Hale got his lessons conscientiously, but found time in addition to read novels, study history, hunt for wild flowers, do philosophical experiments, and take an active part in college student life. I am not sure but that a college course which allowed such students as Edward Everett Hale and Phillips Brooks time for their own independent intellectual activities would not afford better training than the modern course which fills the student's life so full of prescribed readings that he has no time to follow his own literary inclinations. Perhaps the modern method is better for the average boy, the older method better for the eager student. Those pessimists who lament the tendencies of modern college life might do well to compare the college of 1917 with the following experience of young Hale in the college of 1837:

"On conversing this morning with those who had been present at prayers, I found that there had been considerable noise, and that one or two of our class were *drunk*. On going to morning prayers [they] found a good many

panes broken in University window. There was a good deal
of noise in Doctor Ware's recitation-room. There were
one or two apples and a lemon which were being thrown
constantly from one side of the room to the other, to the
imminent danger of the heads they happened to be aimed
at. In the evening after supper . . . I heard a tremendous explosion which I thought was a pump blown
up . . . . I found that either this, or a later explosion which I did not hear, was made by a torpedo put
on the sill of one of the windows of University." Ex-
plosions followed every night for several nights, and these
grew more serious as time went on. Three months later,
"when we went to prayers this morning we found the
chapel in great confusion, owing to the explosion of a bomb
placed in front of the pulpit. The windows were all broken,
almost every pane of glass being destroyed, the front
of the high platform on which the pulpit stands was blown
in, the plastering broken in several places where pieces
of the shell had entered, woodwork of pews, window-panes,
and seats hurt in some places, the clock injured, part of the
curtain inside of the pulpit torn away, and a couple of in-
scriptions in immense letters on the wall to this effect: 'A
bone for old Quin to pick.'"

Graduating at seventeen years of age, young
Hale decided to enter the ministry. His mother
especially, but also his father, had always desired
him to be a minister, and his friends in college
had known of his general intentions long before
his graduation. "He did not, however, desire
to study in the Divinity School. Just why, is not
clear. Perhaps it was in part a piece of his life-

long objection doing anything in a mechanical way, a feeling that made him through life critical of all institutional processes of education." So the son interprets his father's motive, I think correctly. Doctor Hale was by temperament and training an independent. He had no inclination to model himself after any prescribed pattern, and it would have been really impossible for him to be run into a mould. He had to be himself. He was preordained to be the architect as well as the builder of his own mind.

The motive that took him into the ministry was not a profoundly spiritual one. "He was not," his son says, "very deeply impressed by the responsibilities and opportunities of a minister's life." And he says himself: "One prime reason for the choice of my profession was my desire to be in a walk where I might press my general literature." His ambition, however, was not merely a literary ambition. He chose the ministry partly because it offered an opportunity for a literary pursuit, but also partly because it offered an opportunity to be "at the same time useful and helpful to all kinds of persons who were not so fortunately placed in the world as himself." The first of these motives may have been the earlier one, but the second soon became and always remained the dominating motive of his life.

The author of Genesis has described in a figure the secret of man's double nature. He was made of earth, but into him God breathed the breath of his own life. Jesus used this figure in a play upon words which I venture to interpret to the English reader by a paraphrase: "The breath of God bloweth where it will, and thou hearest the sound thereof, but canst not tell whence it cometh and whither it goeth; so is every one that is born of the breath of God." Doctor Hale has left a record of his experience of this breath of God upon his own soul. He was in Albany, where he had gone to aid in an effort which a few were making to establish a Unitarian church in that city. It was before his first pastorate. He was about twenty-two years of age; he was alone, a stranger in a strange city, and doubted whether the people of the so-called parish even knew that he was in town. Sixty years after, he described the experience which then came to him unsought but never to be forgotten:

Perhaps it was to this loneliness that I owe a revelation which stands out in my memories of life. I had been reading in my musty, dark bedroom by an airtight stove. I think I was reading the *Revue de Deux Mondes*. But I put the book down for what people used to call reflection, and I saw or perceived or felt that I was not alone and could not be alone. This Present Power knows me and loves me. I know Him and love Him. He is here, I am here. We are together. And it is a companionship much closer than I could have with any human being sitting in that chair.

The biographer thinks that his father was a believer in theological doctrine. That depends upon what is meant by "theological doctrine." Theology is defined by the Century Dictionary as "The science concerned with ascertaining, classifying, and systematizing all attainable truth concerning God and his relation to the universe." I do not think that Doctor Hale ever was interested in ascertaining, classifying, and systematizing all attainable truth concerning God and his relation to the universe. In 1874, replying to an inquirer who had asked for some books which would explain to him the Unitarian faith, Doctor Hale replied: "What I do or do not happen to think about one thing or another is of very little consequence, if only I have the infinite help of God's holy spirit, which does come to any man who believes God is, that God loves him, and is eager to help him as being indeed his child." It was not the organization of thought but the abundance of life that interested Doctor Hale. To this correspondent he said, "Live with all your might, and you will have more life with which to live."

This consciousness of God was the foundation of Doctor Hale's character and the inspiration of his ministry. "I know," he wrote in one of his letters, "that that divine spirit which guides us always, led me, even in boyhood, to choose such themes, shall I say, as the fit starting-places for the duties of the pulpit. That perfect love casts out fear, and that this love must show itself in action and not in word—this may be said to be a fair foundation for whatever the pulpit has to say or do." It is true that Doctor Hale was always a loyal Unitarian, and did very much to inspire modern Unitarianism. What he meant by Unitarianism he made clear by referring to its origin. "Unitarians," he said, "were first so called [in Hungary, 1563] because they believed in the unity of religion for all Christians, whatever their especial creed, whether Lutheran, Calvinist, or Socinian." His Unitarianism was that of Doctor Martineau, who objected to the title, and permitted it under protest. Not the creed, but the spirit of a church which insisted that unity should depend on the spirit, held both of them loyal to the Church in which they were born. They were Unitarians because they both believed that the unity of Christendom should depend not on a common creed but on the unifying spirit of faith, hope, and love.

But Doctor Hale was much more than a preacher of ethical culture, much more than a social reformer. It is true, as his son says, the

father was one of the pioneers in the modern movement for social work; but that work was always
inspired by his faith in the living God. "Hospitality, education, charity in the life of a church
are all subordinate to worship," he said. This
spiritual faith converted his early desire to be
helpful into a passion for helpfulness. Charles
Lamb and Leigh Hunt ceased to be his models.
He enjoyed literature as a recreation, but he
had no interest in merely playing with ideas.
Thought became his instrument. His stories
were parables. It will be difficult to find anywhere a keener satire of that specious internation-
alism which repudiates love of one's own country
than is furnished by "The Man Without a
Country"; or a better satire on the modern habit
of self-measurement by the mere quantity of
one's activity, than "My Double and How He
Undid Me"; or a more inspiring interpretation of loyalty to Jesus Christ by service
and sacrifice, rather than by profession, than
the story "In His Name." The biographer tells
us that his father regarded that as his best story,
and I agree with him. It is not more popular
than "The Man Without a Country," but it is
the interpretation of a profounder life.

Doctor Hale was naturally an individualist.
The demands made upon him by the needs of the
community in his first parish, the city of Wor-

cester, and the call of his heavenly Father which those needs interpreted to him, made him from the beginning of his pastorate a social worker. Long before Doctor Parkhurst coined the phrase, "The church is the minister's force not his field," Doctor Hale had adopted this principle. Neither church nor pastor was concerned with spiritual experiences alone. "Wherever there were those who had no one else to stand by them in their social life—whether it were to help them to some work that should give them a daily wage or to offer them some association and fellowship which should make their lives happier or more effective —there, in his view, the Church of the Unity should be at hand to counsel and help." His first call to Boston, to a church well established and a congregation made up of older people, but without Sunday-school or benevolent institutions, he declined. The second call to Boston won him because the church was largely made up of young people, energetic, wide awake, eager for work and for someone to guide them. What that church became under his organizing and inspiring ability, and what Doctor Hale became through its influence as a leader in every form of Christian philanthropy, are a part of the history of the American Church.

I regard the Jewish and the Christian religions as essentially one religion, and the Old Testament

111

and the New Testament as essentially one book. Judaism is that religion in the bud, Christianity is that religion in the blossom. What Isaiah promises, Jesus fulfils. And this is the only world religion that lays emphasis on the truth that the way to please the heavenly Father is to work with him for the happiness and welfare of his children. Edward Everett Hale's service of man was his way of serving God; his love of God inspired his love for his fellowmen.

The difference between denominations is superficially a difference in creeds; it is really a difference in temperaments. It appears in the books of the Old Testament and in the Apostles in the New Testament. Matthew has the temperament of an historian; he represents historical Christianity. John has the temperament of a poet; he represents mystical Christianity. Paul has the temperament of a philosopher who is also a poet; he represents doctrinal Christianity. James has the temperament of a moralist; he represents ethical-culture Christianity. His definition of religion interprets his temperament: "Pure religion and undefiled before God and the Father, is this, To visit the fatherless and widows in their affliction and to keep himself unspotted from the world."

Doubtless Edward Everett Hale believed in historical Christianity, in mystical Christianity,

and in doctrinal Christianity, but his temperament led him to put the emphasis of his life
on practical Christianity. He was no agnostic;
he did not substitute for the service of God the
service of man. But his service of man was his
service of God. In that respect he was typical
of his age. The twelfth and thirteenth centuries
were mystical, the sixteenth and seventeenth
centuries were doctrinal, the twentieth century
is practical. There is room in the heart of the
Father for all his children; the time will come
when there will be room for them all in the
Church.

Edward Everett Hale was always loyal to his
denomination. He was a Unitarian partly because he was born and brought up in a Unitarian
home and a Unitarian church, partly because the
climate of the Unitarian church suited his temperament. But the conception of God which
illuminated his life and his writings were more
Christlike than the conception of God which
darkened some of the sermons of Jonathan
Edwards, and his conception of religion as a life
of service was more harmonious with the teaching of Christ than the conception of religion as a
self-conscious godliness which famous saints in
the past have struggled to attain. He never
could have written the "Confessions of Augustine" or "John Woolman's Journal" but

neither Augustine nor John Woolman could have written "In His Name," or the motto which is perhaps Doctor Hale's greatest contribution to religious literature: "Look up not down, forward not backward, out not in, and lend a hand." I wonder whether he realized at the time that he was simply translating into modern phraseology Paul's summary of Christian experience: "Faith, hope, and charity, and the greatest of these is charity." Whatever was the occasion that led to his writing of that now world-famous motto, it is certain that it was the natural expression of his own inner life.

He was care-free to a fault. His loose-fitting clothes indicated a wearer who cared more for comfort than for appearance. To have and to hold did not interest him; to be and to do, did. His eagerness to accomplish gave his work an ease and spontaneity which was the secret of its charm and one of the secrets of his power. Whether he was writing an article for a magazine or a letter to a friend, whether he was speaking to a friend or addressing an audience, he was essentially a conversationalist. Queen Victoria is said to have complained that Gladstone always addressed her as though she were a public meeting. Doctor Hale always addressed a public meeting as though it were a friend. That he put careful thought into his

114

speeches was quite evident, but unless I am
much mistaken he put that thought into what he
would say and not into the form in which he would
say it. Most New England ministers think in
philosophic terms and then endeavour to translate
their thoughts into the speech of the common
people. Doctor Hale thought in the forms and
phraseologies of the common people.

He looked out not in. I do not think in all his
writings is to be found a piece of self-examination
such as characterized the writings of many of
his Puritan forbears. He was more eager to
serve God than to enjoy him, and enjoyed him
by serving him. He neither practised nor ad-
vocated spiritual vivisection.

He was not a partizan of any party in either
Church or State; nor the enlisted adherent of any
cause. He was not an abolitionist, nor a prohibitionist, nor a socialist, nor was he enrolled
in the ranks of their opponents. How catholic
he was as a churchman an incident in my experience illustrates:

When, obedient to the command of my doctor,
I resigned in 1898 the pastorate of Plymouth
Church, I was in my sixty-third year and was
depressed. My life interests had always been
in my work and I thought my life work was over.
It is true that I was still the editor of the *Outlook*, but I had visions of a gradual failure there

also. Edward Everett Hale, before yet I had succeeded in getting my full release from Plymouth pulpit, asked me to preach for him for two successive Sundays, and when I declined because of my wife's earnest request that I take a few months of absolute vacation from all work, Doctor Hale renewed the invitation, extending the request the following year to four Sundays. Then I gladly accepted. The invitation no less than the service was a tonic. I have not been able to find any record of the sermons preached, but my recollection is that I took this opportunity to put before a Unitarian congregation my interpretations of The nature of man, The nature of Christ, The nature of sacrifice, The nature of the Bible. In doing so I omitted, as I have habitually omitted throughout the fifty years of my preaching, the much-battered words of controversial theology, such as Total Depravity, Trinity, Vicarious Atonement, Plenary Inspiration—words conspicuously absent from the Bible and generally from devotional literature. This omission was not due to any concession to Unitarian feeling, but to the fact that my aim in my religious teaching, whether by voice or pen, has never been to advocate a theology but always to promote spiritual life. Nearly twenty years of fairly active work in the pulpit and the press have passed since then, and I am still writing and preaching, but I can never forget the debt of gratitude I owe to the minister of another denomination, often counted a hostile denomination, for the following letter, which Edward Everett Hale wrote me at the close of those four Sunday services.

Jan. 29, 1900, Roxbury
Monday morning.

DEAR DR. ABBOTT:

I shall stay at home this morning—so I shall not see you.

All the same I want to thank you again for the four sermons: and to say that I am sure they will work lasting good for the congregation.

More than this. I think you ought to think that such an opportunity to go from church to church and city to city—gives you a certain opportunity and honour—which even in Plymouth Pulpit a man does not have—and to congregations such a turning over the new leaf means a great deal.

Did you ever deliver the Lectures on Preaching at New Haven?——

With Love always
Always yours
E. E. HALE.

I have said that Doctor Hale was not an adherent of any cause. That sentence requires a word of explanation. He was an advocate of many causes but he did not belong to or train with any organized body of reformers.

117

SILHOUETTES OF MY CONTEMPORARIES

Previous papers in this book, especially the sketches of President Hayes and General Armstrong, have indicated the radical division in the Republican party at the close of the Civil War, one section holding that if the ballot followed emancipation the work would be completed, the other holding that the ballot without education would be a peril not a safeguard. The attempt to follow emancipation with national aid to education after a vigorous and at first hopeful struggle, failed. Doctor Hale's interest in that attempt, in which Senator Hoar was a leader, is interpreted by himself in the following letter, which has an historical as well as a personal interest:

UNITED STATES SENATE,
WASHINGTON

February 23, 1904.

DEAR DR. ABBOTT:

I have read with great interest your study of Mr. Hoar's character. It is an excellent review of the book. If you really want to know who killed the national education plan, when he was in the House, I think I can tell you. Dr. Gilman told me that he thought, and they all thought it was going through. It had the coöperation of some of the best southern men, of all the northern men not impracticable and of the Cabinet; when it was savagely attacked by your friends of the New York *Nation*. It seems as if they acted on the general principle of attacking anything which seemed to promise well. Gilman thinks that but for them we should have had for twenty years a thorough system of education at the South supported by the National Treasury.

I am to speak here one of the last days of March at the inauguration of the new President of Howard University. I believe I shall pronounce in favour of a national endowment of a dozen such schools as Hampton. Mead says, and I rather think he is right, that the seven battleships which they are trying to make us build this winter will cost more than all the endowments of all the colleges. This is so absurd that it seems as if it could be hindered.

Truly and always yours
EDWARD E. HALE.

I have quoted this letter in full partly because it indicates Doctor Hale's possession of a quality with which I do not think he is generally accredited, that of statesmanship.

A great statesman, however wide and diverse his interests, generally accomplishes his result and wins his reputation by concentrating his life energies on some one achievement: Cavour, on the unification of Italy; Bismarck, on the creation of Imperial Germany; Gladstone, on leading England out from a feudalistic into a democratic basis; Abraham Lincoln, on creating a united and emancipated Republic. Edward Everett Hale was not, and in the nature of the case could not be, in this specific sense a statesman. He was a preacher, interested, as all preachers ought to be, in men and in whatever

119

concerned the men of his time. But his clear comprehension of our Reconstruction Problem and our Industrial Problem showed him possessed of that apprehension of fundamental principles and that prevision of future events which constitute at least two essentials of the mind of a statesman.

In 1895 Mr. Albert K. Smiley invited to his hotel on the Shawangunk Mountain at Lake Mohonk a number of gentlemen and ladies to what came to be popularly but erroneously called a "Peace Conference," though at every session Mr. Smiley laid emphasis on the fundamental fact that it was not a mere peace conference but a conference to study the problem how a substitute could be found for war as a means of securing international justice. The name he gave to the meeting was "Conference on International Arbitration." To that question Doctor Hale in the first session offered an answer which has since been practically accepted by the world's greatest statesmen. That speech is one of the very few I have heard in my lifetime which I dare attempt to report, in abstract, without the guidance of any manuscript, more than a quarter of a century after it was delivered.

Arbitration, said Doctor Hale, is not the remedy. The remedy is a permanent court of justice, a supreme court of the nations analogous to the

Supreme Court of the United States. Arbitrators are selected after a controversy has arisen and passions and prejudices are aroused. They represent the two parties, generally with an umpire to hold the balance between them. No fundamental principles are settled by their decision; only the immediate question is settled, and that usually by a compromise. A permanent court exists before the controversy arises, its existence tends to abate the prejudices and passions which that controversy would otherwise kindle, it is selected for the judicial character and impartial spirit of its members, its object is not primarily to secure peace but to establish justice, and by its decision it settles principles that will prevent future disputes of a similar character from arising. And he proposed a plan for such a court which, if I am not mistaken, does not differ essentially from that which Mr. Elihu Root and his colleagues have proposed and the European nations have accepted for the International Court which it may well be hoped will be adopted and in session at no very distant date.

This speech was as a lighted match applied to dry wood ready to be kindled. In May, 1896, the *Outlook* was able to say editorially: "It is considerably less than a year since Edward Everett Hale made his remarkable address before the Peace Conference at Lake Mohonk, urging in lieu of International Arbitration the organization of a permanent tribunal, to which, as of course, all issues of civilized nations should be referred for settlement. The idea seemed then, probably, to those who heard him, that of a poet, who dared to present a moral ideal far in advance of his times, but which a future generation might adopt. To-day it is seriously taken up, approved, urged by as wise and representative an assembly of American jurists, statesmen, diplomats, and educators as has perhaps ever been brought together on our continent." And the *Outlook* added a report of various notable addresses and public meetings called without concert in various parts of the country to urge on Congress and on the country this plan of a permanent tribunal, culminating in a national meeting of the first public importance held that month in Washington.

That from the first a permanent tribunal was in the thought of Doctor Hale no mere poet's dream is clear from the following extract from a letter which he wrote me ten years later, in 1906, preceding the Second International Conference at The Hague:

I am really distressed that I cannot be at the Conference, but I cannot. . . . I wish that your Conference might simply consider itself as preparing for the Hague Conference—and that you could rule out all that did not really help that way. As I have said to Friend Smiley, "Cut off the Frills and Feathers."

Doctor Hale was not an international lawyer, but he had a definite sense of the value of international law and a definite and evidently practicable plan for substituting in the settlement of international disputes an appeal to reason for the appeal to force, by appealing to the judicial department of government in lieu of appealing to the military department. In this he was in 1895 so far in advance of the age that even yet, more than quarter of a century after, the statesmen have not got his simple, and now generally accepted, plan in working order.*

Neither was he a constitutional lawyer. But he had very definite ideas respecting the fundamental principles of the United States Constitution and the rights and liberties both of local communities and of individuals which it was intended to safeguard. To these ideas he gave characteristic expression in a keen but good humoured criticism of some of our public teachers in the press. He put a high value on personal

---

*He preached in 1889 at Washington a sermon in which he foretold the creation of a Permanent International Court, probably to be suggested by the United States. See "The Life and Letters of Edward Everett Hale," by Edward Everett Hale, Jr., Vol. II, pp. 381, 2.

liberty and believed that the development of the capacity for self-government would require time and patience and was worth taking some risks of temporary misadventure. I wonder what he would say to-day to the passion for power which incites in some reformers the desire to regulate by law the cut and length of ladies' dresses and the height of the heels of their shoes. The passion for governing other people is no longer confined to Englishmen, Scotsmen, and Irishmen:

UNITED STATES SENATE
WASHINGTON, D.C.

My Dear Friend: Dec. 14, 1904.

. . . .

So many Englishmen, Scotchmen, and Irishmen are engaged on our newspapers that *editorials* get printed in absolute ignorance of the Principles of the Government or even of Administration. Godkin, for instance, knows as little of the Constitution as I do of the interior of the Foreign Office at Ispahan. I have seen the *Tribune* speak of the President as the *Ruler of America*.

Hearst's paper spoke of the *Nation* as having the original Right to the soil or coal of Pennsylvania. The women think that Congress can make a Divorce Law for Massachusetts. I wish you would make somebody write a stiff article about this.

Always
Edward E. Hale.

To Dr. Lyman Abbott.

This letter was dated, the reader will observe, from Washington. It was written in the eighty-seventh year of his age while he was fulfilling his last public service, that of Chaplain to the United States Senate. He kept his lively interest in public affairs and his boyish humour to the end. He died in June, 1909, eager to the last. On June 6th he wrote in his diary: "Doctor Temple had forbidden my preaching to-day. . . . The first White Sunday in 65 years without a White Sunday sermon."

On June 10th he died.

JOHN G. WHITTIER, MYSTIC

W HITTIER," says Mr. Higginson, "was a politician before he was a reformer." In 1832 he would probably have been nominated for Congress, but had not quite reached the constitutional age of twenty-five years when the election occurred. He was an enthusiastic admirer of Henry Clay, for whom he wrote several spirited campaign poems. But when the Slavery issue arose he was drawn into the anti-slavery ranks. He at first coöperated with Garrison, but could not agree in either temper or methods with that acidulous reformer. If not a leader, he was a wise counsellor in the gradually developing party of liberty. He unsuccessfully urged the Liberty party not to make a separate nomination for President in 1860. "Do not gratify your enemies by making any nomination," he wrote to Elizur Wright. After the Mexican War he urged his fellow-abolitionists not to oppose the admission of Texas into the Union, but to fight against its admission as a slave state. He was mobbed for his anti-slavery utterances and on one occasion his life was in serious peril. If his health had permitted, he might perhaps have been a political leader in those troublous times, for he had principles, courage, tact, and ambition. But he was without means. "My brother and myself," he wrote, "are almost constantly engaged in the affairs of our small farm." And he was without health. In 1830 his physician warned him that he had not a year to live unless he gave up his political work. From the storm and stress of political campaigning he was driven to quieter but more enduring activity with his pen.

When I knew him, this was all past history. The Civil War was over; the slave was emancipated; abolition was an accomplished fact. If my treacherous memory can be trusted, I first met him some time in the 'seventies in the hospitable home of Governor Claflin of Massachusetts. I wonder if there is any man of wealth in our time whose home is dedicated to the uses to which their beautiful home in Newtonville was dedicated by Mr. and Mrs. Claflin. It was a meeting-place of preachers, authors, reformers. I lay down my pen for a moment and recall them —men and women all of whom have now joined the choir invisible. Mrs. Stowe, Henry Ward Beecher, John B. Gough, John G. Whittier, Charles Dudley Warner, Miss Sarah Orne Jewett, are a few of those in the procession that passes before me. Once I attended a house party given by Mrs. Claflin to a selected company, parents and children, gathered from the North End of Boston for their poverty and their need. A gaunt woman, one of the guests, approached the hostess with the question: "What made you think of doing this? Jesus Christ told you, didn't he?" "Yes," said Mrs. Claflin, "I guess he did." "I thought so," was the reply, "I knew you couldn't have thought of it yourself."

Mrs. Claflin in her "Personal Recollections of John G. Whittier" reports a conversation between Whittier and Emerson from which defenders of the faith might well take a lesson in theological tactics:

Whitter. I suppose thee would admit that Jesus Christ is the highest development our world has seen.

Emerson. Yes, yes, but not the highest it will see.

Whittier. Does thee think the world has yet reached the ideals he has set for mankind?

Emerson. No, no, I think not.

Whittier. Then is it not the part of wisdom to be content with what has been given us, till we have lived up to that ideal? And when we need something higher Infinite Wisdom will supply our needs.

I wonder what Emerson replied.

In the summer of 1878 I called on Mr. Whittier in his country home, Amesbury, Massachusetts. Had he invited me when I met him at the

Claflins? Or had I a letter of introduction to
him? Or, being a journalist, had I more enterprise than modesty? I do not know. I only
remember with what hospitality I was received
and how gladly I accepted the invitation to stay
to dinner. Of Amesbury I have no recollection
whatever. Indeed I am not sure whether it was
at Amesbury I found him. That was forty-two
years ago, and the picture I retain is faded. All
I remember is a story-and-a-half New England
cottage by the roadside, simple furniture, a
simple meal, two middle-aged ladies who were
apparently the joint housekeepers, and the poet-
prophet himself. He must have then just passed
his seventieth year. No one would call his face
handsome; it was better, it was beautiful. The
features were homely, though the forehead was
high and the eyes were luminous. The photo-
graph but poorly represents him. For his face
was a transparency; the spirit within lighted it
up; and photographs rarely, the older photographs
never, interpret the spirit. His illuminated face
has made quite real to me the picture given in
Exodus, of Moses when he descended from the
mount where he had talked with God and "his
face shone." Whittier's was a shining face.

Mr. Whittier's friends have told me that he
rarely talked about himself. I can well believe
it. I do not recall that he told me anything

about his early adventures as an anti-slavery reformer. I know that I was surprised when long after I learned from his biographers of his political ambitions and activities. But that afternoon it was the poet and prophet, not the reformer, whom I met; and he talked freely with me of his religious experience. Perhaps he realized that he was talking to a comrade of half his years who was eager to get the light and life he had to give. Perhaps it was because his thought was not upon himself, but wholly upon that light and life, as was my thought also. Why did I not go back to my hotel in Boston and write it all down while it was fresh in my recollection? I do not know, except that I had from my early youth a prejudice against the diaries and journals so popular at that time and never have kept one myself, save in occasional starts, soon abandoned. Nor shall I attempt now to recall that sacred conversation. But it led to some brief correspondence, and that I may put before the reader because in it Mr. Whittier will speak for himself.

Going back to my editorial office, I presently wrote to him asking him for an article on the Religion of the Spirit. The reader must remember that at that time such books as Sabatier's "Religion of the Spirit," Matheson's "The Spiritual Experience of St. Paul," Hoching's "God in

Human Experience," were very few, and such as existed were little known. In reply to my request I received the following letter:

Bearcamp River House
West Ossipee, N. H.
4th 9 Mo. 1878

MY DEAR FRIEND:

I wish that I could comply with thy request, but the state of my health at this time forbids it.

I entirely agree with thee. The only safe and impregnable position in these days, is the doctrine of the Divine Immanence—the inward Guide and Teacher. What Fénelon calls "the inexpressible voice of Christ in the soul." Believing and feeling this we have nothing to fear from the revelation of science or the criticism which assails the letter and the creed.

In the Sept. *Atlantic* I have endeavored to give expression to the mystics of the Romish Church in the 15th century who were believers in a purely spiritual religion, independent of creed, ritual or even the outward letter of Scripture.

The only real proof of the inspiration of the sacred books is that we find the laws and the prophets in our own souls, —that our hearts burn within, as we walk with Christ through the New Testament—that the hymns of David have been sung in our own hearts,—that the Sermon on the Mount accords with our intuitions.

Have thee ever read Barclay's Apology or Dymond's Essays on Moral Philosophy? The subject is well treated in them.

I am very truly,
thy friend
JOHN G. WHITTIER.

The contribution to the *Atlantic Monthly* to which he refers was "The Vision of Eckhard," now familiar to the readers of his works. From it I venture to extract four verses because by this letter he makes it clear that the vision of Eckhard is also the vision of John G. Whittier:

> For the dead Christ, not the living
> Ye watch his empty grave
> Whose life alone within you
> Has power to bless and save.
>
> O blind ones, outward groping
> The idle quest forego;
> Who listens to his inward voice
> Alone of him shall know.
>
> . . . .
>
> My Gerizim and Ebal
> Are in each human soul
> The still small voice of blessing
> And Sinai's thunder roll.
>
> The Stern behests of duty
> The doom books open thrown,
> The heavens ye seek, the hell ye fear
> Are with yourselves alone.

The above letter from Mr. Whittier was written as the reader will see, in April, 1878. In May, 1879, he wrote me again on this subject. The *Friends' Review* had published what was intended to be a commendation of a religious article of mine in the *Christian Union*. What that article was I do not know, and I have not thought it worth while to spend any time in looking it up; for the object of this sketch is not to define or to defend my own theological opinions, but to interpret the spiritual faith of Mr. Whittier or rather to give the reader Mr. Whittier's own interpretation of that faith. The paragraph in the *Friends' Review* to which Mr. Whittier refers and which he had cut out and sent to me in his letter was this. His comment follows the extract:

Lyman Abbott points out how dim is the light given to men by the Spirit compared with the full blaze of the revelation of God and of His truth given in the Gospel. And how the effect of the light vouchsafed to men immediately begets a longing for a personal Saviour—leads to Christ.

5 Mo 6 1879
Danvers

MY DEAR FRIEND:

I enclose to thee a notice of the S.S. Lesson in the Christian Union on Job XXXIII, 14-30 which appeared in the *Friends' Review* (a paper which professes to advocate Friends' principles)—of the 12th ult.

It is evident that the writer has greatly misrepresented thy views, so contrary to those expressed in some of thy Editorials. If the light given *immediately* by the Holy Spirit is *dim*, what must that be which comes to us through the medium of human writers in an obsolete tongue? Is

133

the bible more and better than the Spirit which inspired it? Shall the stream deny the fountain?

The writer in the *Review* evidently has adandoned the root principle of the early Friends and really has no reliance upon anything but the *letter*.

Thy friend
JOHN G. WHITTIER.

In my library there has been accumulated a large amount of material—letters, pamphlets, newspaper reports of sermons and lectures, and the like. In this material I have found a sermon of mine on "John G. Whittier's Theology," preached in Plymouth Church, Brooklyn, in 1893. It is said in this sermon that the faith once delivered to the saints is not a creed or form of doctrine; "it is always a personal experience in the heart of the individual"—"a seed planted which takes on many forms and many growths." I quote here a few sentences from an embodiment or expression of this faith in the biography of John G. Whittier, from which I quoted more fully in that sermon:*

God is One; just, holy, merciful, eternal, and almighty, Creator, Father of all things. Christ the same eternal One, manifested in our Humanity, and in Time; and the Holy Spirit the same Christ, manifested within us, the Divine Teacher, the Living Word, the Light that lighteth every man that cometh into the world.

---

*I presume that this expression of Whittier's faith is to be found in the authorized biography by Samuel T. Rickard, Houghton Mifflin Company.

JOHN G. WHITTIER

The Scriptures are *a* rule, not *the* rule of faith and practice, which is none other than the living, omnipresent spirit of God. The Scriptures are a subordinate, secondary, and declaratory rule, the reason of our obedience to which is mainly that we find in them the eternal precepts of the Divine Spirit, declared and repeated, to which our conscience bears witness.

My ground of hope for myself and for humanity is in that Divine fulness of love which was manifested in the life, teachings, and self-sacrifice of Christ. In the infinite mercy of God so revealed, and not in any work or merit of our nature, I humbly yet very hopefully trust.

I am not a Universalist, for I believe in the possibility of the perpetual loss of the soul that persistently turns away from God in the next life as in this. But I do believe that the Divine love and compassion follow us in all worlds, and that the Heavenly Father will do the best that is possible for every creature he has made. What that will be must be left to his infinite wisdom and goodness.

Writing this sketch as I am approaching my eighty-fifth birthday, I accept this admirably clear and comprehensive statement as an adequate expression of my own spiritual faith, developed by over sixty years of Bible study and Christian teachings; and I gratefully wonder if I am not more indebted for that faith to John G. Whittier's influence than I have ever before realized.

GENERAL SAMUEL CHAPMAN ARM-STRONG, EDUCATIONAL PIONEER

THE Civil War destroyed the industrial system of the South and put nothing in its place. War never does put anything in the place of what it destroys. It does not reform; it only prepares the way for others to reform. The Negroes set free by emancipation gathered in extemporized camps; white refugees gathered with them. In such camps these refugees, outcast by the war, had to be fed, clothed, and sheltered temporarily while a new labour system was organized. The difficulties in the way of such organization seemed at the time almost insuperable.

The slave-holding class had an affection for their slaves, but no respect. Their feeling has been not inaptly compared to that of a good master for a loyal dog. Cotton was the staple product of the South, and it was the prevailing opinion that cotton could be raised only by slave labour. That in half a century Negroes would be lawyers, doctors, merchants, bankers, successful planters, and in increasing numbers landowners, would have seemed as preposterous a prophecy as that men would be outflying the birds. Many in the South believed that some form of serfdom must follow slavery, temporarily if not permanently; more were dazed by the revolution and knew not what to expect or what to prepare for.

The North had no affection for the Negro, was glad that he was in the South, and hoped that he would stay there. But the inherited opinion that labour should be free had been converted by the Civil War into a passionate conviction. That emancipation must be followed by a process of industrial reconstruction was realized by only a few leaders. The dominating political and economic philosophy of the decade might be stated thus:

The Negro is a white man with a black skin. We have struck the manacles from his wrist and made him free. Let him go where he likes and do what pleases him for what wages he can get. Give him the ballot and he can protect his freedom; give him an education and he will use his freedom aright. Meanwhile, public and private charity may see that he does not starve, and the beginnings of education can be attempted by missionary and philanthropic associations. The period of transition cannot be very long.

But the prejudice against Negro education was

not confined to the South. "Nigger teacher" was a term of reproach in some circles in the North as well, and one of the early Freedmen's Aid Societies "was rent asunder by the unwillingness of a part of its members to coöperate in any movement looking toward the education of the Negro, though they were willing to provide him with food and clothing in order to prevent suffering and death."*

Something such was the chaotic state of public opinion when in the winter of 1866 General S. C. Armstrong called on General O. O. Howard, head of the Freedmen's Bureau, and asked for an appointment. He was the son of missionary parents in Hawaii, a graduate of Williams College, had received there inspirational training from Mark Hopkins, author of "The Law of Love and Love as a Law," on graduating had entered the Army, had received a baptism of fire at Gettysburg, and as colonel of a Negro regiment had acquired a familiar acquaintance with the Negro's temperament and character, and had earned promotion by his notable service in the Southern field. General Howard discerned in the young brigadier-general a kindred spirit. Both were brave soldiers, both earnest Christians, both convinced believers in the right of all men

---

*Special Report on the Results of Emancipation by the American Freedmen's Union Commission, 1867.

of whatever race or colour to be treated justly and given an opportunity for self-development. General Armstrong never wore his heart upon his sleeve; but no one could be in his presence fifteen minutes and not realize that he had a heart. General Howard put him in charge of a camp near Hampton, Virginia, an appointment which gave him control as agent of the Freedmen's Bureau over ten counties in Virginia and as Superintendent of Schools over the educational work in a large, loosely defined area embracing those ten counties. His description of his charge is quoted here from one of his early official reports.

Coloured squatters by thousands and General Lee's disbanded soldiers returning to their families came together in my district on hundreds of "abandoned" farms which the Government had seized and allowed the Freedmen to occupy. There was irritation, but both classes were ready to do the fair thing. It was about a two-years' task to settle matters by making terms with the landowners, who employed many labourers on their restored homes. Swarms went back to the "old plantations" on passes with thirty days' rations.

There were seven thousand Negroes within a radius of three miles from General Armstrong's office, thirty-five thousand in his district, and eight thousand rations were distributed every day to those who but for these rations would have died of starvation. By appeals to friends in Boston he found places of domestic service in the North for nearly [a thousand refugees. In October, 1866, three months' notice having been given, all rations were stopped except for those in hospitals, and he was able subsequently to report that "trouble was expected, but there was not a ripple of it or a complaint on that day." He attributes this to the spirit of the Negroes. "Their resource was surprising. The Negro in a tight place is a genius." I attribute it quite as much to the confidence of these children in their new care-taker, a confidence which he won in a surprisingly short time.

From the first General Armstrong seemed to get, as by inspiration, a clear idea not only of *what* had to be done but *how* to do it. Slavery had destroyed industrial ambition in the South. Work done under compulsion, whether from the lash or from hunger, never is and never can be inspiring. To convert slave labour into free labour required a change in the spiritual habits of the Negro. Mr. Lincoln had said that God had given every man one brain and a pair of hands and it looked as though he intended that brain to control that pair of hands. But this statement had secured but little attention. There were no industrial schools in the United States, North or South, unless two or three engineering schools like the Troy Polytechnic and the Stevens Institute may be so regarded. Providing industrial education for the Negro met with bitter opposition. Southern aristocrats thought that any education would spoil him; Northern abolitionists thought that industrial education discriminated against him.

If I had space, I should devote it to an appreciative sketch of the work which, immediately at the close of the war, various missionary societies of the North undertook for the education of the Negroes. An army of teachers entered the South before the army of soldiers left it. Hundreds of men and women, as self-devoted as General Armstrong, offered their services for the difficult and thankless task. Of the societies entering this work the American Missionary Association was one of the first and most important. It was organized before the Civil War because neither the home nor the foreign missionary societies would bear their testimony against slavery, and when slavery was abolished it saw in the hordes of ignorant Negroes its opportunity. In the beginning of his work General Armstrong was dependent both for moral and financial support on this society. But this sketch is a portrait of General Armstrong, and must pass by without further mention the educational army with which he always cordially coöperated.

From the first he saw clearly what not all of his contemporaries saw, that it was not enough to transfer the New England schoolhouse to the Southern states. From the first he had an almost unique vision of the unique need of the hour, and to the realization of that vision he and his successor, Doctor Frissell, gave their lives with single-hearted and untiring devotion. Their object I state here in a sentence from memory as Doctor Frissell once stated it to me. "The object," he said, though I am not quoting his words, "is to give the Negro boys and girls what the State gives by the public school. The public school gives the education; the family provides the support for the pupil while he is studying. Hampton *gives* the education to the pupil; and it provides productive work which enables the pupil to feed and clothe himself." The pupils were paid for the work, not in cash, but in credit on the books of the school.

From the first Hampton Institute was a Christian school—Christian, but not anti-Jewish; Protestant, but not anti-Catholic; industrial, but not anti-cultural. From the first also it preserved Negro traditions and respected the Negro temperament. A satirical writer years ago criticized Christian missions in the East as an endeavour to make middle-class Englishmen out of native Hindus. There was no attempt at

Hampton to make Yankees out of Africans. Every Sunday evening the whole student body gathered in the chapel and spent half an hour singing the Negro spirituals, followed by a brief address. The custom is still kept up. Never has death seemed to me more friendly, or the celestial world only an "Other Room" adjoining this in God's great house, than when I have heard those eight hundred voices join in singing "Swing Low, Sweet Chariot." From the first the school has never officially recognized a difference in the rights or privileges of the races. Hampton is in fact a Negro school. But there is nothing in its constitution or its charter to prevent white pupils from being admitted. A large portion of the money granted to the institution was given on the express condition that all should be admitted without condition as to colour, and the charter granted by a Virginia Legislature in 1870 accepted this condition.

The school was opened in 1866 with fifteen pupils; on April 26th it had thirty pupils doing manual work in the morning and studying in the afternoon and evening. In 1918 I visited the school. It then had 140 buildings; 1,100 acres of land; 1,802 pupils, including those who attended the summer school; 2,098 graduates, besides 7,500 who had gone out from Hampton after having taken a partial course. With the exception of the church, capable of seating about fifteen hundred, and the Robert C. Ogden Auditorium, seating about twenty-five hundred, and possibly two or three cottages, all the buildings have been erected by the students themselves and all the farm work and all the household work of the school, including that of an inn upon the grounds, is done by the pupils.

What has been called, I think without exaggeration, the most efficient and capable industrial school in the United States, if not in the world, is primarily due to an extraordinary corps of co-workers, dominated by the same spirit and guided and inspired by two leaders of singularly different temperament, but inspired by the same spiritual ambition—General S.C. Armstrong and Dr. H. B. Frissell. If life is a campaign, then Armstrong may be compared to General Sheridan and Frissell to General Thomas; if life is a garden, then Armstrong selected the site, ploughed the ground, sowed the seed and planted the seedlings, and Frissell weeded, pruned, trained the growing plant, and harvested the crop; if life is a school, then Armstrong gave life to the pupils, Frissell discovered unconscious life in the pupils and developed it in them. General Armstrong was a pioneer, Frissell a teacher, Armstrong a creator, Frissell an organizer. I wish I had space to essay a snapshot of them both, but I must confine myself here to the one selected to be the subject of this sketch.

I do not find in his daughter's biography any description of General Armstrong's appearance. The faded shadow-picture in my memory is that of a young man, somewhat under six feet, of slim build but broad shoulders, with no superfluous flesh, erect in pose, with keen eyes that looked not at you but into you, and an electric energy at once physical and moral.

I say *young* man, for he had up to the last the charm of youth. To him every day was a new beginning. In every day was the freshness of interest which belongs to youth. He would never have passed the dead line of fifty, not if he had lived to be a hundred. He lived in the present for the future. I never heard him talk of the past, would hardly have known that he had been a general in our Civil War except for the soldier's title which fitted him so perfectly that he could not have laid it off if he had tried. I was surprised when I began the preparation of this article to learn that he was only four years my junior. I had always thought of him as a much younger man. Years, infirmity, failing health, did nothing to abate his unquenchable humour. One day, after paralysis had laid him aside from work and his physician had prescribed for him a walk of a few hundred yards as his only exercise, he was taking the prescription with his intimate friend, Robert C. Ogden. They were talking of the *Evening Post,* and Mr. Ogden asked General Armstrong what he thought of its editor, Mr. Godkin. "I think," said General Armstrong, "that he would begin the Commandments with 'I am the Lord thy Godkin, thou shalt have no other Godkins before me.'"

He was an electric battery, and in his writing, his conversation, his speeches he scintillated. He was unconsciously epigrammatic. Spontaneous epigrams, always kindly, though often keen, made him an intensely interesting conversationalist. When you talked with him, you naturally said only enough to start him talking or to keep him going. From his daughter's biography I select by chance a few of these spontaneous epigrams:

"Laughter makes sport of work."

In a speech to his students—"Spend your life in doing what you can do well. If a man can black boots better than anything else, what had he better do? Black boots."

After a visit to some of the missionary schools in the South in answer to the question, "What was your impression?"—"One sweetly *solemn* thought comes to me o'er and o'er."

To his students—"Doing what can't be done is the glory of living."

To the argument at Lake Mohonk that a cer-

tain policy he had proposed was impossible—
"What are Christians put into the world for but
to do the impossible in the strength of God?"

From letters—"Philanthropy is the thief of
time."

"The chief comfort of life is babies. Institutions are a grind, humanity a good deal of a
bore; causes are tiresome; and men of one idea
are a weariness."

"What you spend on yourself you lose; what
you give you gain."

"When it comes to the scratch, I believe in the
prayers of the unorthodox—why are they not as
effectual as any? From the deep human heart to
the Infinite Heart there is a line along which will
pass the real cry and the sympathetic answer—
a double flash from the moral magnetism that
fills the universe."

"Human life is too weak to be an incessant
flight toward the Sun of Righteousness. Wings
will sometimes be folded because they are wings."

"God's kings and priests must drudge in seedy
clothes before they can wear the purple."

"To get at truth, divide a hyperbole by any
number greater than two. . . . In animated
narratives divide facts by ten."

Such spontaneous epigrams as these are both
revealers of character and inspirers to life. A
"table talk" of General Armstrong on the plan

of the "table talk" of Coleridge and that of Luther would be a classic.

With this freshness of interest in life was combined the courage of youth, but not the rashness. Rashness leaps before it looks; courage looks before it leaps; timidity does not leap at all. The wise man in asking, What shall I do? takes counsel of courage; in asking, How shall I do it? takes counsel of caution. It is because General Armstrong was both inspired by courage and guided by caution that he won the confidence of men who had no ambition to be pioneers. He wanted for his school a building which would cost seventy-five thousand dollars; he had on hand two thousand dollars. He used the two thousand dollars to dig the cellar and lay foundations, and so had a "mute appeal" to speak to the visitors from the North who came down to lay the corner-stone, and it talked to good purpose. The students learned brickmaking by making the brick and bricklaying by building the walls, and at the end he had made both a building and the builders. The vision appealed to the idealists, the method to practical men—and he got the money.

I felt that by the triple task that he had set himself he was killing himself. To overcome race prejudice in the South, to educate for useful service Negroes at Hampton, and to create in the North an understanding of the problem and at the same time the means to carry the work on was too much for any one man to undertake. I joined with other friends in urging him to secure a permanent endowment for Hampton, and so relieve himself from the Northern campaigning. "Yes," he replied in substance, "I would like an endowment for Hampton; we need it. But I do not wish to avoid the begging campaign. To educate the North is as important for the Nation as to educate the South and the Negro." At the same time that the old Abolition Society was formally by resolution disbanding because nothing remained for it to do, General Armstrong was organizing his campaign to carry forward the work which the Abolition Society had only begun. "It failed to see," said he, "that everything remained. Their work was just beginning when slavery was abolished." He was right. No historian can adequately estimate the value of the service to our national development rendered by the campaigns carried on in the North by General Armstrong, Doctor Frissell, Booker T. Washington, and the Christian churches. To these campaigns we owe the consciousness that the race problem is a national problem, and with that consciousness a better mutual understanding between the North and the South and between the white and the coloured races.

With this youthful interest, this cautious courage, this ever-reinvigorated energy, was coupled a spirit of humility which I have not often found in men who do things. He had self-confidence, but was singularly free from self-conceit. I had written in what was then the *Christian Union* an article about Hampton, not then known and honoured as it is to-day, and received from him the following characteristic letter of appreciation:

Parker House
Boston, December 18, 1884.

DEAR DR. ABBOTT:

Thanks for your kind article in the last *Xian Union* on Hampton.

It is very cordial and earnest and will do good. It is not easy to live up to where you place me. The true prayer for a man in a responsible position is—

Lord, help me to not make an ass of myself. I often pray this fervently. . . .

Yours sincerely,
S. C. ARMSTRONG.

I have no doubt that this was true. With all his seeming abandon he walked "circumspectly." Yet his abandon was not a seeming. One of his teachers tells me the following incident illustrating his habitual self-forgetfulness. To one of the Hampton boys was assigned the care of the General's house and waiting on him at his meals, for the General ate with the rest of the teachers in a room in the students' hall. As this teacher was passing out from dinner the General beckoned to her for some consultation and was immediately absorbed in the business in hand. Presently, his eyes fixed on the teacher and his mind on their topic, he took up the mustard pot at his side and, without turning his head, reached it out toward the waiter. The boy took it, for a moment was puzzled, then smiled, put down the mustard pot, took up the General's tea-cup and brought it back refilled, and the General took it and went on with his meal and his conversation, quite oblivious of the little comedy in which he had taken a part.

He did not live in a "fool's paradise." "Mere optimism," he said, "is stupid; sanctified common sense is the force that counts." But neither did he live in a fool's purgatory. "It remains to make the best of things. Those who are hopeless disarm themselves and may as well go to the rear; men and women of faith, optimists, to the front." The cynic scoffs at those who will not face facts; but there is no man who so persistently refuses to face facts as the cynic. General Armstrong saw the evil in men, but also saw the good, and instinctively, and without knowing it, gave life and power to the good. There is no work which seems to me so discouraging as "raising money"—the need seems so imperative, the public so apathetic. General Armstrong apparently believed that if you know how to strike the rock in the desert you can always get water. "Begging trips," he called them, and he rejoiced to escape from them to the more congenial companionship of the school at Hampton, but his habitual attitude toward the apathetic North was one of cheer. "I never cease to wonder," he wrote in one of his reports, "at the patience and kindness of those who daily listen to appeals from here [Hampton] and some other quarters, the wear and tear of which can be hardly less than that of those who solicit aid from these overtaxed givers."

He carried the same spirit into his campaign appeals for teachers to give themselves. The difficulty of his job appealed to him, and he believed that it would equally appeal to others. Life was to him what a game is to the chess player —the more difficult the problem, the more interesting it is. Thus his appeals were what Christ called a fan; they separated the wheat from the chaff, discouraged the timid and self-distrustful, inspired and attracted the courageous and self-denying. Professor Peabody in his story of Hampton quotes the following summons from General Armstrong to Miss Helen W. Ludlow, which he rightly calls "one of the classic passages of Hampton literature."

GENERAL SAMUEL CHAPMAN ARMSTRONG

Hampton, September 27, 1872.

DEAR MISS LUDLOW:

Five millions of ex-slaves appeal to you. Will you come? Please telegraph if you can.

There's work here and brave souls are needed. If you care to sail into a good hearty battle where there's no scratching and pin sticking but great guns and heavy shot only used, come here. If you like to lend a hand where a good cause is shorthanded, come here.

We are growing rapidly; there is an inundation of students and we need more force. We want you as teacher. "Shall we whose souls are lighted?" etc. Please sing *three* verses before you decide, and then dip your pen in the rays of the morning light and say to this call, like the gallant old Col. Newcome, "Adsum."

Sincerely yours,

S. C. ARMSTRONG.

Miss Ludlow responded to the bugle call "as though called into action," and was in the school from 1872 until 1910, some years after the General's death.

My impression is that General Armstrong was a Congregationalist; but he did not *belong* to the Congregational denomination; he did not belong even to Hampton Institute. He belonged to God and to God's world. So far as I know, he never talked about his spiritual experience. I find in his autobiographic fragments two very significant sentences. One: "I would rather minister than be a minister." The other: "True

153

worship is a gentle, sensitive, shrinking emotion that steals softly into hearts in quiet moments, often in response to some beautiful scene; sometimes it comes to us from the faithful true ones near us."

Two favourite religious books of his are said to be Thomas à Kempis's "Imitation of Christ," the most archaic and ecclesiastical of devotional literature, and "Amiel's Journal," the most modern and least ecclesiastical.

After his death a memorandum was found among his papers from which I quote three paragraphs:

Few men have had the chance that I have had. I never gave up or sacrificed anything in my life—have been, seemingly, guided in everything.

Prayer is the greatest thing in the world. It keeps us near to God—my own prayer has been most weak, wavering, inconstant, yet has been the best thing I have ever done. I think this is universal truth—what comfort is there in any but the broadest truth?

I am most anxious to get a glimpse at the next world. How will it seem? Perfectly fair and perfectly natural, no doubt. We ought not to fear death. It is friendly.

To this glimpse of his inner life, the source of his charm and of his power, no friend would wish to add anything.

GENERAL WILLIAM BOOTH, HOME MISSIONARY PIONEER

WHEN the Salvation Army first made its appearance in the United States, I shared the hostile prejudices of most Christian people. The military organization, the uniforms, the cheap music, the street meetings, and the public prayers arrayed against the Army my democratic principles, my Puritan tastes, my temperamental reserve. The theology seemed crude, the preaching emotional, the piety loud, exhibitory, pretentious. But when a little later I spent several winter months in England, I found there the saloon keepers and the gamblers to a man arrayed against the Army; and the moralists and churchmen divided in opinion concerning it. The naïve confessions of Salvation lads and lassies uttered between the drum beats in the street had not been convincing evidence of its value; but the fact that generally where it went saloon habitués and drunken brawls decreased in number outweighed all criticisms of its offences against taste. And when on one of General Booth's visits to America, I think in 1886, I was invited with half-a-dozen

other gentlemen to meet him at "breakfast" I
gladly accepted the invitation.

At this breakfast I found myself a guest of an
Englishman unmistakably of the so-called middle class, but one who possessed in a notable
degree the qualities which Stormonth's (Eng-
ish) Dictionary attributes to a gentleman: "a
man in any status of life who is possessed of good
breeding and refined manners, strict integrity
and honour, kindness of heart and such-like
qualities." I found in him, moreover, a man
singularly free from that moral partizanship
which is a common defect in moral reformers.
One of his principal reasons for inviting the half-
dozen men who gathered about his breakfast
table to meet him was that he might get at the
truth respecting the drinking habits in America.
One of his guests was the editor of a weekly journal of national circulation, one an author whose
volume on American life and manners had a more
than national reputation, one a journalist whose
connection with the newspaper fraternity gave
him special advantages for knowing the social
customs in every section of the country. And
it was a noteworthy circumstance that all agreed
in the testimony that there was more drinking
and less drunkenness in America than there had
been in our boyhood.

The desire to get at the exact truth on a question of vital interest, the capacity to receive and weigh it, and the ability to keep his own counsel were three characteristics in General Booth which impressed me as preëminent in that memorable interview. His biography by Harold Begbie portrays a man in his earlier years of great intensity of feeling. To one who criticized him for going too fast he replied: "What do you mean? I know no 'Flying Dutchman' or 'Flying Scotchman,' or any other kind of flying railway train that goes fast enough for me. Time is so precious that unless it can be spent in sleeping or working, every minute of it is begrudged, and my feeling whenever I seat myself in a train is, 'Now, engine driver, do your best and fly away.'" But when I met him, probably in 1886, his natural impetuosity was tamed and harnessed. The impression he left on me was that of a man of great power, both physical and spiritual, but power under absolute control.

This introduction seemed necessary in order to inform the reader that the following shadow-picture of General Booth, based on Mr. Harold Begbie's interesting Life of the General, is sketched by one who might perhaps call himself not an unprejudiced historian but a bi-partizan historian, one who is accustomed to measure all religious movements not by their conformity to traditions and conventions but by their practical effect on conduct, and whose first inherited prejudices against the Salvation Army have been conquered by some study of its fruits and some acquaintance with its personnel. Some of its methods I could never employ, most of its work I should be incompetent to undertake, to its military discipline I should find it very difficult as a member to submit, but ever since that memorable interview with its founder I have been, whenever the opportunity afforded, a hearty and even enthusiastic supporter of its beneficent work.

William Booth was born on April 12, 1829. His father was an unsuccessful business man whose disappointed ambitions were almost wholly materialistic. The son described him significantly but irreverently in the sentence: "My father was a Grab, a Get." He lost his money and died brokenhearted. His mother was probably of Jewish origin. After her husband's death she set up one of those little shops which the traveller is almost sure to see in any English town or village, perhaps wondering how the shopkeeper gets enough out of it to pay the rent. The boy was apprenticed to a pawnbroker because his father thought this business would give the son the best chance to make money; and in the first years of his life he was divided between a commercial ambition and a

spiritual aspiration. "The three steady things
in his mind were," says his biographer, "first,
the determination to get on in the world; second,
the ambition to work for political change; and
third, a longing to right himself with God."
The longing to right himself with God was
strengthened and intensified by his attendance
at Methodist meetings, and particularly by the
preaching of one evangelist by the name of
Caughey, but the origin of his spiritual restlessness neither William Booth nor his biographer
attempts to explain. "How I came," says Mr.
Booth, later, "to this notion of religion, when I
saw so little of its character manifested around
me, sometimes puzzles me." It was not, however, only his own lack of religion that oppressed
him. He was made by his business familiar
with poverty and was burdened, not merely by
the material poverty but even more by the
spiritual poverty which was constantly before
him. He felt more and more the call of the
streets; more and more he realized that spiritual
poverty was the real cause of the wretchedness
with which in his business he was continuously
in contact; and this restlessness in himself and
this realization of the wretchedness of others
about him became at length an irresistible call
to the ministry.

At that time in England, especially in London,

humanitarianism was regarded as the hobby of a few fussy philanthropists. Little concern was shown by the churches for the bodies of men. There was no system of national education; no idea of housing reform; no factory legislation; no provision for poverty but the poorhouse. There were voices crying out, sometimes with pity, sometimes with indignation, for reform—Dickens, Lord Shaftesbury, Carlyle, Ruskin, John Stuart Mill, Cobden, and Bright; but none of these had the support of the churches, and none of them was inspired by any recognized and avowed religious motives. These reformers all addressed themselves to the cultivated and comfortable people of England. The voice which was to compel the attention of the English people to conditions at once shameful and dangerous came, curiously enough, from an evangelist whose education had been in the pawn-shop.

William Booth was able afterward to fix on the day when this change in his life from the pawn-shop to the pulpit took place, a change which was to have so extraordinary an influence on the religious life, not only of England, but of the world. A Methodist minister offered him financial support for three months if he would devote himself to preaching. The youth accepted the offer, notified his master of his purpose, packed his portmanteau, and went out to begin a new life. Three things, he afterward wrote, marked this day: It was Good Friday; it was his birthday; and, "most important of all, was that on that day I fell over head and ears in love with the precious woman who afterward became my wife." Catherine Mumford became not only a devoted wife and an inspiring companion but a wise counsellor, and by her wisdom and devotion earned the title of "Mother of the Salvation Army." Mr. Begbie characterizes her in a few sentences as "an able, masterful, and brilliant young woman, who delighted in table controversies, who was somewhat proud of her logical adroitness, and was able, brilliant, daring, and righteous to a fault; but one doubts if her heart at that time had asserted its equal partnership with her brain."

William Booth, before formally entering on the ministry, had attracted attention in the Methodist Church by occasional and not infrequent lay preaching, and was from the first a real though somewhat rude and unconventional orator, who moved his audiences by his profound conviction, his passionate faith, and his power of dramatic interpretation. His theology he had imbibed from the Christian Church of that epoch. "This earth occupied the central place in the stellar universe; man, created in perfection, had chosen sin and had rejected God; God, in his mercy, had visited and redeemed man; man had it in his power, every man, to accept or to disdain that redemption; everlasting happiness would be the lot of those who accepted, everlasting misery the lot of those who rejected the divine mercy." "This was," says his biographer, "the absolute and indubitable theology of the whole of Christendom."

The preachers of that time believed that they believed it; but William Booth realized it, and in his preaching it was apparently simplified to this: The human race is in rebellion against God; Jesus Christ has come to conquer that rebellion; Christianity is war against the devil and all his works; the duty of every individual is to lay down the weapons of his rebellion and join the forces of Christ; and the duty of the preacher is to call for recruits. This with William Booth was not a theological opinion, but from the first a vivid experience. He believed that this war was going on in his own soul, that it was going on in the souls of all men, and that this revolt against God was the cause of the poverty, the wretchedness, the degradation, and the sin which were at once the shame and the peril of England. I cannot see from his biography that he ever preached what would ordinarily be called theological sermons—sermons the object of which was to prove or to define the Trinity or the divinity of Christ or the vicarious atonement or the infallibility of the Bible. Theological theories did not interest him. What he sought after was the rescue of human life from the degradation and misery which were the results of the revolt against God and the rejection of God's law and God's love.

This applied Christianity he pressed home upon audiences with passionate earnestness and with dramatic power. His biographer quotes an account which General Booth has given of one of his earliest sermons:

I described a wreck on the ocean, with the affrighted people clinging to the masts between life and death, waving a flag of distress to those on shore, and, in response, the lifeboat going off to the rescue. . . . I reminded my hearers that they had suffered shipwreck on the ocean of time through their sins and rebellion; that they were sinking down to destruction, but that if they would only hoist the signal of distress Jesus Christ would send off the lifeboat to their rescue. Then, jumping on the seat at the back of the pulpit, I waved my pocket handkerchief round and round my head to represent the signal of distress I wanted them to hoist.

One reads this account without a thrill, perhaps even with amusement; but if the reader had been one of an emotionl audience under the spell of this orator's passionate faith and believed that this grotesque act was the natural expression of the orator's genuine feeling, it would not seem to him grotesque.

Crowds flocked to hear this new preacher. The Methodist chapels would not hold them. Scores crowded to the altar to seek for prayers or to confess themselves converted. Young Booth went to London to pursue some studies better to fit himself for his life-work, but the call of the congregations followed him and proved irresistible. Doubtless the peculiar fascination of an audience for a born orator attracted him; but far greater was the impelling power of the young preacher's faith that really the world of men were doomed to perish in an endless conflagration unless they were rescued by the instant and energetic efforts of individuals who had been already rescued. Inspired by that faith, he could not refuse to respond to calls which came to him from many quarters. To the woman who was about to become his wife he writes of his reception in Lincolnshire: "My reception has been exceedingly pleasing. Even the children laugh and dance and sing at my coming, and eyes sparkle and tongues falter in uttering my welcome. Yesterday I had heavy work. Chapel crowded. Enthusiasm ran very high. Feeling overpowering, and yet not the crash we expected. My prospects for usefulness seem unbounded. But God knows best, and where He

wants me, there He can send me." And again:
"Yesterday I preached to crowded congre-
gations, and we had a crushing prayer meeting.
Some splendid cases."

But his sermons were not merely dramatic,
they were apparently well thought out. He
thanks Catherine Mumford for an outline that
she sends him and asks for more: "I want a sermon on the Flood, one on Jonah, and one on the
Judgment. Send me some bare thoughts; some
clear, startling outlines. Nothing moves the
people like the terrific. They must have hell-
fire flashed before their faces, or they will not
move. Last night I preached a sermon on
'Christ weeping over sinners', and only one came
forward, although several confessed to much
holy feeling and influence. When I preached
about the harvest and the wicked being turned
away, numbers came. We must have that kind
of truth which will move sinners." In this request he indicates what was always the purpose
of his preaching. It was not to instruct men in the
truth. It was to move them to instant decision.

Pages of Mr. Begbie's Biography of General
Booth are taken up in describing the problems
the young preacher met, the difficulties he encountered, and the courage and energy with
which he encountered them. He was always
subject to what would now probably be called

nervous dyspepsia. He married a wife who was always an invalid, and he divided his time unevenly between nursing her and ministering to the public. He was too independent to submit to ecclesiastical authority which endeavoured to curb his impatient spirit, or to accept money on conditions which required from him submission to any kind of authority. At one time, later in his ministry, money and, the author thinks, probably a fine hall in East London at a cost of something like 7,000 pounds, were offered to General Booth, together with a generous settlement upon both Mr. and Mrs. Booth if he would consent to settle permanently in East London and not roam about; and the offer was promptly declined.

No man can enter upon such an undertaking as that of General Booth in such a spirit as his without awakening strong opposition. The greatness of his spiritual ambition appalled some, the intensity of his faith rebuked others; some of his methods provoked not unreasonable criticism; the very greatness of his popular successes excited jealousy in his contemporaries. Greater than any of these obstacles, perhaps greater than all combined, was the coldness of the churches and the hardness of the world. "If," says Mrs. Booth, writing to her mother, "the present effort disappoints us, I shall feel quite tired of tugging with the churches and shall insist on William

166

taking a hall or theatre somewhere. I believe
the Lord will thrust him into that sphere yet.
We can't get at the masses in the chapels."
At one time he thought sincerely of uniting with
the Congregational churches for the sake of the
larger liberty which the Congregational policy
would give him. But the theology of the Con-
gregationalism at that time was Calvinism, and
the Calvinistic theology held that man could
not repent without the *special* grace of God. Its
honest acceptance would have required a fundamental reconstruction of William Booth's
message. When in reading a theological treatise,
which a Congregational minister lent to him, he
reached this conclusion, he threw the obnoxious
book to the other side of the room, and never
after considered the proposal to accept a theological servitude in order to escape an ecclesiastical servitude.

When the Methodist Conference decided to
recall him from the work of an evangelist and
assign him to a circuit, he left the Methodist
Church, went to London, and started there the
"Christian Mission." It appears to have been
a purely individualistic enterprise; where the
funds came from is not clear. Out of this
Christian Mission, which continued its work in
London for a year or two, grew, by a natural
process, the Salvation Army.

Having once laid off the harness of the Church William Booth never took it on again. At one time prominent dignitaries in the Episcopal Church desired to make an alliance with the Salvation Army, so that it would become, if not a branch, at least a recognized instrument, of the Church of England. But this would have required a tacit, or at least an apparent, recognition of the principle that acceptance of the two historic creeds of Christendom and the two sacraments, Baptism and the Lord's Supper, were necessary to complete acceptance of Christianity.* To this General Booth would not consent. Many, probably most, of the crowd were gathered from the slums. To them the sacraments were obstacles, not aids, to the Christian life. Mr. Booth's attitude toward the sacraments was the attitude of Paul toward circumcision: neither Baptism and the Lord's Supper nor the absence of Baptism and the Lord's Supper profiteth anything, but a new creature in Christ Jesus. Though Mr. Booth had been baptized and doubtless had often partaken of the Lord's Supper, his study of the Bible convinced him that neither Baptism nor the Lord's Supper was required by Jesus Christ, and he would not re-

---

*In 1833 the High Church party in the Church of England had agreed upon the statement "that the only way of salvation is the partaking of the Body and Blood of our sacrificed Redeemer, that the means of this is the Holy Sacrament of His Supper, and the security for the due application of this is the Apostolical commission." See "John Keble: A Biography," by Walter Loch, M.A.

quire them of his converts, although he cordially assented to their voluntary use by those who desired them.

But neither did kneeling for prayer and professed Christian conversion satisfy him. He wanted to see a changed life, and often he did see a changed life. Gradually experience drove him to the conclusion that the only way in which he could lastingly change men and women was to make them from the moment of their conversion seekers and savers of the lost. From almost the birth of the Salvation Army its two fundamental principles were: Work with men if you would work for them, and work to make them Christian workers.

Mr. Booth had been in London over twenty years before the Christian Mission took on the name of Salvation Army and adopted substantially an army organization and General Booth assumed the title and the powers of a commander-in-chief. For ten years more it remained largely a recruiting organization, though carrying on important philanthropic work. Then the philanthropic work received a new impulse and a new importance.

Late one night in the year 1888 William Booth, returning to London from a campaign in the south of England, crossed one of the bridges on the Thames, and was thunderstruck to find sleeping there men and women in huddled forms on the stone benches. In the morning he greeted Bramwell, his oldest son, who had become his chief-of-staff and his understudy, with an imperious demand that something be done. "Do something, Bramwell," he cried, "do something. Get a shed for them, anything will be better than nothing; a roof over their heads, walls around their bodies." Almost simultaneously sentence of death from cancer was pronounced upon Mrs. Booth by the doctors after a careful consultation. Watching at the bedside of his dying wife, while the shelter- and food-depots which he had set up were inadequately meeting the demand of outcast humanity, he wrote what was to prove an epoch-making book, "In Darkest England." Upon its publication in 1890 I wrote in what was then the *Christian Union* that "the essential principle of this volume lies at the foundation of any effective and far-reaching philanthropy; this, namely, to use the waste of modern civilization in providing for the men and women whom modern civilization wastes."

By this volume William Booth knocked at the door of rich, comfortable, and complacent England, and pointed her to the beggar who lay at her threshold uncared for. The publication was the sensation of the hour. Its author met with a storm of abuse. He was declared to be un-

truthful, an exaggerator, an alarmist, a vision-
ary, impracticable, demanding the impossible,
seeking to cure the incurable, and at the same
time he was denounced by Single-Taxers and
Socialists for seeking only to alleviate what society ought to cure. He was even accused of
being an ambitious self-seeker aiming to create
an organization of which he would be the head
and which would be dangerous to the State, a
covetous self-seeker aiming to secure vast sums
of money of which he could have the absolute
control. Most important, or at least most prominent, among these accusers was Mr. Huxley,
whose extraordinary charges the curious reader
can find to-day in one of the volumes of his
Essays.

The charges of Mr. Huxley against the Salvation Army may be briefly stated in two sentences: First, that it is a military organization
in which "everyone has taken service on the
express condition that he or she will obey without
question or gainsaying the orders from headquarters"; second, that "the process of degradation of the organization into a mere fanatical
intolerance and personal ambition, which I declared was inevitable, has already set in and is
making rapid progress."

The first criticism assumes that Christians
may never unite in a military organization in

order more effectively to fight organized evil.
That is a proposition which I hold to be entirely
untenable. The Salvation Army is not a church;
General Booth made this very clear: "I do not
want to found a sect," he said. It is an instrument which offers itself to the churches to
carry on certain aspects of their work for which
their organization does not adapt them. If a
free state may have an army to protect the legal
rights of its citizens, the churches may have an
army to resist the subtler but equally dangerous
attacks against the innocent and the ignorant by
forces of evil which a state has not made illegal and
perhaps cannot make illegal. The Church is not
merely a worshipping and teaching organization;
it is also a working and at times ought to become
a fighting organization. The cross is in some
places a summons to war, and in no place more
so than in the great cities in our civilized States.

A liquor saloon in London was carried on for
the purpose of coining money by creating beasts
out of men. Mr. Booth raised the necessary
money, partly out of contributions by the poor,
bought the saloon and turned it into a Salvation
Army hall. No sooner had the conversion been
made than such a storm broke upon him as we
in these days can scarcely imagine. "Hooting
mobs besieged the place by day and by night,
the worst pimps and crimps of London stoned it;

drunken and savage gangs armed with sticks and stones assailed it; for some months the place had to be guarded by police, on many occasions with drawn truncheons. William Booth was many times in grave danger of his life."

A body of Christian men and women form a league for the purpose of promoting purity, temperance, and honesty in a community where law has allowed such conditions to grow up. The object of the league is not merely to control these conditions; it is to abolish them. Have they a right to organize a society on military principles and give to the leader the authority of a commander-in-chief? To that question who will not reply "Yes!" And such conditions, though in less aggravated form, are to be found in every great city in the civilized world. To conduct a successful campaign against them may well be thought to require an army. Those who think so and have enlisted in a campaign whose most warlike implements are a drum and a fife, deserve our whole-hearted support, not our cynical hostility.

Mr. Huxley's second criticism—that the process of degradation of the organization into a *mere* engine of fanatical intolerance and personal ambition—received its answer from the "jury of the vicinage" in William Booth's lifetime. The violent campaign of abuse which even Mr. Huxley's honoured name was unable to make respectable, burned itself out in less than a score of years.

A committee of prominent Englishmen investigated the administration of the "Darkest England Funds," gathered and administered for the conduct of its campaign by the Salvation Army, and after thorough examination reported in detail the careful, thorough, and adequate provisions which had been made against any misappropriation of money. Since the last edition of the Encyclopædia Britannica announces that "the opposition and ridicule with which Booth's work was for many years received gave way, toward the end of the nineteenth century, to very widespread sympathy as his genius and its results were more fully realized," I do not think it necessary to give any further attention to this transient, heated, and sometimes violent campaign of calumnity. It burned itself out in less then a score of years.

General Booth's history of the conditions in England and of the Army's campaign against them, entitled "In Darkest England," was published in 1890. In 1905, fifteen years later, the Freedom of the City of London was presented to General Booth, together with a subscription of one hundred guineas to the funds of the Salvation Army, and he lunched with the Lord Mayor and a select company. It was character-

istic of the man to take advantage of this occasion to make a plea, not for himself nor for the
Army, but, to use his own words, "for the drunkard, the harlot, the criminal, the pauper, the
friendless, the giddy, dancing, frivolous throngs."
A little later he was asked to be a vice-president
of the Bible Society and was given the degree of
D.C.L. by the University of Oxford. His visits
to America during these later years of his life
were an ovation. At the request of royalties
he had interviews with the sovereigns of Den-
mark, Norway, and Sweden, the Emperor of
Japan, Queen Alexandra, the Dowager, Empress
of Russia, the Prince and Princess of Wales in
England. I imagine that of all these receptions and testimonials two must have preëminently impressed him: One, a letter from the
well-known skeptic Goldwin Smith, who wrote,
"It is a signal testimony to the spiritual power
of the founder of Christendom that so many
centuries after His death such a work should be
done under His inspiration and in His name";
the other, the popular reception given to him at
Japan, a feature of which was two prayer meetings in which no less than five hundred people
came on to the stage, seeking with cries and
tears the salvation of God.

To the end of his life General Booth continued a profoundly religious man. He lived

and died believing that the salvation of society depended on the salvation of the individuals of whom society is composed, that men would never be brought into right relations with each other unless they were first brought into right relations with God. But as he grew older his creed became simpler. In his speech to the Lord Mayor of London, delivered in 1905, when he received the Freedom of the City of London, he defined, not indeed the creed, but the religion of the Salvation Army in terms which not all Christian believers would regard as adequate but to which it is scarcely possible that any Christian believers could object as erroneous:

> The religion of the Salvation Army is very simple; any one can understand it. It says to a man: "You must worship God, consecrate yourself to his service, and do what you can for the benefit of those who are around you. You must be good and true and honest and kind and do all you can for the benefit of your family and friends. You must persevere as the days go by, and so shall you have a peaceful dying-bed and a blissful immortality."

Having exerted perhaps as wide an influence on the religious thought and life of the world as any man in his time, he died in England in the eighty-fourth year of his age, honoured by his country, revered by his followers, and beloved by his friends. There might well be inscribed upon his tombstone as the motive of his life the words: "A friend of publicans and sinners."

DANIEL BLISS, FOREIGN MISSIONARY PIONEER

I LAST saw him probably seven or eight years ago. He had passed his eighty-fifth birthday and was about returning to his home in Syria. He had been a missionary in that land for more than half a century, and for thirty-six years president of the Syrian Protestant College. The graduates of that college gave him a farewell supper in New York at a downtown Syrian restaurant. I had the good fortune to be one of the comparatively few American invited guests. He sat in an easy chair that had been provided for his comfort. His body was aged and getting beyond possible repair. But he had all the intellectual courage, the welcoming sympathy, the broad interest, the unfaltering courage, and the genial humour which had made him as a young man a pioneer and a chosen leader among pioneers. When it came time for him to reply to the cordial farewells that had been spoken, his son helped him to his feet, and, leaning upon his crutch, his beautiful face fully framed by his long white hair, he began his speech thus:

"Boys! in this last speech that I shall ever make to you I will repeat the first speech I ever made as a schoolboy:

"'You'd scarce expect one of my age
To speak in public on the stage.'"

He was born to be a teacher. No one is fitted to answer the questions and solve the problems of youth who has not in his own youth formed the habit of asking questions and facing problems. When he was eight or nine years old he cut off one of his toes with a scythe in the hay-field. This started in his mind the question what would become of that toe in the resurrection. His father could give him no better answer than that the resurrection was a great mystery, but God was able to raise the dead. He had patience as well as curiosity, and the question remained unanswered for twenty years, when he reached the conclusion: no resurrection of the body; God shall give a new body. In narrating this incident, he adds: "Since studying Paul I have never, except in memory, seen bones flying in space in search of the old body."

In the first half of the nineteenth century asking questions about religion was generally regarded as dangerous. An old minister remonstrated with the youthful inquirer. "Dan," he said, "you are the most dangerous boy in town."

178

"Why, what evil have I done?" "None; that is the trouble. If you were drunk half the time, your influence would not be so bad. You neither lie, swear, drink, nor quarrel, and others point at you and say, 'Dan Bliss is not a Christian, and yet what a good boy he is.'"

He carried the same spirit with him to college. Graduating in 1852, when the anti-slavery agitation was at its height and Congress had passed a resolution that there should be no agitation of the Slave question during the session, he took for the subject of his graduating address: "Agitation." The spirit of the address is sufficently indicated by a single sentence: "Truth can lose nothing by agitation but may gain all; and Error can gain nothing but lose all."

It indicated both the spirit of the American Board and the non-combative spirit of the young collegian that, three years later, young Bliss, still engaged in that quest for truth which every success converts into a braver quest, obtained an appointment as a missionary to Syria and set sail with his bride in a sailing vessel of three hundred tons burden. Mrs. Bliss has left a graphic description of the perils of what proved to be a perilous voyage.

In 1843 Doctor van Dyck had established a high school in Syria, which in three years had developed into an academy for the training of

teachers and preachers. In 1855 it had twenty-
four students and its curriculum included physics
and the higher mathematics taught from Arabic
textbooks prepared by Doctor van Dyck himself.
Little attention was paid to the English language, but much to the study of the Bible.

It was the success of this school or academy
probably that led to the suggestion in 1862 of an
institute for the higher learning in Beirut. It
was resolved at a gathering of missionaries to
attempt it, and Mr. Bliss was chosen as its principal. Its object was to be, not proselytizing, but
education; its aim, to furnish an education equal
to that of the better American colleges; the
language of the lectures and the textbooks,
Arabic. It was an undertaking that required
an audacious faith and an inexhaustible patience.
The undertaking was sure to meet bitter hostility from the Turkish Government, for apos-
tatizing from the Moslem faith was punishable
by death. "A delegation of Druses called on
the wife of a Druse seminary student who was
seeking admission to the Church and asked her
permission to kill him." Even to this day very
few of the students either in the Syrian College
in Beirut or in Robert College in Constanti-
nople are of Turkish parentage. It could have
at first little welcome from the Syrian Christians,
for they were divided into bitterly hostile sects.

"Mr. Bliss's maidservant, who was a member of the Greek Church, was threatened with death by her own family when she encouraged a Protestant suitor." There was no money, for these missionaries had no notion of taking mission funds to support an educational institute which was not the object for which the funds were given. The money must be raised in England and in the United States, and there was opposition to the enterprise in both countries. To train ministers was all very well, but to prepare boys for other callings—business, law, medicine, engineering, literature—was quite another matter. Sectarian differences at home as well as sectarian differences abroad had to be overcome. The movement was interesting to *all* Christians and therefore did not interest any particular denomination.

Not least of the burdens to be borne was the great variety of tasks imposed upon those who were now proposing to add to them the task of building a college in a community which did not even know what a college was. "You ask about Abby's health," writes Mr. Bliss to his wife's mother. "You must know that she is much better than when she was in America, for could she then take care of a large baby, keep a house, and attend to a houseful of company, make clothes for her husband, self, and baby, besides fitting dresses for others, and in addition to all this carry on a correspondence extensive enough to weary out a common mind?" Nor where his labours less diversified. "A missionary in those days had to be a jack-of-all-trades. To the ordinary life of preacher and pastor he was obliged to add the function of a lawyer in case members of his flock were denied their legal rights; he daily acted as school superintendent; he had to understand the arts of land purchase, building, carpentry; he was indeed often helpless if he did not know something of medicine. In dealing with the government he could hope for little success if he did not know something of diplomacy."

The college was devised in 1862. In 1871 the corner-stone of the main building was laid by William E. Dodge, one of its principal founders, and on that occasion in the following characteristic utterance Doctor Bliss interpreted its spirit:

This college is for all conditions and classes of men without regard to colour, nationality, race, or religion. A man, white, black, or yellow, Christian, Jew, Mohammedan, or heathen, may enter and enjoy all the advantages of this institution for three, four, or eight years, and go out believing in one God, in many gods, or in no god. But it will be impossible for any one to continue with us long without knowing what we believe to be the truth and our reasons for that belief.

182

Upon his retirement in 1902 his son, Howard Bliss, was elected his successor, and continued the work of his father for eighteen years in his father's catholic spirit and with his father's courage. Then, worn out by the tragic experiences through which the college passed during the World War, he came home to die. But the college lives. Under the administration of the father and the son it has grown to a university with seven departments; nine hundred students, drawn from a territory extending from the Ural Mountains to Abyssinia, and from Greece and Egypt to Persia; eighty instructors; twenty-six buildings of stone, crowning a hill overlooking the Bay of Beirut and having 2,860 graduates, many of them occupying positions of commanding influence in the various communities from which they came and to which they have returned. They are its epistles known and read of all men; and the college itself is an enduring monument to the missionary pioneer who had the idealism to see, the courage to undertake, and the patience to accomplish so great an achievement.

DWIGHT LYMAN MOODY, EVANGELIST

WITHOUT office in Church or State; without theological, collegiate, or even high-school education; without a church or society behind him to support him or a constituency, except such as he himself created, to afford him moral support; without any of the recognized graces of oratory; and without any ambition to form a new ecclesiastical organization or a new school of theological thought, and perhaps without the ability to do so; nevertheless, Dwight L. Moody probably spoke to a greater number of auditors than any man of his time in either Europe or America, unless possibly John B. Gough may be an exception, and he spoke on spiritual themes to audiences which were less prepared therefor by any previous spiritual culture than those addressed on such themes by any preacher since Wesley and Whitfield.

More fundamental than the much-discussed question, Are the churches losing their power? is the question, What is the secret of such power as they possess? What is the attraction that draws to the churches, with such regularity, so many men and women of different stations and

184

of varying degrees of moral and intellectual culture? To markets people go to procure food required to support physical life; to dry-goods stores, for clothing necessary for comfort; to theatres, to forget their toil in an hour of amusement; to art galleries and concert rooms, attracted by æsthetic desires; to schools, that they may obtain the results of the experience of the past, and so may avoid the blunders of their fathers. But why do they go to church? What do they expect? What have they a right to expect? What must the churches give to them if the congregations are not to go away disappointed? These questions Mr. Moody's character and career help at once to emphasize and to answer.

Dwight Lyman Moody was born on February 5, 1837. His father's death when he was four years old left his widowed mother with nine children, a mortgaged New England farm, and no money. They were so poor that the creditors, with incredible heartlessness, took from the widow everything she possessed, including the kindling wood from the wood-pile. All the schooling the boy ever had was given to him by the average village school, and that average never was, and is not now, very high. He never became a good speller nor a great reader. At seventeen years of age he went to Boston, got a business position through an uncle on condition that he would go to church and Sunday-school, accepted the condition and loyally fulfilled it, was converted and wished to join the Church but was kept out for a year because one of the deacons did not think he knew enough of the essential doctrines; and two years later went to Chicago, which furnished a more congenial atmosphere for his energetic spirit. Here he applied to a mission for a Sunday-school class, was told he could have one if he could get the scholars together, and appeared the next Sunday with a complete outfit of ragamuffins, "an embryonic Falstaffian army."

His interest in his Sunday work rapidly increased; his interest in his week-day work as rapidly diminished. He was born to be a missionary, as Beethoven was to be a musician or Millet to be a painter. It is a very common experience for business to encroach upon religion; in young Moody's case, religion encroached upon business. He was a creature of enthusiasm; and for making money he had no enthusiasm, for teaching ragamuffins a boundless enthusiasm. When he had saved a thousand dollars, he cut loose from the store and gave himself unreservedly to the mission. His thousand dollars was soon exhausted; but he was not disturbed. When asked what he was doing and how he was supported, his ready reply was, "I am working for God, and he is rich."

No man can understand Mr. Moody who does not appreciatively understand the meaning of enthusiasm. He was an enthusiast, as were Paul, Luther, Wesley. His whole life might be summed up, his whole character portrayed, in three phrases from one of Paul's letters: "In diligence not slothful; in spirit aflame; serving the Lord." To a remarkable degree and in a remarkable measure he united a practical judgment with an enthusiastic spirit, both directed by absolute singleness of purpose.

He possessed, or, to speak more accurately, was possessed by, a miraculous energy. I use the word "miraculous" advisedly. A miracle, as that word is used in the New Testament, indicates a work that excites wonder and is accepted as an indication of extraordinary power. Mr. Moody's work to the end of his life excited the wonder of all who knew him, and the more they knew him the greater was the wonder. To them his work was a demonstration that he possessed a very extraordinary spiritual power. He might be defined as a spiritual athlete. Of course his energy was not literally tireless, but to those who worked with him it seemed so. Life is the best interpreter of the Bible. Mr. Moody's life interpreted to his friends and co-workers the meaning of Christ's words to his disciples: "I have meat to eat that ye know not of."

With this energy, and inseparable from it, was an adventurous spirit. He was never afraid of risks. If he had speculated, he would have made or lost great fortunes—perhaps both lost them and made them. If he had become a "captain of industry," the industry would have been a large one and the workers well organized and to a man loyal to their captain. The greatness of an undertaking always fascinated him. Difficulties in its accomplishment never daunted him. The word "impossible" was not in his vocabulary. There was a curious psychological resemblance between Moody and Grant. One was speechful, the other taciturn; one was a soldier, the other an evangelist. But to both difficulty, opposition, danger were a challenge; neither surrendered to a defeat; both were inspired with incredible courage by the greatness of the service to which they had been called.

Out of his Sunday-school in Chicago grew a Congregational church of which he was pastor, although he was never ordained to the ministry. The Congregational churches habitually use, but their principles do not require, ordination, nor does their ordination confer any ecclesiastical authority. The Chicago fire destroyed his

188

church; at the same time two not particularly conspicuous English Nonconformist ministers invited him to go to England and begin an evangelistic work there, but made no provision for the trip. Doctor Goss in his biography of Mr. Moody thus narrates the result:

That first trip will be long remembered for the incredible manner in which it was undertaken. He set the day for his departure, but did not have a cent with which to pay his expenses. However, this did not seem to disturb him in the least, for he went on with his preparation as if he had millions in a vault. There were still but a few hours left before the departure of the train, and yet the funds were not in sight. The trunks were packed and his family waiting. It was about time for someone to turn up with money, one would think! And sure enough he did! A friend who thought that he would need some "*after he reached England*," handed him five hundred dollars! There have been too many such strange events in his life to make it easy to call them mere coincidences.

The evangelistic mission was successful, although when Mr. Moody reached England one of the two ministers who had invited him was dead and the other dangerously ill, so that he was left without any point of contact with the English except such as he himself could make.

Quite as noteworthy was his undertaking the publication of the "Gospel Hymns." Music had for him no special attraction. But he realized its emotional power, and, perceiving that power in a young man who led the singing at a religious convention, he called on Mr. Sankey to become his co-worker in his evangelistic enterprise and pledged him a financial support. Pretty soon the need of hymn-books that could be scattered through the audiences was felt. If they were needed, they must be had. He went to a London publisher. The publisher refused; he had made the experiment, published a book of revival hymns, and the books had been left unsold on his hands. He went to another publisher, who would publish only in case Mr. Moody would assume all the financial risks. Mr. Moody proposed the venture to Mr. Sankey, and Mr. Sankey prudently declined. But the books were needed as ammunition for the campaign and Mr. Moody was determined to have the ammunition. He had no money, but he had courage. He assumed the entire financial responsibility without knowing where the money would come from if the publication proved to be a commercial failure. It proved to be a commercial success; the "Gospel Hymns" sold by the million; they made a fortune. For Mr. Moody? No! The first profits were given to benevolent enterprises; and when the fortune waxed great it was by a legally executed instrument permanently devoted to endowing schools at Northfield, Massachusetts, organized by him for the purpose of giving the higher education to pupils of moderate means.

This artless faith that all money belongs to the Lord and that it can be had for the Lord's work if one goes about it in the right way to get it, was the secret of Mr. Moody's remarkable success as a money raiser. He started out one day with "the best minister in Edinburgh" to raise money for a mission in that city, the minister taking the lead and asking from ten to fifteen pounds at each call.

"I saw," said Mr. Moody, "it was going to take all winter at that gait, and so (not daring to criticize him) when we came to the next house (that of a very grand and wealthy woman) I said, 'How much are you going to ask *her* for?'

"'Oh, perhaps fifty pounds.'

"I kept still, but when the door opened into the room where she was I just pushed ahead and said:

"'Madam, I have come to ask you for two thousand pounds to help build a new mission down at Carrubers Close.'

"She threw up both hands and exclaimed: 'Oh, mercy! Mr. Moody, I cannot possibly give more than *one* thousand.'

"This reply astonished the timid minister so much that he almost fainted and when they got outside he said: 'You'd better go ahead.' And I did!

The result was that at the end of the day they had raised the $100,000. Not long after, Mr. Moody received a note saying, 'Well, Moody, you raised the money but you used up the best minister in Scotland, and we had to send him off for a three-months' vacation.'"

This story is matched by one in America. He called once on a wealthy man who had made the principle of systematic giving a protection against excessive generosity; he made it a rule never to give more than one hundred dollars at a time. Mr. Moody wanted a large amount—I believe, ten thousand dollars. "But," said Mr. T——, "you know my rule, don't you?" "Yes," replied Mr. Moody, "but I thought it would save your time and mine to give it at once and not require a hundred calls." He got the whole amount. "Father gave all he had," said his son in narrating the incident to me, "and he asked the same from other people."

This miraculous energy, this adventurous courage which characterized Mr. Moody were born of his spiritual faith—faith in God, faith in himself as God's child engaged in doing his Father's work, and faith that in ordinary men there are somnolent spiritual forces which will respond to the call of conscience and aspiration if one only knows how to voice the call. The engineer builds a bridge in serene confidence that he can rely upon the attraction of gravitation, though he neither knows what it is nor why it works as it does. The physician prescribes for his patient with the hope that the disordered body, despite the disorder, will respond to the remedy. As there are laws of the material world in which the engineer has faith, as there are laws of the body in which the physician has faith, so there are laws of the spiritual universe in which the evangelist has faith. Like the serene faith of the engineer in the laws of nature, like the less serene faith of the physician in the laws of the body, was Mr. Moody's faith in the laws of the spirit, and it was one very important element in his extraordinary personality.

In 1885 he was conducting some evangelistic meetings in London. A young physician of the city, who had been confirmed in the Established Church but to whom public worship was little more than a method of paying proper public respect to the Great King, was one day passing the hall where Mr. Moody's meetings were being held. Impelled by a mild curiosity and having a leisure half-hour, he stepped inside to see what a "Moody meeting" was like. The hall was crowded. Someone on the platform was offering a volunteer prayer. It had not the ripened beauty of the Episcopal ritual and did not appeal to the young doctor. The prayer went on—and on—and on—and seemed likely never to come to an end, and, the curiosity of the doctor more than satisfied, he was about to slip out as quietly as he had entered, when a sturdy and rather plain-looking man occupying a chair in the centre of the platform rose and said: "While the brother is finishing his prayer we will sing hymn number ——." The young man stayed. This was not only novelty, it was reality. And then and there Dr. Wilfred Grenfell received the impulse which has made him an apostle of spiritual faith not only to the fishermen of Labrador but to unnumbered thousands in England, Canada, and the United States.

I was once a witness of a somewhat similar illustration of Mr. Moody's personal power, though one not so striking and dramatic. Mr. Moody was holding, with the coöperation of the churches, a series of meetings in Brooklyn. One day had been set apart to be observed as a day of fasting and prayer. Henry Ward Beecher spoke in a quiet, conversational tone and followed with a prayer in the tenderest and most spiritual mood. It recalled Christ's prayer at the Last Supper. Then there arose just behind me a shouting revivalist. He was oratorical, waxed louder and louder, grasped the back of the pew in which I was sitting and shook it in the vehemence of his real or artificial emotion. It recalled to me Elijah's scornful address to the priests of Baal: "Cry aloud: for he is a god;

either he is musing, or he is gone aside, or he is
in a journey, or peradventure he sleepeth, and
must be awaked." When at length the orator
stopped, out of breath with his vociferous devotion, I thought the meeting was destroyed; that
nothing could bring back to it its devotional
atmosphere. Mr. Moody rose and said, with
that strangely quiet and penetrating voice of his:
"Now let us have three minutes of *silent* prayer."
And the silence which he summoned erased the
disturbing oration and restored the spirit of devotion.

This penetrating personality of Mr. Moody
made him a great bearer of a great message.
What was that message which he believed would
meet the great but unconscious or half-conscious
hunger of the souls of men? I shall not undertake here to analyze this spiritual hunger or to
describe the elements which enter into it, or all
the causes which especially and notably excite
it. It must suffice for my present purpose to
indicate two elements, neither of which is ever
wholly wanting from any man who is not himself wholly lacking in some of the elements
essential to a normal manhood; the first relates
to his past, the second to his future.

Every healthful man sometimes—some men
at all times—looks back regretfully upon his
past. He is conscious of blunders in judgment,

aberrations of will, deliberate acts of wrong-doing, which have brought injury upon himself and upon others. He wishes that he could live again his life, or some particular crisis in his life. Sometimes this is a keen sense of shame for some specific deed done or duty neglected; sometimes a vague feeling of self-condemnation without clearly defined specific cause; sometimes a passing shadow, evanescent and uninfluential; sometimes a morbid self-condemnation, depressing the spirits and tending toward despair. He who has never felt this sense of remorse in some one of its various forms is singularly lacking either in his memory, his ideals, or his power of sitting in judgment upon his own conduct and character. It is doubtful whether any desire which the human soul ever possessed is keener or more overmastering than the desire sometimes possesses us, in certain phases of our experience, to be rid of our ineradicable past and to be permitted to begin life anew, unclogged and unburdened.

The other spiritual hunger of the soul relates to the future. The soul is conscious of undeveloped possibilities in itself; it is spurred on, to it knows not what future, by unsatisfied aspirations. It longs to do and to be more, and rather to be than to do. It suffers what I may call "growing pains." It has in the sphere of moral experience aspirations that may be compared to those which have summoned the greatest musicians and the greatest artists to their careers. This sense of unsatisfied aspiration differs from the sense of remorse in that it relates to the future, not to the past; the one is a consciousness of wrong committed or duty left undone, the other of life incomplete. The cry of the soul in the one experience is that of Paul. "Who shall deliver me from the body of this death?" The cry of the other is that of Tennyson:

> Oh, for a man to arise in me
> That the man that I am may cease to be.

The one is a craving for peace, the other for achievement.

It is because the Christian religion is able to satisfy these two passionate desires of the human soul—the desire for peace and the desire for achievement—that it possesses the attraction which the failures and the folly of its adherents may diminish but cannot destroy.

The Church of Christ declares to men that God bears no ill-will toward them; that he desires for them that they shall be good men and true; that to accomplish this, his good will toward them, Jesus Christ has come for his Father and our Father into the world, and that this fact is attested by the joyous experience of unnumbered millions of different eras, creeds, and races. At the same time the Church inspires with hope for the future. It tells the story of a Man who in himself fulfilled the spiritual desires that are in all noble men, and then, departing, left as his legacy the command, which is also a promise: "Follow me." It answers the question, "What is human nature?" by pointing to the character of Jesus of Nazareth, with the assurance that, what He was every man can become, and it answers the question, "Is life worth living?" by pointing to that life and declaring that, as He laid down His life for us, so can we lay down our lives for one another.

This is the message of the Christian Church reduced to its simplest form; the message of the Roman Catholic ecclesiastic and the Protestant preacher, of Cardinal Gibbons and General William Booth. I think its briefest statement in religious literature is that of Isaac Watts:

> But he forgives my follies past
> And gives me strength for days to come.

I lay down my pen, close my eyes, and lean back in my chair, and the scene of my childhood is before me—our Sunday-evening service of song in my grandfather's home; and I hear again the treble voice of my aged aunt, singing in our closing hymn as her own experience, this confession of faith which her favourite hymn writer had phrased for her. Then the scene disappears and her song is taken up by a great chorus, a host like the sands on the seashore for multitude, whom no tongue can number and no imagination can picture, and in which all lands and all generations, the living and the dead, have a part.

This was Mr. Moody's twofold message—forgiveness for the past, strength for the future.

His theology was very simple. Asked by an orthodox Churchman for his creed, he replied: "It is already in print and circulation, the fifty-third chapter of Isaiah." One verse from that chapter suffices for one article of his creed: "All we like sheep have gone astray; we have turned every one to his own way; and the Lord hath laid on him the iniquity of us all." The other article of his creed is comprised in a verse which he often quoted and which he always lived: "As many as received him, to them gave he power to become the sons of God, even to them that believe on his name." I think his message might all be summed up in one sentence: You can leave all your past for God to take care of, provided you will give yourself unreservedly to him and his service for the future. The whole object of his ministry, whether he spoke to a thousand from the platform or to one in the inquiry meeting, was to bring individuals to self-surrender and self-devotion. He was a recruiting officer; and he neither asked as to the life of the past nor as to the opinions entertained or the feelings experienced in the present; his one and only question was: "Will you devote yourself unto death for the future to Christ and his cause?"

Mr. Moody had none of the arts of the orator. He had a carrying voice, and without apparent effort on his part could be heard throughout the largest halls. He was intense in spirit but quiet in method, generally conversational in tone, never shouted, rarely was dramatic, never theatrical, his gestures simple. One of his co-workers reports that once, to emphasize his picture of a man refusing to take the medicine that would cure him and then blaming the physician, "he actually took the tumbler that was on the table and dashed the water on the floor." But whenever I heard him, and I heard him frequently, he depended entirely on the spiritual power of his message and his own intense conviction of its truth. I venture to transcribe here the impression of his appearance and method on the platform as I wrote it at the time of his death:

As he stood on the platform he looked like a business man; he dressed like a business man; he took the meeting in hand as a business man would; he spoke in a business man's fashion; he had no holy tone; he never introduced a jest for a jest's sake, but he did not fear to use humour if humour would serve his purpose; he never turned a sentence neatly to catch that applause of the eye which is substituted in religious assemblies for applause of the hands; and whether they believed in him or not, his auditors were always sure that he believed all that he said, and, indeed, said less than he believed because no language could express fully the experience of his own life.

His sermons abounded in illustrations but they were never used for ornament; were seldom taken from either nature or literature; with rare exceptions were concrete biographical accounts borrowed from his rich and varied pastoral experience, and used not to enforce a theory but always to make vivid a fact. He aroused the emotions of his audience, but not by an emotional appeal. The notion disseminated during his life by his critics that he pictured hell-fire to excite men's terror and a celestial heaven to excite their sensual delight was absolutely untrue; was the reverse of the truth. I think the most terrifying sermon on future punishment I ever heard was one on "Son, remember." But it was wholly psychological; a vivid portrayal of what was here and what would be hereafter the anguish of a soul who, looking back, could remember only a life of wasted opportunities, sensual excesses, selfish cruelties. There lies before me, as I write, a volume of "Twelve Selected Sermons," apparently selected by Mr. Moody himself, published in 1880. One of these sermons is on the words "The Gospel." It is his definition of the Gospel as he understood it. No condensation can adequately interpret its illustrative quality and its spiritual power, but a few lines may suffice to indicate to the thoughtful reader the essential nature of his simple message. He says:

I like the Gospel because it has been for me the very best news I have ever heard. It has taken out of my path four of the bitterest enemies I ever had.

It has taken away the fear of death. The Conquerer bursts the bands of death and shouts: "Because I live ye shall live also."

It takes away the burden of sin. It tells me: "As far as the East is from the West so far has he removed our transgressions from us."

It takes away the fear of judgment. Christ declares: "He that believeth on Him that sent me is passed from death unto life."

It takes away bondage to sin and gives me the spirit of liberty. Do I speak to a man who is a slave to strong drink? Christ can give you strength to hurl the cup from you and make you a sober man, a loving husband, a kind father.

It is a free Gospel. This Good News I am bid to proclaim to "every creature."

In an important respect the spirit of this sermon characterized all Mr. Moody's preaching.

His sermons were never expositions of a theological theory; they were always interpretations of a present experience. In this sermon he says nothing about a future punishment from which the sinner is saved by the Gospel. He believed and habitually preached a hell on earth and a heaven on earth. Lost and saved were with him present facts. To live without God and without the glorious life that companionship with God inspires is to be lost, to live in that companionship and inspired by that hope and love is to be saved. That there is an eternal lost which lies in the future of the one condition and an eternal saved which lies in the future of the other condition was implied in his teaching, but this was not the truth on which he laid chief emphasis. I once studied with care a published volume of his sermons to endeavour to get the secret of his power. The examination confirmed his own summary of his preaching: "I used to think," he says in one of his sermons, "of God as a stern judge on the throne, from whose wrath Jesus Christ had saved me. It seems to me now I could not have a falser idea of God than that. Since I have become a father, I have made this discovery: That it takes more love and sacrifice for the father to give up the son than it does for the son to die."

His method of preparation for his sermons was

unique. He had no background of material for preaching prepared by a course of school, college, and professional education. So he prepared his own background by a method of his own creation. He had a number of large manilla envelopes labelled topically to suit the method of his own thinking, such as Repentance, Grace, Love, and the like. Into these envelopes he put all sorts of material—sometimes his own thoughts, sometimes a copy of something he had read, sometimes clippings from a newspaper or a periodical. When an envelope was full, he would open a new one. In time he accumulated five or six hundred of these envelopes, often two or more on the same topic. These constituted his pulpit material—his library, so to speak—and from them he prepared his sermons, generally in vacation. These sermons were mere notes, written in a very large hand, not more than three or four words on a line. They were usually filed in his Bible, kept in place by a rubber band, generally at the text he had chosen. These notes he took to the pulpit or platform with him, but he never read his sermons; he used the notes merely as memoranda.

He never "got up" a revival. He was generally invited to a church, or to a town or city, by a coöperation of churches, and to the committee spontaneously organized by the church or the combination of churches he left all preliminary arrangements. Nor did he ordinarily make any effort at the close of his mission to organize its results. The work of preparing the ground and the work of gathering in the harvest he left to others. But his preaching was almost invariably accompanied by inquiry meetings, and these were always carried on under his immediate supervision. He himself selected his co-workers. Partly by temperament and partly by long experience, he had acquired an intuitive judgment of spiritual character. His supervision of these meetings extended to the minutest details, such as a draught from an open window or a buzzing gas jet.

He had an enormous correspondence, many of the letters asking counsel on ethical or spiritual or perhaps theological problems. Writing was always a great physical effort for him and he never learned to use a typewriter. Mr. Paul Moody, to whom I am indebted for some of these incidents, has given me an interesting picture of his management of this phase of his ever-growing work:

He handled his correspondence at home, which was the only place where I saw it. It was very interesting. He entertained more or less. There were usually people stopping at the house, and he would sit at the desk opening his letters, glancing at them, and then would throw them across the room to some member of the family with the direction: "Answer that." Sometimes it was a difficult letter which demanded quite a little thought, and if you brought it to him and asked him what he wanted to say he always replied by saying: "I do not intend to buy a dog and then do the barking myself. If I were going to answer it I would, but I want you to answer it." Very seldom would he take a letter back. Once in a while an unknown person made a confession a matter of the soul, and that I refused to handle. My mother did a great deal of his correspondence. My mother was the buffer between himself and the world. She was the "shock absorber." She stood between him and things.

Mr. Moody did not have that broad intellectual outlook which scholarship sometimes, but not always, gives to the scholar. But he had that broad human outlook which almost invariably characterizes the man who possesses both a living spiritual faith and catholic human sympathies, who estimates men not by the accidents of their creed, their race, or their social culture, but by their character, and can therefore recognize real spiritual worth in men of differing theological opinions. This catholicity of spirit led him to welcome the coöperation in his evangelistic labours of men whose intellectual outlook was very different from his own, and made him indifferent to theological theories which men of less catholic temper regarded of vital importance.

In the book of "Selected Sermons," from which
I have already quoted, are two on "The Blood."
In these sermons Mr. Moody lays great emphasis
on the passion and death of Jesus Christ as at
once a fruit and a proof of God's forgiving love,
but it would not be easy for any theologian to
deduce from them which one of the conflicting
theological theories of the atonement he held.
He accepted the Bible as an infallible rule of
faith and practice; but he habitually used it as
the Epistle to Timothy affirms it should be used
—for reproof, correction, and instruction in
righteousness. I do not think that he ever discussed the supposed bearing of the Bible on such
questions as the age of the world and the processes of creation. It was wholly as a book of
spiritual experiences that he used it, and its
adaptation to that use was for him an adequate
verification of its authority. In the little booklet
on the use of the Bible which he published I do
not find any discussion concerning the nature of
inspiration. His question to George Adam
Smith: "Why do you make such a fuss about
two Isaiahs when most people do not know that
there is one?" indicates his comparative indifference to the so-called "Higher Criticism." And
the fact that certainly with his consent, if not at
his request, I gave in the eighties a course of
winter lectures on the Bible at the two North-

field Schools, crossing the Connecticut River on the ice with the thermometer ten degrees or more below zero, indicates his entire readiness to welcome for his pupils any light on the Bible provided it came from one who was seeking to find in it for himself and others inspiration for the Christian life.

Another incident in which I participated showed how little sympathy he had with the heresy hunters. At the time of the World's Fair in Chicago an arrangement was made for the coöperation of the Evangelical churches in their Sunday services under the direction of Mr. Moody. An invitation to preach on my visit to the Fair I declined, because I was unwilling even to seem to interfere with this coöperative movement. The invitation was then renewed through Mr. Moody, and I preached, not in the Evangelistic service, where I might have been a misfit, but in the Congregational Church to a congregation which filled all the pews and sat on the floor in the aisles. The notion somewhat widely circulated that Mr. Moody was narrow-minded, and in his methods mechanical, was due probably less to the malice of enemies than to the ignorance of the public misled by the folly of some of his defenders. He habitually refused to defend himself.

A more striking illustration of this breadth of

spiritual sympathy is afforded by two incidents narrated by Mr. Paul Moody:

Mr. McKay, who went with us through Palestine, was converted late in life, when he was middle-aged; for a few years was a Protestant, then became a Christian Scientist, and finally went over to Catholicism. His one desire was to get my father to come over also. He arranged a meeting between Archbishop Corrigan and my father. They had a conference, and it is said that they prayed together. After this meeting with the Bishop in Chicago I had a number of Catholics tell me that they always felt that he was going to come over to the Church because he was so sympathetic with them. Later he gave a substantial donation to the Catholic Church in Northfield and also an organ, and the dear old pin-head people attacked him in print and otherwise. For years afterward he received letters saying, particularly those from England, that he had been fellowshipping anti-Christ and they consigned him to the outermost hell. He chuckled over these. When we rebuilt our Congregational Church in Northfield, the Catholics in the town turned in and hauled all the stones free of charge as their contribution.

Mr. Moody was too catholic ever to become a member of the Catholic Church. But his fellowship with the priests of that Church ought not to surprise us. For the message of this unordained preacher in the newest of the Protestant churches and the message of the Apostolically ordained archbishop in the oldest Church in Christendom was the same: Divine forgiveness for the past and divine strength for the future.

I say nothing in this paper about Mr. Moody's establishment of the Northfield Schools, though that is in some respects the greatest piece of work he ever did. But here I am sketching Mr. Moody the Evangelist. The work of an evangelist he always regarded as the greatest of all forms of service, the work of the ministry as a cramping and confining occupation. He urged his son not to go into the ministry but to become an evangelist. He had a great admiration for Phillips Brooks and was always sorry for him because he could not be an evangelist. He had a great affection for Anson Phelps Stokes and Henry Sloan Coffin, and wanted them not to go into the pastorate but to prepare themselves for an evangelistic ministry. He made a vigorous endeavour to persuade Henry Ward Beecher to leave his church, at least for a season, and join him in an evangelistic mission. He was not interested in teaching a system of theology; he was interested in inducing men to accept God's gift of a divine life.

Mr. Moody died in 1889. The radical changes in theological thought which had begun before his death have continued since. They will always continue. Theology, if it is a living thought, will be, must be, a progressive thought. But religion, the life of God in the soul of man,

the life of faith and hope and love, the life of
doing justly, loving mercy, and walking humbly
with God, the life of accepting his forgiveness for
the past and of devoting ourselves in joyous self-
sacrifice to his service in the future, remains to-
day what it was when Abraham obeyed the voice
of God and went out not knowing whither he
went. For myself, I believe neither in the
authority of the ecclesiastical organization with
the Church-man, nor in the infallibility of the
Book with Mr. Moody. The authority to pronounce absolution and remission for the sins that
are past and to proffer this gift of life to fulfil
the aspirations of the soul for the future, I believe to be spiritual, not ecclesiastical nor traditional, and to belong equally to every one who
has received such absolution and remission and
such gift of spiritual life. But I am sure that
if we of the so-called liberal faith hope to retain
in these more liberal days the attractive power
of the Church, we can do it only by holding fast
to the great spiritual fact that in the God whom
Jesus has declared to us there is abundant forgiveness for all the past, and an abundant life
for all the future; and this we must affirm not
as a theological opinion, to be defended by philosophical arguments as a rational hypothesis,
but as an assured fact, historically certified by
the life and death of Jesus Christ and confirmed

out of the mouth of many witnesses by the experience of Christ's disciples and followers in all churches and in every age. If we fail to do this, men will desert our ministry for Romanism, Anglicanism, or the old orthodoxy, or, in despair of spiritual life in any quarter, will desert all that ministers to the higher life and live a wholly material life, alternating between restless, unsatisfied desire and stolid self-content. And the fault and the folly will be ours more even than theirs.

HENRY WARD BEECHER,
PROPHET OF THE LOVE OF GOD

IT IS difficult to realize the condition in which the old Puritanism had left the churches of New England at the close of the eighteenth century. There were no missionary societies, home or foreign; no Young Men's or Young Women's Christian Associations; no anti-slavery, temperance, or other reform societies. Yale College had only four professing Christians in its student body and had two Tom Paine societies.

Many causes have combined to overthrow the theological system which produced this moral and spiritual decadence. Chief among them were four Puritan divines leading without conscious coöperation a revolt against it: William Ellery Channing, who taught the essential goodness of man and interpreted sin as a curable disease; Charles G. Finney, who taught that man was a free moral agent, and therefore ought to repent of his sins; Horace Bushnell, who applied the doctrine of development to religion and taught that sin is not natural but unnatural; and Henry Ward Beecher, who taught that God treats men, not collectively as a king treats the community, but individually as a father treats his children. The difference between the old and the new, the Puritanism of the eighteenth century and the Puritanism of the twentieth century, is a difference between a religion of law and a religion of freedom—a religion that is artificial and calls itself supernatural and a religion that is natural because it is life, a religion which with Lyman Beecher repudiates "nateral virtoos" and a religion which with Sabatier declares that man is incurably religious. In the promotion of this spiritual revolution no one exercised a more profound influence than Henry Ward Beecher.

He was singularly equipped for the mission which was given to him. Professor Fowler, a famous phrenologist of that time, correctly called him "a splendid animal." He was not an athlete; when I knew him, he neither fished nor hunted, nor took long tramps, nor rode horseback for exercise; his chief, if not his only, outdoor game was croquet. I asked him once to give me an article on how to keep well. "There are but three rules," he replied: "Eat well, sleep well, and laugh well." I wonder if he got them from Robert Burton, the author of "The Anatomy of Melancholy," who is reported by one of his admirers as saying: "There are only three doctors to be really trusted—Doctor

Merryman, Doctor Diet, and Doctor Quiet."
They were Mr. Beecher's doctors, and he followed
their directions habitually and conscientiously.

He not only slept well, he scrupulously maintained periods of rest. He had, says his intimate friend, Rossiter W. Raymond, "three distinct mental states—the passive or resting, the
receptive and inquiring or filling up, and the
spontaneously active or giving forth state."
That he was so full of superfluous energy in the
giving out state was largely due to his conscientious maintenance of hours for resting as
well as for receiving. "In the resting state
he loved to be alone with birds or flowers or
precious stones or pictures—things that asked no
questions and called for no active reciprocities."

He was full-blooded; for that reason eschewed
the red meat. A rich arterial system may not
cause an emotional nature, but generally accom-
panies one that, like Mr. Beecher's, is both emotional and demonstrative. His religion was not a
theology, it was the spontaneous outflow of his
whole being. His beliefs rested not upon argument but upon experience. He has given a characteristic description of "that blessed morning of
May when it pleased God to reveal to my wander-
ing soul that it was His nature to love a man in his
sins for the sake of helping him out of them; . . .
that He was a Being not made mad by sin, but

sorry; that He was not furious with wrath toward the sinner, but pitied him—in short, that He felt toward me as my mother felt toward me, to whose eyes my wrong-doing brought tears, who never pressed me so close to her as when I had done wrong, and who would fain with her yearning love lift me out of trouble." From that day to his death his faith was in a human God, a Spirit interpreted to us through our own spirits, and in Jesus Christ as the personification in human history of this invisible Spirit. Criticized for preaching in Theodore Parker's pulpit, he replied: "Could Theodore Parker worship my God?—Christ Jesus is his name. All that there is of God to me is bound up in that name. A dim and shadowy effluence rises from Christ, and that I am taught to call the Father. A yet more tenuous and invisible film of thought arises, and that is the Holy Spirit. . . . But Christ stands my *manifest* God. All I know is of him and in him."

This combination of an emotional nature and faith in an Incarnate divinity on whom he could freely bestow it endowed him with a passionate piety. Its nature will be best interpreted by two incidents in his life.

In 1877 he preached a sermon which was subsequently published in the *Christian Union.**

---

*Christian Union, Vol. XVI, No. 26, p. 582 (December 26, 1877).

I believe, though I am not sure, for he never told me, that it was called forth by a visit made the day before upon a mother whose son had died without any evidence of evangelical conversion, and who was almost crazed by the belief that he had been consigned to hell. This sermon contained the following paragraph:

If now you tell me that this great mass of men, because they had not the knowledge of God, went to heaven, I say that the inroad of such a vast amount of mud swept into heaven would be destructive of its purity; and I cannot accept that view. If, on the other hand, you say that they went to hell, then you make an infidel of me; for I do swear, by the Lord Jesus Christ, by his groans, by his tears, and by the wounds in his hands and in his side, that I will never let go of the truth that the nature of God is to suffer for others rather than to make them suffer. If I lose everything else, I will stand on the sovereign idea that God so loved the world that he gave his own son to die for it rather than it should die. Tell me that back of Christ there is a God who for unnumbered centuries has gone on creating men and sweeping them like dead flies—nay, like living ones—into hell, is to ask me to worship a being as much worse than the conception of any mediæval devil as can be imagined; but I will not worship the devil, though he should come dressed in royal robes and sit on the throne of Jehovah.

For this sermon he was bitterly attacked by theological critics. He was "a Universalist," "a heretic," "irreverent," "a blasphemer."

Talking with me afterward, he said: "When I read the horrible caricatures of my God by ministers of the Church in some of their sermons, I understand how the Hebrew prophets felt toward the pagan religions. I can't stand it; something has to give way." Of course at this distance of time I cannot vouch for the verbal accuracy of my report; but the phrase "something has to give way" has remained in my memory ever since. Irreverent? It was the passionate reverence of a son that broke over all restraints in his flaming indignation at the pagan misrepresentations of his Father.

The other incident was radically different, but it none the less indicates Mr. Beecher's forgetfulness of self and emotional absorption in his Master at times when one might at least anticipate a divided interest.

In the summer of 1874 an investigation on behalf of Plymouth Church of certain charges against Mr. Beecher's moral character was conducted by a special committee of six gentlemen of the highest character and some of them of national reputation. They presented on August 28th their report, which was wholly favourable to Mr. Beecher's Christian character and integrity. When Mr. Beecher returned at the close of his summer vacation, expecting to meet his people in the usual Friday evening prayer-meeting, he found assembled a throng which the lecture-room could not contain, and which therefore by a kind of spontaneous movement had adjourned into the church audience room. Mr. Beecher at first insisted that the meeting should be held, as usual, in the lecture-room, but finally, convinced that the lecture-room would not contain one half of those present, he reluctantly consented to the transfer which had been made. When he entered the crowded church, he was greeted with demonstrations of enthusiastic attachment by his people, and an extemporized choir sang an anthem, the words of which, if I ever knew them, I have forgotten. When the choir began this anthem, Mr. Beecher retreated from the platform and did not return until the anthem was concluded. Then, resuming his seat upon the platform which constitutes the pulpit in Plymouth Church, he said in a quiet voice full of suppressed emotion something like this: "We have not come here to look or to be looked at. We have come to worship Him whose name is above every name," and then, taking his hymn-book in his hand, read the hymn:

> When I survey the wonderous cross,
>   On which the Prince of Glory died,
> My richest gain I count but loss,
>   And pour contempt on all my pride.

This hymn he made his own expression of consecration to the crucified Christ, and when he had finished, the assemblage was converted from an audience of hero-worshippers to a congregation of Christ-worshippers. A more startling illustration of the power of a great soul inspired by a clear vision and a divine passion I have never witnessed.

Someone has defined genius as "a capacity for hard work." That is exactly what it is not. I do not venture to define genius, but I am very certain that in all geniuses there is one common quality: spontaneity. Most of us are like a pump—we must work to bring our thoughts to the surface. But there are occasional men who are like a bubbling spring—the ideas rise to the surface spontaneously, and if there is no one to catch them they flow off and are lost. This quality of spontaneity is charactistic of every man of genius. Whether he is orator, poet, artist, novelist, or musician, the truth he utters, the picture he paints, the story he tells, the music he writes seems to him to be given to him. It comes to him unsought. He may spend much time in polishing the diamond; but he does not make the diamond. If he is an executive an inward voice seems to counsel his action and he cannot always explain to others the reason for his course. This spontaneity was very distinctly characteristic of Mr. Beecher. The fact is very clearly indicated by what he once told me of his method of pulpit preparation.

"I always have," he said, "floating in my head half-formed thoughts I would like to utter. Saturday is my day of rest. I am apt to spend it on my farm at Peekskill under the trees. I sleep soundly Saturday night; I sleep vicariously for my congregation. After breakfast I go into my study, feel of my different themes, the one that is ripe I pluck, select my text, organize my thought, and go into the pulpit with my theme fresh, my mind and heart full of it." In his earlier ministry he would write and read parts of his sermon and extemporize parts. In his later ministry his notes were mere hints. These were sometimes so fragmentary as to be meaningless to any one but himself, but sometimes these rough fragments were as thought-provoking as if he had wrought them with care. There lie before me as I write the manuscript notes of one of his sermons, so rough that I cannot determine the proper order of the sheets or find either text or indication of peroration. But there are two hints worth preserving as epigrams:

I. Consider your Past a Treasury. What has been laid up in it?

III. What are called Repentances, Reformations, are

New Growths or New Leaves; do not change old evils—
but overlay with new growths.

Sometimes his mind would refuse to work and
he had to *make* the sermon. Then was he least
successful. Sometimes a hint, an intellectual
jar, would wake him up; then he was often at
his best. "I remember," says Doctor Raymond,
"that at one of his last public appearances—the
dinner of the Polytechnic Alumni, in Brooklyn—
he whispered to me as I passed behind his chair,
'I can't say anything to-night; I am perfectly
empty.' 'Never mind,' I replied; 'the boys are
glad to see you. Thank them for their greeting,
anyhow, and sit down again, if you like.' But
by the time he was called upon, after several had
spoken, he had found enough to say; and the
mingled humour and eloquence of his address
that night will not soon be forgotten."

I do not recommend young ministers to adopt
Mr. Beecher's methods. Imitation never yet
made an original thinker. We are sometimes
exhorted to follow in Christ's footsteps. But
we cannot do it. We must follow him as the
bird follows its leader, making its own path
through the air. But I am quite sure that Mr.
Beecher's principles are well worth careful study
by all men engaged in creative work. We all
recognize the necessity of the two periods—the

giving out and the filling up. But not many recognize the equal necessity for the resting period. Physical rest is the period of physical digestion when the food we have taken becomes flesh and blood. Intellectual rest is equally necessary for intellectual digestion, when we transform thought into experience; without it the preacher or author is simply a reporter of other men's thoughts. I am not a psychologist; but I am inclined to think that unconscious cerebration is not the least valuable part of our intellectual activity.

Whether true as a general principle or not I am sure that his conscientious observance of rest periods was one secret of Mr. Beecher's oratorical power. Rarely was he a reporter of other men's thoughts. He preached, not theories, but experiences. I called on him once with a young man who was preparing for the ministry. "I am studying theology," said the student, "at —— Theological Seminary." "No objection to that," said Mr. Beecher, "if you don't believe it."

Mr. Beecher was a pragmatist without knowing it; I doubt whether the term was invented then. But he tested all theological theories by the question: Does it work well? "Calvinism," he said to me, "is like a churn: it turns out a little very good butter, but it wastes a lot of buttermilk." He took his theories wherever he found them, quite careless where they came from. For example, his *theory* of the divinity of Christ he took from Swedenborg—the divine spirit in a human body. Evolution he accepted because of its religious value; it threw light on problems which had perplexed the Christian Church and which the current theology left in darkness. It was said of him that he was no theologian. It was true. His religious teaching could be reduced to philosophic forms, but he was not interested to reduce it. Asked once for his theology, he replied: "Ask Abbott; he knows." Only late in life, and then to correct misunderstandings among his own brother ministers, did he even attempt to formulate his theological beliefs. For his preaching was not a product of his theology. His preaching was always an endeavour to meet human needs. "I never in my life," he once said, "shot an arrow at a venture. I have always aimed at a mark, though I have very often aimed at one bird and brought down another." His theology was always subject to correction; it was tested and corrected by life.

Was Mr. Beecher a scholar? The answer depends upon the meaning attached to that somewhat ambiguous word. But if George Crabb is right, if to study means to desire eagerly to learn, Mr. Beecher was a student. One more eager to learn I never knew. The learning which interested him was that which could be directly applied in practical life. If he had been a scientist, he would have been a student not of pure science but of applied science—an Edison, not an Einstein.

As a student he had extraordinary facility in the use of books. "One does not read a book through," he once said to me. "You read a book as you eat a fish: cut off the tail, cut off the head, cut off the fins, take out the backbone, and there is a little meat left which you eat because it nourishes you." He made constant and systematic use of phrenology, chiefly as a convenient system for the classification of mental and moral phenomena. I took over to him one day a new volume in philosophy based on that system. I wanted to get his estimate upon it. He took the book with him to the dinner table and read while he ate, turning over the leaves with remarks such as: "Nonsense! . . . Of course. . . . Everybody knows that. . . . Borrowed from Spurzheim. . . . That's new and well worth thinking about." At the end of the meal he had finished the book and handed it back to me with a ten-minute comment which made the basis of my editorial review.

But his use of books was not always like that. He habitually used the Greek, his favourite commentary being Alford's Greek Testament, which I still think is, for the practical use of the preacher, the best commentary we have on the New Testament, better than either Meyer or "The International." He studied Curtis's "History of the Constitution," and his loyalty to that document, because "there is health in it," set him apart from the Abolitionists, whose leader, William Lloyd Garrison, pronounced it "a covenant with death and an agreement with hell." His democratic principles were grounded on a careful study of fundamental authorities such as De Tocqueville and Francis Lieber, with both of whom he was familiar. I do not think he used the Hebrew language; but if he wanted to get at the exact meaning of an Old Testament text he went to his friend Doctor Conant, a well-known Hebrew scholar, who lived only a few blocks away. So he went to his brother, Edward Beecher, for information on scholastic theology when he wanted such information, and to his friend Rossiter W. Raymond for information respecting the scientific aspects of evolution. But he studied the writings of Darwin, Spencer, Tyndall, and Huxley, and it was partly as the result of his influence that the republication of their writings in this country was brought about. In his recreative reading he was more systematic than most of us are. I think that he read

modern novels and current magazines but little.
Instead he laid out early in the year three or four
series of authors—for example: for fiction, George
Eliot; for poetry, Tennyson; for history, Green;
for essays, Milton; for drama, the Greek tragedies
in translation—and then read as the mood invited him. As a result, at the end of the season
he had made a real acquaintance of some worth-
while authors.

His habit of getting knowledge from all sorts
of experts, in all sorts of places, is too well known
to need exposition here. A striking but not
singular illustration is afforded by his getting
acquainted with a professional gambler, in the
early years of his ministry, in Indianapolis, and
using his information so effectively in a graphic
picture of the methods of the fraternity that a
young man, thinking to crack a joke at the expense of the preacher, asked him: "Mr. Beecher,
how could you describe a gambling-hell so accurately if you had never been in one?" and got
for reply: "How could you know it was accurate
if you had never been in one?"

The impression that Mr. Beecher was not a
scholar was partly due to a habit both natural
and deliberately cultivated: he studied his theme
until he believed he had made himself master of
it, then in public speech he gave himself to the
exposition, illustration, and enforcement of what

he believed to be the truth with absolute intellectual, imaginative, and emotional abandon. He gave weeks to the careful study of the issues, personal and political, involved in the Blaine-Cleveland campaign; but when his mind was made up, he took the stump for Cleveland, without reserve, qualification, or limitation.

He was a friend of man, and most of all a friend to men who needed him and whom he thought he could serve. He was curiously unsuspicious, always saw the good in men, and sometimes imagined it when it did not exist. He obeyed too literally and with some disastrous consequences the saying: "Love thinketh no evil." He had many devoted friends who would gladly have laid down their lives for him; but, like all men of genius, he was at times a lonely man. He had a tinge of melancholy, such as, I suspect, all idealists have at times, who instinctively contrast their aspirations with the realities of life. He generally kept this melancholy to himself, though sometimes one felt it in his public speech, and even more in his prayers. He gave me a glimpse of it once. "My father," he said, "wrote his sermons with the angel of hope looking over his shoulder and inspiring his pen. I have never expected to succeed. Success has come to me always as a surprise."

He began life as an individualist, and while in the West conducted with great effectiveness some revivals of religion in the old-fashioned method. He brought with him to the East the spirit of eagerness for immediate personal results, and some remarkable revivals of religion followed his preaching. But his point of view gradually changed. After the Civil War Mr. Moody once urged him to leave his pulpit, at least for a time, and join him in an evangelical mission. In speaking to me about this invitation afterward he expressed in the warmest terms his affection and admiration for Mr. Moody, but added: "We could not work together. For Mr. Moody thinks this is a lost world, and he is trying to save as many as possible from the wreck; I think Jesus Christ has come to save the world, and I am trying to help him save it." When he definitely adopted this theory I do not know, but I am quite sure that he acted on it long before he consciously adopted it.

It was this principle that made him a reformer. When he was criticized for preaching politics and told that he ought to confine himself to the Gospel, his answer was: "I hold that it is a Christian minister's duty not only to preach the Gospel of the New Testament without reservation, but to apply its truths to any question that relates to the welfare of men."

Whoever acts on that principle will always be ahead of his age, because Jesus Christ is ahead of all ages; the world has not yet caught up with Christ. It made Henry Ward Beecher an anti-slavery preacher in Indianapolis before he came to Brooklyn in 1847; and in Indiana, when I was there during the Civil War, abolition was more bitterly and more widely abhorred than slavery. It made him a temperance advocate when drinking habits were still common and prohibition was unknown. It made him heartily indorse Gavazzi and Kossuth in their unsuccessful attempts for the liberation of Italy and Hungary. It made him an advocate of woman suffrage; he believed in the equality of the sexes, and he contended that equality in character involved equality in political power. It gave him an inspired courage in his unplanned mission to England in 1863, and inspired his appeal to the conscience of the plain people of England in five ever-memorable addresses, which did so much to defeat the endeavours of the aristocracy to lend England's moral support to the Southern Confederacy.

Mr. John R. Howard has edited with an admirable introduction a volume of Mr. Beecher's "Patriotic Addresses." The reader of this volume will find in them two characteristics. They are not merely political; they do not discuss

merely questions of economic expediency or
political policy. Always by their essential
spirit, though not always in express terms, they
consider the relation of the subjects discussed to
the kingdom of God. And they are generally, I
think always, free from the bitterness of invective which so often marred the addresses of
both the temperance and the anti-slavery reformers of that period. In one of these addresses Mr. Beecher says: "I have not meant
to be severe. If I should meet a slaveholder in
conversation, I should say just the same. He
might reply: 'I don't believe all you do, but you
say what you think, and I like you; you are no
doughface.'" What Mr. Beecher imagined a
slaveholder saying I heard one say. He was
with me in a pew in Plymouth Church when Mr.
Beecher pictured in his sermon a slave escaping
from his chains, crossing the Ohio River, and
finding in Ohio the Fugitive Slave Law waiting
to catch him there. "Has he a right to flee?"
cried Mr. Beecher. "Shall I help to turn him
back to slavery again? If he were my son and
did not seek liberty, I would write across his
name, 'Disowned.'" And the slaveholder sitting at my side as we went out from the church
said to me, "I cannot agree with all your preacher
said, but he is a great and good man."

In his "Yale Lectures on Preaching" he said

231

to the students: "Never preach two sermons alike if you can help it." He rarely did. But he always expressed himself. His sermon was always an echo of his own experience, and was recognized by his congregation to be an interpretation of his own life. The sermon might be a Biblical exposition, or a devotional meditation, or a philosophical essay, or a chapter in ethics, but, whatever it might be in form, in its spirit it was always true to himself. And this inimitable spirit of life was the secret of his power as a man, not merely as a preacher. His life illustrated his saying, "You cannot pray cream and live skim milk."

For Mr. Beecher preached as he lived and lived as he preached. The faith that gave power to his sermons controlled him in his life, and because it controlled him in his life, gave power to his preaching. His faith in his fellowmen was latent but always ready to be called into action. In his travels he once came to a junction where all the passengers had to change cars. The passengers, with characteristic eagerness to get good seats in the new train, were pushing forward each one for himself. Among them was a woman rather poorly dressed, with three little children and several bags, parcels, and wraps, who waited timidly her chance. Mr. Beecher, grasping the hand rail on each side of the car and blocking up all entrance by his somewhat burly presence, called out: "Isn't any gentleman going to help this lady in?" Instantly the mind of the crowd was changed. Two gentlemen picked up the children, two others helped the lady to the car platform, two others handed up her bags and packages. "I venture the guess," said Mr. Beecher, in telling me the incident, "that that poor woman never before had so many cavaliers attending on her. There's good will enough in the world; all that is necessary is to call it out." He could and did. But as he told me the incident I had to confess to myself that I could not and probably should not have tried.

His sympathies were not confined to men of any race or creed, social class or moral character. They were not even confined to men. To Paul's question: "Does God take care of our oxen?" Mr. Beecher's reply would have been "Certainly." He enjoyed flowers and precious stones, but he was fond of birds, horses, and dogs. When I was looking for my first parish he advised me to notice what kind of horses the farmers drove when they came to town. "Wide-awake teams," he said, "indicate a wide-awake community." He drove a good pair himself. His sympathy with animals in distress, his readiness to come to their relief, and his resourcefulness are illustrated by an incident told to me in a letter by a correspondent which I cannot better tell than in the words of the narrator, now ninety years of age, but written by him when he was a boy in the Indianapolis Seminary. How Mr. Beecher appeared on the scene the boy does not tell in his composition.

It was the first day in the year 1847. The rain had been pouring down with undescribable fury; as if the clouds had been shedding tears and thundering their requiem on account of the sad parting which they had so lately taken of the "Old Year." Being obliged to go over into the city, I saddled my horse, called my dog Ben, and started off (By the way Ben was a large "Bulldog" and it is stated that he was born without a tail, which as far as I know was the truth, for even at the time he was shot for killing sheep it was not larger than a hickory nut). Proceeding through mud and water we soon came to the creek. There I by dint of getting the most of my body on the top of the horse passed through unseated by the tide. But Ben was not so fortunate, for having no horse to ride he was obliged to swim. We passed on but soon came to another bayou even worse than the former. This Ben tried to pass over on top of the fence, but having arrived about the middle of the fence was unable either to return or proceed. There he remained all that day and night and half the next day. In the mean time I had gone on, not knowing what had detained him and had it not been for Rev. H. Beecher, the poor dog would have died. He made a raft of wash tubs, much in the Swiss-Family-Robinson fashion, but this did not succeed, for having launched it, it turned over and left him floundering in the water. He next made a common board raft; but forgot to make allowance for the weight of the dog, so that when he took him on, the raft sunk and both were obliged to choose the alternative sink or swim, live or die, survive or perish. On reaching the shore Mr. B. looked back to see how Ben had fared but to his sorrow found that he had clambered back to his old situation. But Mr. B. was not to be disheartened by these failures, for he went to a neighbouring board yard and made a stout raft and thus brought the shivering dog to shore. Ben was so glad to land on "terra firma" that he frightened Mrs. Beecher, ran over the children, and bedaubed Mr. B. from head to foot with his dirty paws. And ever after when his benefactor would come to our house, the first thing he would do would be to endeavour to throw his paws around his neck and embrace him.

Nor were Mr. Beecher's deeper spiritual faiths in immortality and in what men have called the impracticable precepts of Jesus Christ less a part of his inward experience nor less manifest in his daily life.

At a prayer meeting once, in the time of his greatest prosperity and his unclouded fame, he said something to this effect: "I am very happy; I have a home rich in love; a devoted people; am surrounded by my friends; with everything to make me joyful. But nothing could give me greater happiness than to hear my heavenly Father say to me to-night: 'Your work is done. You can come home.'" His aged father, who was no longer able to preach, sitting directly in front of his son, sprang to his feet with a vehement rebuke. "Henry," he cried, "I am ashamed of you. You ought not to be willing to stop. Would that God would call me back to go on with the war!" The son made some gentle reply, and called for a hymn to close the meeting. But the contrast emphasized the constant message of the son that there are not two worlds but only one, that the curtain that separates them is easily brushed aside; that death is "friendly."

When some years later he was put on trial for what was more than his life, his honour as a Christian minister, he continued preaching every Sunday morning, refused any other relief than ceasing his public lecturing and his Sunday evening sermons, refused to talk about the case with any one but his lawyers, and refused to talk with them on Saturday, because, as he said, "You cannot raise cream if you keep the milk in the pan always stirring." And the people reported that never had his sermons a deeper spiritual tone. While his friends, though their faith in him was never shaken, still feared for his good name, he maintained an untroubled mind and had, I believe, very rarely a wakeful night. He once expressed his assurance of the inefficiency of wickedness to achieve its aims by saying to me, with a scorn which no type can possibly portray: "I tell you, Abbott, the

236

name of the wicked shall *rot!*" But when later one of his accusers had left the country and was living self-exiled in Paris, and another was reported to be involved in business difficulties and in danger of bankruptcy, he said to me, with tears in his eyes and in his voice: "I would like to lend some money to —— and I think I could raise it, but I suppose it would not do. It would be misunderstood."

History has justified his confidence and illustrated the whole of the text: "The memory of the just is blessed; but the name of the wicked shall rot." Never in my lifetime, nor I think in the history of the world, has so great honour been paid at death to a purely private citizen, who never held a public office in the nation, and never a higher office in the state than that of pastor in a local church.

He died from the breaking of a blood-vessel in the brain on March 8, 1887. From the hour of his death until the day of his funeral the flags in Brooklyn were at half mast and the public buildings were draped in token of the loss that the community had sustained. The coloured clergymen of Brooklyn expressed the desire to attend his funeral in a body, which privilege was accorded them. The New York Legislature appointed a committee to attend the funeral, and both Houses were adjourned. In Brooklyn on

the day of the funeral the public offices were
closed and business was in a large measure suspended. Plymouth Church could not contain
the congregation that gathered. Four other
churches in the neighbourhood were filled to
overflowing with men and women who had come
to pay their respects to the deceased preacher,
and it was estimated at the time that had double
the number of churches been opened they would
all have been filled. Among those attending
were several Roman Catholic priests. Not the
least significant incident in connection with
these services was the fact that there was no
black drapery used in the church or in the home;
instead were flowers. The family put on no
mourning. Mr. Beecher had often said: "Strew
flowers on my grave, but let no heathenish use
of black be used as a token of sorrow when I
have passed from death into life eternal."
This desire, so characteristic of the man, was
faithfully observed.

Mr. Beecher was a great preacher because
he was a great and good man; pure as a woman;
simple as a little child; frank to a fault. His
most intimate friend never heard from his lips
a suggestion of a salacious jest; I never knew the
man bold enough to venture on one in his presence. He was incapable of deceit or artifice.
He could conceal, when concealment was nec-

essary, only by maintaining an absolutely im-penetrable reserve. His life was more eloquent than his speech; he was most eloquent when he most failed to say what he wished to say. He was not logical; the seer never is. He was a revelator. What he had seen in the closet he disclosed in the pulpit. He was a man of God and walked with God. These phrases are so contaminated with cant that the pen shrinks from writing them. But they are phrases full of a divine meaning. It is possible to walk with God; to have a personal acquaintance with him through his Son, Jesus Christ; to be a tabernacle for God's indwelling. No one who knew Mr. Beecher intimately, in the varieties of his experience from hours of the lightest merriment to experiences of the deepest sorrow, could question that this companionship with God was the secret of his power.

PHILLIPS BROOKS, PROPHET OF THE
SPIRITUAL LIFE

IN THE spring of 1889 I received the following letter from Phillips Brooks:

> 233 Clarendon Street, Boston,
> May 30, 1889.

MY DEAR DR. ABBOTT:

Professor Peabody tells me that there is some sign of a
prospect that you may join our Company of Preachers at
Harvard College.

I cannot help saying how thoroughly delightful I should
think it if such a thing should come to pass. It is the most
interesting work that I have ever had to do. I am sure
that, done as you could do it, it would be full of new value
and satisfaction.

This being the case—and you having nothing on Earth
to do at present—I dare to hope that what the Professor
suggests may really come. God grant it!

> Ever sincerely yours
> PHILLIPS BROOKS.

REV. DR. LYMAN ABBOTT.

The "Company of Preachers" to which Phillips Brooks alludes was a group of six, one of
whom was a university professor who had over-
sight of the religious life of the University; the

other five were non-residents invited for the current year. Each minister usually preached for four Sundays, conducted morning prayers for four weeks, and after prayers held morning conferences with such students as wished to call upon him. The call to share in this service delighted me. But engaged then in both ministerial and editorial work, I hesitated to take on a new responsibility. Phillips Brooks's letter decided me. From that time until the day of his death in 1893 I was a co-worker, though not continuously, with Phillips Brooks in the Harvard "Company of Preachers."

I have known greater orators than Phillips Brooks. Henry Ward Beecher had more stops in his organ; Daniel Webster was more massive, his sentences were more heavily weighted; Abraham Lincoln was more persuasive—no utterance of Phillips Brooks's had the effect on the Nation of Abraham Lincoln's Cooper-Union address or the immortality of his Gettysburg address. But no orator I ever heard was more inspirational. A friend of Phillips Brooks, who knew him well, admired him greatly, and possessed rare psychological insight, indicated in the one word "abundance" his distinguishing characteristic. "You will find," said he, "the word 'abundant' in almost every sermon: abundant life, abundant light, abundant grace, abundant goodness." The trees of the Lord, said the Psalmist, are full. Phillips Brooks was one of the trees of the Lord.

Physically he was an impressive specimen of manhood—stood, I am sure, something over six feet in his stockings and could not have weighed less than two hundred and fifty pounds. But he was not corpulent; had not the appearance of carrying an ounce of superfluous flesh. He enjoyed marvellous health. Two years before his death he told me that he had never known what it was to be tired. More's the pity! If he had rested more, he might have lived longer. He never apparently spared himself; rarely, if ever, declined to render a service to the public or to a friend if acceptance was possible; did not, I think, use a shorthand writer in his correspondence until after his election as bishop; all his letters to me were written with his own hand. His beautiful library was on the ground floor of his bachelor home on Marlboro Street in Boston, and visitors were apparently always welcome. When and where and how he read and studied I do not know, but that he was both a careful student and a wide reader is abundantly indicated by his sermons. I asked him once when he did his reading. His reply was characteristic of a man who never talked about himself. "I have," he replied, "a cottage at Andover where I go in the summer. And every year I take up a book and read it there; and—well—the next year I take up another book."

His body was a fit tabernacle for a large mind. He had a wide horizon, intellectually lived in the open country, was interested in large themes. But no themes seemed to him large unless they concerned human life. His thinking was always suffused with feeling; but his feelings were always under his control. He was never an indifferentist and never an enthusiast.

He was a loyal, consistent, and conscientious Churchman. But ecclesiastical questions did not interest him. In the meetings of the House of Bishops the newly elected bishops sit in the rear of the church, the older ones in front. In the first meeting after Phillips Brooks's election, toward the close of the session Bishop Henry C. Potter was passing out. Bishop Brooks stopped him with this whispered question: "Henry, is it always as dull as this?"

Mr. Beecher once said in my hearing: "Scholars talk about *essential* truths. Essential to what? Essential to a perfect system, or essential to a perfect life?" The only truths that Phillips Brooks regarded as essential were the truths that contributed something to life. I do not know what Phillips Brooks thought about evolution as a biological theory or whether he thought about it at all, nor what sociological theory of industrial and political development he held, or whether he had ever formulated for himself any theory. But this I do know: That in the seed he saw the flower, and in the babe the man, and in the tribe the nation; that he believed that life is an end in itself not a means to some other end, as happiness either here or hereafter; that this life of God, this divine life, this Christ-life is possible to men here and now; that it is not something external to man, but an experience in man. Phillips Brooks believed in this life because he possessed it; and it so abounded in him as to overflow, as water out of a great fountain, so irradiated him as to shine out, giving light and life always and everywhere.

It was this life of God in his own soul and this faith that it broods over all men and is manifest in all the natural and healthful activities of man that made him the inspiring preacher that he was. I sat next to him once at a public dinner where we were both to speak on a semi-political topic. He said to me: "I don't know what to say on this theme to-night. Religion is always easy to talk on; it is so natural. Don't you think so?" He was fond of and familiar with architecture. "They say," he said, "that the grotesque gargoyles were put on the outside of the cathedrals to represent the evil spirits

244

being driven out from the house of God. I think it far more likely they were expressions of that humour that is innate in all men and finds expression in our time in newspaper caricatures." And he told me that when his own church was being decorated it was discovered that the painter had put a grotesque figure on the ceiling, and I believe it became necessary to put the scaffold up again in order to take this figure out.

Thus his faith in the universal presence of God in all innocent and healthful human activities is illustrated by his understanding of children. No grown-up, I think, ever understood them better. He had in some respects a child's mind, which is very different from a childish mind. Jesus said that one must become as a little child if he would enter into the kingdom of heaven. Phillips Brooks remained as a little child after he had entered that kingdom. Staying with a friend, he went up to his room to get ready for supper and did not return. After some delay the lady of the house went up to call him, and found him in the nursery sitting on the floor with the children as his hosts, having afternoon tea out of their toy cups and saucers. This was no act of condescension on his part. He enjoyed it as much as they. In his charming letters of travel none are more charming than those to his nephews and nieces.

One incident in my own association with Phillips Brooks which brought us into very close fellowship illustrates his catholicity, his comparative unconcern about ecclesiastical and theological theories, his interest in the various phases of the spiritual life, and his understanding of children.

On January 16, 1890, a Congregational Council was to be held in Plymouth Church to ordain to the Christian ministry my associate, Howard S. Bliss, and to instal him and myself as co-pastors of that church. After the death of Henry Ward Beecher there was no man in the Christian ministry whom I revered and loved as I did Phillips Brooks. With some hesitation, I wrote to him, telling him of the expected service and that there was no man whose presence and participation I so much desired as his, yet I did not want to ask him to violate a canon or rubric of his Church, and with them I was not familiar. Could he and would he come? I received in reply the following letter:

Wadsworth
December 2, 1889.

DEAR DR. ABBOTT:

I know you will not think it indifference or carelessness which has left your kind & welcome & surprising note so long unanswered. It has been only the waiting for that leisure half hour which never comes & which we always keep the delightful delusion of expecting. But I must not wait for it any longer & so, between the students' visits, I will tell you first how truly I thank you for the friendly impulse which made you wish that I should come and take any part in the most interesting service of your installation. I value that impulse of yours very deeply and I always shall. I may most frankly say that there is no man from whom I should more joyfully receive such a token of confidence & affection.

I should like exceedingly to come, I would make every effort to do so. There is nothing I am sure in any Canon or Rubric which would prevent my coming. I am not very wise in Rubrics or Canons, but I do not remember one which says a word about our ministers sitting in Congregational Councils. The only questions in my mind are two. First, about the date. Your letter is not by me here but I think you do not give the exact date, and there are so many foolish promises which I have made to do foolish things in the early part of January that I do not dare to feel absolutely sure of escaping during that time.

The other question is as to the function of a member of an Ordaining Council. I am disgracefully ignorant. I have been nothing but an Episcopalian all my life. What does an Installer do, I wonder. And what would the Congregationalists say when they saw me there?

Would it not be better that I should come, if possible, and utter the interest which I really deeply feel by giving out a hymn or reading a Lesson from Scripture at the Installation service? And then if at the last moment something here made it impossible for me to come, perhaps another man might do my important duty in my place and I should be with you in spirit and bid you godspeed all the same.

These are my questions. In view of them, do with me what you think best. I hope I have written intelligently, but since I began to write several of these boys have been in with their big questions which they ask with as much apparent expectation of an immediate & satisfactory answer as if they were inquiring the way to Boston. How delightful they are! We are all rejoicing in the good work which you did here and left behind you. It was a distinct refreshment & enlargement of all that had been done before. We will do our best to keep the fire from going out until you come again.

Meanwhile, I hope I have not written too vaguely about the Council & I am,

Ever faithfully yours,
PHILLIPS BROOKS.

He came and made one of the four addresses of that occasion. It was a characteristic interpretation of the life of the spirit; but nothing in it so much endeared him to us all as an incident in our home, which I have asked my daughter to write for insertion here:

At the time of my father's installation, there was held at our house a luncheon for those who were of the Ordaining Council. I was about twelve years old at the time, and I suppose that my mother thought that it would be a valuable memory for me to have, so she insisted that I should come and sit in a chair at my father's side during the dessert. Naturally, I was not very enthusiastic about the prospect, for I much preferred playing out of doors to listening to a number of ministers talk theology. Shortly after I

248

had come into the room and taken the appointed place I noticed a big man who sat, if I remember rightly, about half way up the table. He was telling Father all about the games the little Japanese girls played, and also giving Father a description of the Japanese toys. I thought to myself that at least one minister knew what was interesting, for all the others stopped talking and listened, too. After the luncheon I tried to slip out of the way, so as to attract as little attention as possible, when I saw the same big man come round the end of the table toward me and I soon found my hand lost in his.

"Would you like to go to Japan?" said he.

"Yes, sir," I gasped.

"We'll go then," said he.

He then took me into the front room and told me more about that part of his travels in Japan which would interest a child. The one thing that remains in my mind is that he said that in greeting each other the Japanese bowed way down to the ground (I think it was the Japanese), and that it was not so hard for them to do it, as they were not so very tall. "It was harder for me," said he, "and very hard for my friend Doctor McVicker, who is just exactly twice as tall as I am."

From that time Phillips Brooks was in my mind a "truly friend of mine," although I did not see him again until I was about sixteen. I was staying in Cambridge with my father, when one day he asked me if I would like to go into Boston with him and leave my card on Phillips Brooks in addition to doing some sight-seeing. We had very little idea that we would find Bishop Brooks at home, but, to our delight, he came to greet us immediately on our sending in our cards. He took us to his study, and what impressed me more than anything else was the contrast between him and some other ministers on whom Father had taken me to call. They all were cordial and friendly, but very soon after the greeting they would talk with Father about theology and I would wait with as much patience as I could summon until the call was over. Not so Bishop Brooks. He, from the beginning, talked about things in which both Father and I could be interested. That day, I remember, he told us how the carvings in many of the cathedrals in Europe were the only means by which the artists of olden time could express their sense of humour and he cited instances of the humour in those carvings. After a short call Father said we must not keep him any longer. This is my recollection of that conversation:

Bishop Brooks. People think that because I am a bishop I am busy. I'm not busy.

My father. I feel sure that we have taken as

much of your time as we should, and besides I want my daughter to see your church.

Bishop Brooks (to me). Now, wouldn't you rather see me than see my church? (*To my father.*) You surely have nothing to do here. It is just because you are so busy at home that you think you must be busy here, too.

However, my father insisted that we must go. Then Bishop Brooks turned to me and said: "The next time you come to Boston, bring your knitting work and spend the afternoon."

In both cases—the first time when I was twelve and the next time when I was sixteen—I was impressed by the fact that he took the trouble and was able to understand the interests of others, and so could establish at once friendly relations. He died not long after our last call upon him, and, like thousands, I felt I had lost a personal friend. I had seen him but twice.

How far he was a pastor in his parish I have no means of knowing. To have called systematically on stated days so as to visit every family once a year would have been foreign to his nature. But his acquaintance with God and his sympathetic understanding of men made him a wise counsellor in spiritual perplexity and a strength-giving comforter in time of sorrow. The number of students who called upon him in his university ministry evidenced the first; the following incident narrated to me, though not by him, illustrates the second:

A young man who was living with his wife and their infant child in a boarding-house in Boston trying to save money with which to buy an interest in the business in which he served, attended Trinity Church irregularly on Sundays, sitting in the gallery. His child died suddenly. The young wife was heartbroken and half crazed by the suddenness of the blow. She would not relinquish the babe, but held it in her arms and rocked it as though it were asleep. Nothing he could say had any effect. The motherly landlady suggested that he call on Phillips Brooks. He was reluctant; had never met him, was not a member of his church, nor even of his regular and recognized congregation. But despair for his wife reinforced the counsel of his landlady. He went to the rector's house; found access easy to the rector's study, as did all callers; and before he had finished his story was interrupted. "I will go with you," said the rector. They went together to the house of sorrow, and found the wife and mother still rocking the babe in her arms as though in sleep. Phillips Brooks leaned over and looked on the sleeping babe. "What a beautiful child!" he said. "Would you let me rock him for a little while?" The mother laid the babe in the rector's arms and he took the mother's chair. Then, responding to a gesture of Phillips Brooks, the husband led the mother from the room. When he returned, Doctor Brooks asked when the funeral was to be, himself proposed to attend it, and an hour after he had gone there came a bunch of lilies with his card for the morrow. The man who wrote: "The priest should be, above all things, a man with an intense and live humanity," illustrated his definition by his deeds. Never, I think, was priest more honoured and loved than he.

I at first had intended to entitle this chapter "Phillips Brooks, A Catholic Priest." But a wise friend advised me to change the title. "To the average reader," she said, "it will suggest ideas that you do not wish to suggest and it will arouse prejudices that subsequent explanations in the chapter will not easily allay." I think she was right and I changed the title. But if it is true that a catholic is one whose mind appreciates all truth, and whose spirit appreciates all that is good, and if a priest is one who by his conduct of public worship interprets the unspoken experiences of a silent congregation to themselves by speaking for them to a listening Father, then Phillips Brooks was preëminently a catholic priest. Almost the last act of his life illustrated, because it unconsciously expressed, his catholic spirit. A correspondent in a letter to me has narrated this act with such beautiful simplicity that I transfer it here to my pages:

Readville, Mass.
June 13, 1921.

REV. LYMAN ABBOTT, D.D.
DEAR SIR:

I read with the deepest interest your tribute to Phillips Brooks in a recent number of the *Outlook*. The last sermon he preached was in our little Union chapel—not 200 feet from my home where I am now writing. It was my pleasant duty to secure the various preachers who ministered to us (we had no pastor). I learned that he was to preach in Hyde Park Sunday morning Jan. 15 [1893] and was to give a "talk" in the evening in East Dedham. He had never heard of our chapel, and certainly had never heard of me, but I wrote him a brief note telling what a joy it would be to us, if in the afternoon, he would preach to our little congregation of Methodists, Baptists, Congregationalists, Presbyterians, and a *few* Episcopalians. I didn't expect he would come, I simply cherished a forlorn hope that he might.

To my great surprise and intense delight I received in a few days a card from him, accepting the invitation and closing with the beautiful words I can never forget: "I thank you for inviting me." He came, and preached a sermon which those who heard must still remember. Had he stood in some grand cathedral before a throng of the rich and great, he could not have been more earnest, or more *eloquent*. In a week our hearts were broken when the morning papers told us the great man, preacher, and bishop was dead. Two splendid portraits of him in his prime hang on the walls of our chapel, and his memory still makes the place sacred.

After Doctor Brooks's death a unique meeting was held in New York City which was an unconscious tribute to the catholicity of one who had endeared himself to men of all faiths and to many who appeared to have none at all, by his appreciation of all truth and of all that is good. A young man called at the office of the *Outlook* to suggest to me that a public meeting should be held in New York in memory of Phillips Brooks. I have since learned that he was a teacher in one of the public schools of the city, that he was not a churchman and was by no means a regular attendant at any church, but was a grateful admirer of Phillips Brooks because of the inspiration which the spirit of Phillips Brooks had imparted to his spirit. He represented no church, no organization, no committee, and had never spoken with Phillips Brooks, but urged that there ought to be a spontaneous and unsectarian expression of the universal reverence and the universal sorrow. I sympathized with his desire but discouraged his attempt. To organize a great meeting in a great conglomerate city like New York is never easy. To do it without support previously pledged seemed to me impossible. Would I attend? Yes. And speak? Yes.

A week later I received notice that a meeting would be held and that Carnegie Hall, the largest hall in the city, had been secured. There was still no organization, no committee. There was no extraordinary advertising. But when, on the appointed evening, I reached the place, the hall was crowded to its utmost capacity, and the speakers included a Jewish rabbi, a Roman Catholic priest, New York's most eloquent lawyer, and four Protestant clergymen. The young man was not to be seen; and I have never seen him since. The speeches were as simple, as spontaneous, and as catholic as the audience. Rabbi Gustav Gottlieb said of the man we came to honour: "He was not bishop of his Church only, he was my bishop also by divine calling and consecration." The Roman Catholic priest said of him that he "was about his Master's work. He seemed emancipated from all human vanity." And I venture to bring this tribute of affectionate reverence to a close by quoting a sentence from my own closing address on that memorable occasion:

"We have been wondering, Is there any God? And we have been reaching out in nature to find the evidence of him. And suddenly there appears before us the divine shining in one great illuminated nature, one that is full of God; and while we stood in his presence, while we heard his voice, while we were looking in his eyes and he was looking into ours, then did God come again; then did we realize that God is; then did we feel that God speaks to the heart of man through the heart of man."

BOOKER T. WASHINGTON, STATESMAN

MR. ROOSEVELT once sent me a newspaper clipping which Mr. Washington had sent to him with a note affirming its truth. I returned the clipping to Mr. Roosevelt and quote it here from memory.

A Southern gentleman, meeting Mr. Washington in Florida, said to him, "Professor Washington, you are the greatest man in the country."

Mr. Washington. Oh, no, sir! you mustn't think that. There are many men much greater than I am.

Gentleman. Name one.

Mr. Washington. Well, sir, President Roosevelt is a much greater man than I am.

Gentleman. No, sir! I used to think he was a great man until he invited you to luncheon.

This testimony from a Southerner to the greatness of Mr. Washington was by no means unique. It represented a considerable sentiment of respect throughout the South for Mr. Washington's character as a man and as a publicist.

A number of years ago, during Mr. McKinley's presidency, I was in a Southern town in one of the border states where I had gone to preach or to lecture. Half a dozen prominent citizens were invited by my host to meet me. They were all Southerners. I was the only one in the company who resided north of Mason and Dixon's line. The conversation at the supper table drifted toward politics and then to estimates of some of our public men. The question was raised who our greatest statesman was. Each gentleman present gave his estimate. With one exception they all declared Booker Washington to be the greatest statesman. The one exception put Mr. McKinley first and Booker Washington second.

If comparisons are odious, superlatives are impossible. There is no greatest poem, or greatest statue, or greatest picture, or greatest book, or greatest text in the Bible; though these are constantly being asked for by writers to the newspapers. Every useful product of human effort has its own peculiar value. Which is the more important in a watch?—the hair spring or the main spring? Both are essential. I would not, therefore, agree that Booker Washington is the greatest statesman; but he was, certainly, one of the great statesmen of his century.

What do I mean by statesman?

I shall not assume the office of a lexicographer or go to the dictionaries to get the meaning of the word, but give the meaning which I attach to it in estimating the public men of history. Hegel says, "God governs the world; the actual working of his government—the carrying out of his plan—is the History of the World." He is a statesman who understands that plan, reads aright the enigma of his age, and successfully coöperates in achieving the divine purpose. Cavour was a statesman; Bismarck was not. Both worked to accomplish a national unity; one in Germany, the other in Italy. But Bismarck thought that national unity could be accomplished by uniting different governments under one imperial head through the power of a great army. Cavour saw that national unity could be accomplished only by uniting a dissevered people in one community by inspiring them with a common spirit and a common purpose. Italy, united from within, was never more a unit than it is to-day. War, the fickle patron saint of Germany which gave to her Alsace and Lorraine in the nineteenth century, has given them back to France in the twentieth century, and what is to be the fate of shattered Germany no one can foretell.

Booker T. Washington was a great statesman because he understood the meaning of his age and gave himself a willing and intelligent instrument to the beneficent solution of his nation's problem. The Civil War had established the authority of the National Government, but it still remained to unite North and South by a common spirit and a common purpose; it had set free the slave, but it still remained to establish new relations of mutual friendliness and respect between the races; it had abolished the old system of compulsory labour, but it still remained to create a new system of free labour; it had stricken the shackles from the limbs of the slave, but it still remained to strike the shackles from his mind and to teach him and his neighbour the rights, the duties, and the responsibilities of freedom. To this task Booker Washington devoted his life with singleness of purpose, clearness of vision, and patience of endeavour.

He has told the story of his life very simply and very modestly in his autobiography: "Up from Slavery"; a book which is a valuable addition both to American history and to American literature. It is preëminently a book for American boys and girls and ought to be in every school library in the country. Out of this book the thoughtful reader can easily get some impression of the spirit that animated Mr. Washington and the principles that governed him during his extraordinary career. How far these principles were carefully thought out and accurately defined by himself to himself;

how far they were unconsciously imbibed from the great leaders whose examples he emulated— General Armstrong and Doctor Frissell; and how far they were born in him and cultivated by his own reflection upon the experiences and observations of his own life I do not know, and I do not think he knew. Nor is it important for us to inquire.

Booker T. Washington was born in 1858 or 1859—he does not know the day or the month. His mother was a slave and a woman of unusual character. He does not know who his father was. After emancipation and he began to go to school he found the other boys had two names while he had but one. To meet the dilemma he adopted his surname. "When the teacher asked me what my full name was, I calmly told him 'Booker Washington,' as if I had been called by that name all my life. . . . I think there are not many men in our country who have had the privilege of naming themselves in the way that I have." From the very first he shared the ambition common to his race: he was eager to get an education. His mother aided him; his stepfather did not. The boy was earning money by his work in a mine and it was with difficulty that he got permission to attend school at all, and much of the time could attend only a night school. "Often," he writes,

"I would have to walk several miles at night in order to recite my night-school lessons. There was never a time in my youth, no matter how dark and discouraging the days might be, when one resolve did not continually remain with me, and that was a determination to secure an education at any cost." He chanced to overhear two miners talking about a great school for coloured people somewhere in Virginia and resolved at once to go to it, although he had no idea where it was, nor how many miles away, nor how he was going to reach it. The distance was about five hundred miles. The little money that he had been able to accumulate partly by his saving, partly by gifts to him from Negro neighbours, was entirely exhausted by the time he had reached Richmond. He slept under a wooden sidewalk with his satchel for a pillow, earned a little money by working in unloading a ship, and finally reached Hampton with fifty cents in his pocket with which to begin his education. The story of his unique examination, though probably familiar to many of my readers, is so significant and so simply and graphically told by Booker Washington that I quote from his narrative here:

I presented myself before the head teacher for assignment to a class. Having been so long without proper food, a bath, and change of clothing, I did not, of course, make a very favourable impression upon her, and I could see at once that there were doubts in her mind about the wisdom of admitting me as a student. I saw her admitting other students and felt deep down in my heart that I could do as well as they if I could only get the chance to show what was in me. After some hours had passed the head teacher said to me: "The adjoining recitation room needs sweeping. Take the broom and sweep it."

I swept the recitation room three times. Then I got a dusting-cloth and I dusted it four times. All the wood-work around the walls, every bench, table, and desk, I went over four times with my dusting-cloth. Besides, every piece of furniture had been moved and every closet and corner in the room had been thoroughly cleaned. I had the feeling that in a large measure my future depended upon the impression I made upon the teacher in the cleaning of that room. When I was through, I reported to the head teacher. She was a "Yankee" woman who knew just where to look for dirt. She went into the room and inspected the floor and closets; then she took her handkerchief and rubbed it on the woodwork about the walls, and over the table and benches. When she was unable to find one bit of dirt on the floor, or a particle of dust on any of the furniture, she quietly remarked, "I guess you will do to enter this institution."

He had exemplified one of the lessons which he was to spend his life in teaching to others: the way to secure respect is not to demand it, but to earn it.

His successful passing of this examination won for him the position of janitor which he gladly accepted because he could thus work out nearly all the cost of his board. How little familiarity he had with the elements of what we are accustomed to call civilization is indicated by the fact that he had never before slept in a bed with sheets and they were a puzzle to him. "The first night I slept under both of them, and the second night I slept on top of both of them, but by watching the other boys I learned my lesson in this, and have been trying to follow it ever since and to teach it to others." Another lesson which he learned in those Hampton years, not from the textbooks, but from the life, was the value of unselfish service. "One of the things that impressed itself upon me deeply, the second year, was the unselfishness of the teachers. It was hard for me to understand how many individuals could bring themselves to the point where they could be so happy in working for others. Before the end of the year I think I began learning that those who are happiest are those who do the most for others. This lesson I have tried to carry with me ever since." He learned also the use and value of the Bible. "I learned to love to read the Bible, not only for the spiritual help which it gives, but on account of its literature. The lessons taught me in this respect took such a hold upon me that at the present time, when I am at home, no matter how busy I am, I always make it a rule to read a chapter or a portion of a chapter in the morning before beginning the work of the day."

On graduating from Hampton he taught for two years and then decided to spend some months in study at Washington, D. C. Here he got a glimpse of the effect of the so-called higher education upon the men of his race; the result was not appealing to him. A large proportion of the students by some means had their personal expenses paid for them. They were, in most cases, better dressed, had more money, and often were more brilliant mentally, but they were less self-dependent, gave more attention to outer appearances, knew more about Latin and Greek, but less about life and its conditions as they would meet it at their homes, and were not as much inclined as were the Hampton students to get into the country districts of the South and work for the members of their own race.

At the end of his term in Washington he received from a committee of white people in Charleston, West Virginia, an invitation to canvass the state in support of the proposal to transfer the capitol from Wheeling to Charleston. The reputation he acquired in that canvass brought him an urgent invitation to engage in political life. At that time it was a popular notion among the coloured people that activity in politics was the sure method to win both influence and fame. There was one Negro in the Senate of the United States and he had made there an excellent record. But Mr. Washington, young as he was, did not think that the best service to his race could be rendered in a political career. "Even then," he writes, "I had a strong feeling that what our people most needed was to get a foundation in education, industry, and property, and for this I felt that they could better afford to strive than for political preferment. . . . A very large proportion of the young men who went to school or to college did so with the expressed determination to prepare themselves to be great lawyers or congressmen, and many of the women planned to become music teachers; but I had a reasonably fixed idea, even at that early period in my life, that there was need for something to be done to prepare the way for successful lawyers, congressmen, and music teachers."

Declining the seductive call to a political career, he went back to Hampton Institute to take up there the work of a teacher and to pursue some supplementary studies. A night school was presently started by General Armstrong for the purpose of opening the way for the education of young coloured men and women who were too poor to be able to contribute anything toward the cost of their board or even to supply themselves with books. They were received on the condition that they were to work for ten hours during the day and attend school for two hours at night. Only those who had an eager desire for education would attempt such a school; only those who had patience would persist in it. Mr. Washington, by one of those inspirations which are a part of the furnishing of such a man, gave to his night school the title of "The Plucky Class," and after a student had been in the night school long enough to prove what was in him, he received a certificate: "This is to certify that James Smith is a member of The Plucky Class of the Hampton Institute and is in good and regular standing." This night school which started with only twelve students numbered three or four hundred when, in 1900, Mr. Washington wrote his autobiography.

Mr. Washington's administration of the night school was his final preparation for his life work. One year of that preparation sufficed. In 1881 the Legislature of Alabama had appropriated two thousand dollars for starting a school for coloured people in Tuskegee, which had been previously an educational centre for the whites. The committee having this matter in charge wrote to Hampton Institute to recommend a principal. General Armstrong, the principal of

Hampton Institute, recommended Mr. Washington and to Tuskegee Mr. Washington went.

He had expected to find there a building properly equipped for school work. He found nothing of the kind, but did find "that which no costly building and apparatus can supply— hundreds of hungry, earnest souls who wanted to secure knowledge." There was no provision for securing land, buildings, and apparatus, and the annual appropriation made by the Legislature of two thousand dollars could be used only for the payment of the salaries of the instructors. The best accommodations for the school Mr. Washington could discover in the town was the Coloured Methodist Church and a rather dilapidated shanty standing near it, both of them in so bad a condition that during the first month of school whenever it rained one of the students would leave his lessons to hold an umbrella over the teacher, and on more than one occasion the landlady held an umbrella over him while he ate his breakfast.

There was plenty of need for the kind of education in which Mr. Washington believed and which it was his eager desire to furnish to the members of his race. In the county in which Tuskegee is situated the coloured people outnumbered the whites by about three to one. In the plantation districts, as a rule, the whole family slept in one room and guests shared the apartment with them. He writes that on more than one occasion, "I went outside the house to get ready for bed or to wait until the family had gone to bed. They usually contrived some kind of a place for me to sleep, either on the floor or in the special part of another's bed." Land about the cabin homes could easily have been used for kitchen gardens, but such gardens were practically unknown. The only object of the Negroes was to plant cotton which in many cases grew up to the very door of the cabin. Sewing machines, showy clocks, and parlour organs were often to be found in these cabins—clocks that did not keep time; sewing machines that no one knew how to use; organs on which no one could play. "On one occasion when I went into one of these cabins for dinner, when I sat down to the table for a meal with the four members of the family I noticed that, while there were five of us at the table, there was but one fork for the five of us to use." In general the crops were mortgaged and the coloured farmers were in debt.

Such schools as existed were taught in churches or in log cabins, by teachers inadequately prepared for their work, and inadequately provided with books and apparatus. "I recall," says Mr. Washington, "that one day I went into a schoolhouse—or rather into an abandoned log cabin that was being used as a schoolhouse— and found five pupils who were studying a lesson from one book. Two of these, on the front seat, were using the book between them; behind these were two others peeping over the shoulders of the first two, and behind the four was a fifth little fellow who was peeping over the shoulders of all four."

Of the thirty students who reported for admission when Tuskegee Institute was opened, a greater part were public school teachers who came in order to be able to earn a bigger salary. Some had studied Latin, and one or two Greek; some thought they had mastered arithmetic and knew about banking and discount, but had not mastered the multiplication table. The girls could locate the Desert of Sahara or the capital of China on an artificial globe, but could not locate the proper places for the knives and forks on an actual dinner table, or the places on which the bread and meat should be set. That there was a lack of any acquaintance with the simplest rules of health, or any provision for complying with them, might not unreasonably be expected. There was generally no provision for washing in the one-room cabins, though there existed some sort of provision for washing at least the face and hands outside. Toothbrushes were unknown even at a much later date, though in time, and after much repetition, pupils seeking admission to the school learned that the possession of a toothbrush was part of the required equipment. "I remember," writes Mr. Washington, "that one morning, not long ago, I went with the lady principal on her usual morning tour of inspection of the girls' rooms. We found one room that contained three girls who had recently arrived at the school. When I asked them if they had toothbrushes, one of the girls replied, pointing to a brush: 'Yes, sir. That is our brush. We bought it together yesterday.' It did not take them long to learn a different lesson."

In such circumstances the introduction of industrial education was attended with great difficulties. The greatest difficulty, however, was not the lack of equipment. It was the lack of desire on the part of the students for an industrial education. Slavery, by making labour compulsory, had dishonoured it. The whites had disdained to labour; the blacks when emancipated were eager to escape labour. Pupils objected to use their hands in school work; they had come there, as one of them expressed it, to be educated, not to work. Letters came from parents protesting against their children engaging in labour while they were in school.

Students brought requests from their parents to the effect that they wanted their children taught nothing but books. Religious teaching was summoned to the support of this inherited prejudice. An old coloured minister undertook to convince Mr. Washington from the story of Adam and the Garden of Eden that God had cursed all labour and therefore it was a sin for any man to work. But great difficulties seem never to have discouraged Booker Washington. Looking back upon his experiences in those first years at Tuskegee, and at details I have not space here to report, he writes:

As I look back now over that part of our struggle, I am glad that we had it. I am glad that we endured all those discomforts and inconveniences. I am glad that our first boarding-place was in that dismal, ill-lighted, and damp basement. Had we started in a fine, attractive, convenient room, I fear we would have "lost our heads" and become "stuck up." It means a great deal, I think, to start off on a foundation which one has made for one's self.

In April, 1906, the twenty-fifth anniversary of the founding of Tuskegee Institute was celebrated by appropriate exercises at Tuskegee. A special train from the North and local trains from the South brought to that celebration some two hundred distinguished visitors. Among them were such educational leaders as President

Eliot of Harvard University, Principal Frissell
of Hampton Institute, and President J. W. Aber-
crombie of the University of Alabama; such
business leaders as Andrew Carnegie and Robert
C. Ogden; such reformers, philanthropists, and
publicists as George McAneny, J. G. Phelps
Stokes, and William H. Taft; the latter was
supposed to represent the views of Mr. Roosevelt's administration of which he was an honoured member. They found in place of the
dilapidated coloured Meeting House and its
companion shanty an institute possessing 2,300
acres of land, upward of ninety buildings, more
than twelve hundred pupils, more than one
hundred and fifty teachers, an aggregate endowment, including real estate, of more than two
million dollars in value and involving a current
expenditure of about one hundred and eighty
thousand dollars a year. From its gates six
thousand women had gone out to carry with
them a leaven of intelligent industry throughout
the South and some of them into distant lands;
nearly five hundred had been trained in its
Bible Training School for direct Christian work;
upward of two thousand were engaged in teaching; and as a result of their efforts there had
sprung up sixteen incorporated schools animated
by its spirit and extending its work. It was stated
then, and we think the statement is still true,

that it was not known that a single graduate of the Institute had ever been convicted of a crime.

Here we might bring this article to a close, for the building of Tuskegee Institute is rightly regarded as Mr. Booker Washington's great achievement. But to justify our characterization of him as a great statesman one other dramatic incident, and the incidents that led up to it, must be briefly narrated.

Public speaking has formed a larger part of Mr. Washington's work than he intended. "I never planned," he says, "to give any large part of my life to speaking in public. I have always had more of an ambition to *do* things than merely to talk *about* doing them." But when the invitations came to him to speak he carried into this new development of his work the same spirit of thoroughness and of trust in divine guidance which had animated him from boyhood. He has given some insight into the secret of his power as a public speaker in a few sentences which are well worth the meditative study of all who desire to influence by public address their fellowmen, whether from the pulpit or the platform. "I make it a rule," he says, "never to go before an audience, on any occasion, without asking the blessing of God upon what I want to say. I always make it a rule to make especial preparation for each separate address. I care little how what I am saying is going to sound in the newspapers, or to another audience, or to an individual. At the time, the audience before me absorbs all my sympathy, thought, and energy."

In 1893, when the International Meeting of Christian Workers was held at Atlanta, Georgia, an invitation came to him at Boston to give at that meeting a five-minute address. It was, I believe, his first invitation to speak to an audience of whites in the South. Was it worth while to travel so far to do so little? But was it little? A great deal can be done by the right man on the right occasion in five minutes. In five minutes he can plant an acorn out of which will grow an oak. He accepted the invitation, went to Atlanta, made the five-minute speech, and returned to Boston. Two years later he was invited by telegram to accompany a committee from Atlanta to Washington for the purpose of presenting to a committee of Congress reasons for granting government help for an international exposition which was to be given in Atlanta in September. His speech before the Congressional Committee confirmed the favourable impression produced by his five-minute speech two years before. And as the opening of the Exposition drew near, he was invited to deliver one of the opening addresses, as a representative of the Negro race. With considerable hesitation, he accepted the invitation. The situation which that acceptance created was correctly diagnosed by a white farmer, one of his neighbours in Tuskegee: "Washington," he said, "you have spoken before the Northern white people, the Negroes in the South, and to us country white people in the South; but in Atlanta, to-morrow, you will have before you the Northern whites, the Southern whites, and the Negroes all together. I am afraid that you have got yourself into a tight place."

The committee gave him a perfectly free platform. "When the invitation came to me, there was not one word of intimation as to what I should say or as to what I should omit." The public interest upon this occasion was very great. The public excitement was indicated by the act of Mr. William H. Baldwin, one of the trustees of Tuskegee Institute, and a warm personal friend, who "was so nervous about the kind of reception that I would have, and the effect that my speech would produce, that he could not persuade himself to go into the building, but walked back and forth in the grounds outside until the opening exercises were over." The gist of Mr. Washington's speech was expressed in one homely metaphor that went the rounds of the country. Rarely does a single figure re-

ceive from so large an audience so intelligent
and enthusiastic a response. Holding up his
hand with his fingers extended and separated he
cried: "In all things that are purely social we
can be as separate as the fingers," then closing
the hand he continued, "yet one as the hand in
all things essential to mutual progress." The
sentiment was received with enthusiastic applause in which the members of both races
heartily joined, and the entire speech was well
characterized subsequently in a single sentence
by Mr. Clark Howell, the editor of the Atlanta
Constitution: "The whole speech is a platform
upon which blacks and whites can stand with
full justice to each other."

I have characterized Booker T. Washington
as a great statesman. Perhaps to justify that
statement the story of his life ought to be more
fully told and the condition of the problems with
which he dealt and of the state of public opinion upon them more fully described. Here it
must, however, suffice to state, however inadequately, the principles which he inculcated by
his speeches and illustrated by his action.

He interpreted the North to the South and the
South to the North, for he never modified his
opinions in order to adapt them to the current
opinion of the geographical section in which he
was speaking.

He interpreted the Negroes to the whites and the whites to the Negroes; drew sharply the distinction between social equality and industrial equality; never demanded more for the Negro than an opportunity for self-development and useful service, and never conceded that anything less than this would be justice.

He spent no time in discussing dead issues; but he unhesitatingly condemned slavery when he spoke of it at all, pointed out the evils it wrought upon the white race as upon the black race, and urged his own people to justify emancipation by demonstrating the superior value of free labour.

He made no demands upon the white race to respect the Negro; but he pointed out to the Negroes how they could earn that respect, and this he did not only by his words, but by his life of unselfish and devoted labour.

He saw no hope for the Negro in conferring upon him political power until he had the capacity to use it intelligently. Looking back upon the past he declared his belief that it would have been better to make the possession of a certain amount of education or property, or both, a test for the exercise of the franchise, but that test should be made to apply honestly to both the white and the black races. In other words, while seldom discussing the political question, he made it clear that he believed taking part in the government of others is a responsibility to be earned, not a natural right nor a privilege to be universally granted.

When he began his public labours I do not think there was any organized industrial education in the nation save in exceptional cases, such as Hampton Institute. That we now have industrial education as a part of our public school system in every state in the Union is very largely due to three men far in advance of their times: General Armstrong, Doctor Frissell, and Booker Washington.

In building the Tuskegee Institute Mr. Washington built his own monument. Greater educators there may have been; but it would not be easy to find in the history of any race the story of a life more Christ-like in its patient devotion to an unselfish cause than was his. This monument is a witness to the possibilities of the Afro-American. For the possibilities of a race are to be always measured, not by their averages but by their leaders, and Doctor Washington is a conclusive answer to the ignorant assertion that the Negro is incapable of great things. Nor is Tuskegee less a monument to the white people of the South. It was called into existence by them; received its first appropriation from a Southern legislature; and so hearty and unanimous has been the support awarded to it by the community in which it is situated that Doctor Washington was able to say that he had never asked anything of his white neighbours which they did not cordially grant to him if it was in their power so to do. Finally, Tuskegee affords conclusive demonstration that it is possible to unite both races in a common effort to promote the common welfare.

RUTHERFORD B. HAYES, PEACEMAKER

THE spirit in which General Lee and General Grant met at Appomattox Court House when, after four years of skilful and courageous fighting, the Southern leader surrendered to his chivalric antagonist, augured well for the early establishment of friendly relations between the South and the North. These leaders truly represented their respective sections.

But the assassination of Abraham Lincoln, which so quickly followed that surrender, wrought an almost instant revolution; it inspired bitterness in the North and despair in the South. President Johnson combined hatred of the ex-slaveholder with contempt for the ex-slave. For four years a new political battle raged between the South and the North after the four years of military battle had ended. There were statesmen who welcomed Grant's "Let us have peace," and saw clearly how it could be attained. If the ex-slaveholder and the ex-slave were to live prosperously together in the same community, mutual respect and mutual friendship must be cultivated between

282

them. Years of education would be needed to prepare the uneducated Negro for full citizenship. The burden of that education must not be thrown upon the South alone. Federal aid must be given to Southern education. But there were radicals of a different opinion. They held that suffrage is a natural right and that democracy means government by the majority. Their policy was: "Give the Negro the ballot and he will take care of himself. His late masters will be his enemies. If he cannot protect himself against them, the Federal Government must protect him."

The incompetence and corruption which this policy inflicted on the South surpasses belief. James Ford Rhodes in his history of this period tells us that at first Southern men attempted to coöperate with the Republican party in rebuilding a new civilization on the ruins of that which slavery and war had destroyed. But they soon gave up the endeavour in despair. Nine tenths of the Republican party in the South were Negroes; one tenth were white; and the one tenth were rarely wise and not always honest. The inevitable effect of this policy on the Republican party Henry Ward Beecher foretold in a graphic figure. "The radicals," he said to me once, "are trying to drive the wedge into the log butt-end foremost, and they'll only split their beetle." This they did. By the second term of Grant's administration the Republican party existed in two bitterly hostile factions. Meanwhile, the corruption which the radicals had unwittingly fastened on the South returned to plague the North. A successful war is almost inevitably followed by corruption. Germany suffered more from her victory in the Franco-Prussian War than France suffered from her defeat. The most corrupt period in our national history was that which followed the Civil War. It was the period of the carpet-bag government in the Southern states, of the Tweed Ring in New York State, of the Crédit Mobilier in the Federal Government. The most corrupt election in our history was that which followed the second term of General Grant. Charges of intimidation, of fraudulent registration, of flagrant bribery, were preferred by each party against the other and were substantiated by indubitable evidence.

When the election was over, it was very doubtful who had been elected. Threats of civil war were freely made by partizans; fears of civil war were seriously entertained by men behind the scenes. It was solemnly affirmed that 145,000 well-disciplined troops were ready to fight to seat the Democratic candidate. An army of men not disciplined and not organized, who had been thrown out of employment by one of the worst panics that ever struck the American market, were believed to be ready for a campaign of plunder. Three circumstances conspired to ward off the danger: the assurance that General Grant would use all the resources of the Nation to preserve order; the dread of civil war by a generation just emerging from one; and the poise of both the Presidential candidates who showed equal anxiety to secure a peaceable decision of the issue.

In the election Mr. Hayes had taken no such active part as has now become the fashion of Presidential candidates. In the post-election controversy his influence is indicated by a letter he wrote to Senator Sherman at New Orleans: "We are not to allow our friends to defeat one outrage and fraud by another. There must be nothing crooked on our part. Let Mr. Tilden have the place by violence, intimidation, and fraud, rather than undertake to prevent it by means that will not bear the severest scrutiny." Finally, by an almost unanimous consent, a tribunal was created to determine the issue; and when this tribunal, by a majority of one, declared Mr. Hayes duly elected, the decision was accepted by the Congress and by the country—sullenly, but still accepted. To this day history is doubtful whether this decision was right or wrong.

When Mr. Hayes was inaugurated President in March, 1877, the conditions that confronted him were these:

He held his office with a clouded title. More than half of the white citizens of the United States believed that he had not been constitutionally elected; less than half the voters had voted for him. He was called to administer the government over a nation divided not more by the Civil War than by the undemocratic reconstruction policy, the effect of which had been to incite jealousy and suspicion between the sections and hostility between the races. Corruption in local, state, and national governments had brought government into contempt, given to the term "politician" an odious meaning, destroyed some reputations and besmirched others. During the first two years of his term the Democrats had a majority in the House; during the last two years a majority in both House and Senate. And he had the hesitating and reluctant support of a divided party and the bitter hostility of some of its most influential and prominent leaders. During his stormy administration he never lost his temper, never answered abuse with abuse, never sacrificed principle to policy, never fought fire with fire, retained the respect of his friends in defeat and compelled the respect of his enemies in victory.

RUTHERFORD B. HAYES

At the very beginning of his administration he foreshadowed his break with the "Old Guard" of his day by the personnel of his Cabinet, selected upon the following simple principles, stated in his diary:

1. A new Cabinet.
2. No Presidential candidate.
3. No appointment to "take care" of anybody.

Seven weeks later he emphasized the break by abandoning military rule in the South. In both Louisiana and South Carolina were two state governments—one Republican, the other Democratic. He withdrew the Federal troops from both states, and in both states the Republican governments collapsed. The wrath of the militant Republicans was unbounded. To them this was a surrender to "unrepentant rebels." His reply to the fierce invectives in the Senate was confided to his diary, which was dumb. "My policy," he wrote, "is trust, peace, and to put aside the bayonet. I do not think that the wise policy is to decide contested elections in the State by the use of the National army."

In his inaugural address he declared that a thorough, radical, and complete reform in our civil service was a paramount necessity. He emphasized this conviction by removing two of Senator Conkling's wards from the Custom House in New York. The Senate rejected his nomination of their successors, and Conkling's wards held over. "I am right," said Mr. Hayes to his diary, "and shall not give up the fight." He did not. A year later his nominations were renewed and confirmed. His withdrawal of troops from the South had made Blaine his enemy; his removal of Conkling's appointees made Conkling his enemy. Mr. Conkling had no use for what he called "snivel service reform." The President confided to his silent diary the political principle which compelled his course. "I stand," he wrote, "for the equal and Constitutional independence of the Executive. The independence of the different departments of the Government is essential to the progress and existence of good government."

A plan to increase the money of the country and lower the standard by remonetizing silver he vetoed. Democrats and Republicans, responding to a popular demand, reinforced undoubtedly by silver-mine owners and silver-producing states, were able to overrule the President's veto. In the tangle of that hour, when financiers were themselves perplexed, Mr. Hayes gave to his diary in a sentence the conclusion to which years after the whole country came: "I cannot consent to a measure which stains our credit."

The Democratic party attached a rider to the Appropriation Bill which would have made it impossible for the President to fulfil the duty laid upon him by the Constitution and preserve order in the States if necessity should arise. The President called an extra session, laid the facts before Congress and the country in a message so short that busy men could read it, so simple that men unskilled in politics could understand it, and so free from combativeness that partizans could not complain of it, and then waited for Congress to hear from the country and retire from its impossible position; and this it did, after a long controversy with the patient President.

Men will face a lion who will flee from a swarm of bees. So men will face a political cabal who will hesitate to challenge social conventions by disregarding a long-established social custom. Mr. and Mrs. Hayes had never served wine on their home table. They resolved to carry their habit of abstinence into their new home in the White House. Their action aroused a thunderstorm of criticism—lightning that did not strike and thunder that did not terrify. The criticism took on every variety from the good-natured *bon mot* of Mr. Evarts: "At the President's reception water flowed like champagne" to the irritating accusation of a disappointed office-seeker that what made the President a total abstainer was his parsimony. The only serious argument advanced against his course was that as host of the nation he should in his hospitality represent the sentiment of the nation. It proved a boomerang. For presently the White House was deluged with letters, telegrams, resolutions, thank-offerings of flowers, from every section of the country. Only a very small number of Americans served wine on their tables; the President was conforming the hospitality of the White House to the habits of the American people. His action was the more significant because he had not been a strict total abstainer before his election, and he never was a prohibitionist. As his biographer has given to the world his statement of his views of this subject as they were communicated to his father confessor, the diary, I violate no confidence by giving to my readers his definition of them in the following letter to me:

Private

Fremont, O.
22 Sept., 1880.

REV. LYMAN ABBOTT
  N. Y.
DEAR SIR:
  Your note of the 16th instant is before me. With very decided opinions as to the value of "temperance legislation" I am yet persuaded that their publication would, if any attention was given to them, provoke profitless

controversy. Certain experiments must, as I see it, be tried before there will be any general concurrence of sentiment among the sincere friends of the cause. The tendency to division and discord is already so strong that I am averse to doing anything which will add to it. The true agencies for good in this work, as I look at the subject, are example, education, discussion, and the influences of religion.

Sincerely,
R. B. HAYES.

I met President Hayes personally twice. Once during his Presidency, in company with Governor and Mrs. Claflin and Mr. and Mrs. Lawson Valentine, I spent an evening at the White House as quietly as if we had been in a rural home ten miles from a railway station. The President's "shop" was by common consent excluded. Politics were not discussed. One incident I recall: the President took me upstairs to show me his children asleep in the nursery. I had two boys of about their age at home; and for a few moments our fatherly pride and our fatherly love united us in a very sacred fellowship.

The other incident was later. After his retirement from the Presidency he was elected president of the Prison Reform Association. At its annual meeting in Saratoga—I forget the year—I was preacher and took as my text: "If thine enemy hunger, feed him; if he thirst, give him drink," and as my theme the doctrine that the only justice that the state can rightly administer is a *merciful* justice and the only punishment it can rightly inflict is a reformatory punishment. After the service the President, with a cordiality that was more than official, requested the sermon for publication, and it was printed from the stenographer's notes. He gave expression—I think subsequently to the Saratoga meeting, but I am not sure—to the same principle in a characteristically well-balanced statement:

The chief aim in the treatment of convicts is to protect society against its avowed enemy, the criminal. The advocates of improved prisons and prison discipline add to this a more specific statement. They would reform all criminals whom they can reform by wise systems wisely administered. Those who cannot be reclaimed should remain under sentence of conviction where they can support themselves by labour and do no harm to society.

The principles laid down by Mr. Thomas Mott Osborne in "Behind Prison Bars," and illustrated by his own prison administration, are all implied in this statement of President Hayes, made some forty years ago.

President Hayes did not heal the wounds inflicted by war and by a misconceived policy of reconstruction, but he set the broken bones, and

Time is knitting together again the North and
the South; he did not solve the race problem, but
he did much to create that era of good feeling
which has enabled the best men in both races
to understand each other and to coöperate in
movements for their mutual welfare; he did not
accomplish the purification of government, but
he did give a new impulse to that movement for
political purity carried forward subsequently
by his successors in office, preëminently by
Grover Cleveland and Theodore Roosevelt,
until "A public office is a public trust" has come
to be recognized, at least in theory, as a sound political principle; he did not succeed in wholly preventing the endeavour to give us all plenty of
money by making it cheap, but he halted that
proceeding and gave the sober second thought of
the American people time to develop and assert
itself; he did not fall into the error of thinking
that a people will be made temperate if they are
prohibited from drinking, but his example did
more than perhaps we know toward cultivating
in the nation a habit of total abstinence from
intoxicating liquors which laid the foundation for
national prohibition.

During Mr. Hayes's Presidency I, an editor,
was studying and interpreting current history.
My admiration for Mr. Hayes steadily grew
while he was making history. I admired his

masterful conscience, his gentle strength, his non-combative courage, his unconquerable patience. I admired him for the men he brought about him as his counsellors and for the success he achieved against great odds. And when I planned this series of "Silhouettes of my Contemporaries," I eagerly embraced the opportunity it gave me to sketch the portrait of a statesman whose character and difficulties the country too little realized then and whose service the country has too little appreciated since. Both are indicated by the title I have ventured to give to him: Rutherford B. Hayes—Peacemaker.

ABRAHAM LINCOLN, LABOUR LEADER

O F COURSE I cannot give a portrait of the greatest statesman of his time in a score of pages. But these are not portraits: they are silhouettes, shadow pictures, faded photographs, half-awakened memories of impressions left on the mind of an octogenarian by some of his contemporaries. Some of them I knew intimately, some of them personally not at all, not one of them gave me a sitting. Not one of them did I sketch at the time. But all of them I studied. Their places and current history I endeavour to discern; the divine meaning of their lives I endeavour to read.

William Lloyd Garrison, John Brown, John C. Fremont, General David Hunter, all attempted to be emancipators. But none of them saw what Abraham Lincoln saw so clearly, that slavery was an unjust form of labour and that any form of so-called free labour, if dominated by the same spirit of greed, was also unjust. He was the first, and still remains the greatest, American Labour leader.

In 1856 Buchanan defeated John C. Fremont for the Presidency. The election took

295

place in November; I was not of age until
December. Therefore, I could not vote. But
I could do the work of an enthusiastic boy in the
campaign, and I did. Fremont's defeat was
a disappointment, but not a discouragement.
The pitiable affair of Buchanan's administration
added unnumbered recruits to the Republican
party, and converted the party enthusiasm of
the previous campaigners into a religious enthusiasm. I was never an admirer of Seward;
he was too canny. I had no use for Stephen
Douglas; I think better of him now than I did
then. I had barely heard of Abraham Lincoln.
In those days "the Wild and Woolly West" was a
long way off from New York City. And when
in 1860 he lectured in Cooper Union I managed
to get a ticket. I was then in my twenty-fourth
year.

The city was not pro-slavery, but it was anti-
abolition and anti-agitation. King Cotton ruled
the market place, the press, the schools, the
churches. There was a conspiracy of silence.
Everybody said, "Hush!" No! Not everybody. There were voices of protest here and
there: from a merchant, a lawyer, a newspaper,
a clergyman. The violence of some of these
protests intensified the general apprehension.
An opinion quite commonly entertained was expressed with uncommon clearness and courage

ABRAHAM LINCOLN

by Charles O'Connor, a leader of the New York bar, who said of slavery:

It is fit and proper; it is in its own nature, as an institution, beneficial to both races; and the effect of this assertion is not diminished by our admitting that many faults are practised under it.

But faint echoes of the Lincoln-Douglas debates, in Illinois, had crossed the continent. Curiosity, but not conscience, was aroused. Cooper Union was packed with an expectant audience which had come, much as the audience on Mars Hill went to hear St. Paul, not hostile, not sympathetic, simply curious. I recall the scene, and as I describe the present faded picture, I wonder how far it truly portrays the reality— the hushed expectancy of the audience, the orator on the platform, a tall figure, ungainly but erect, virile, with no trace of that slouchiness which tradition attributes to him, a homely face but a compelling presence, a carrying voice easily heard but never vociferous, little movement, few gestures, no stories, no jests, no pictures, no concessions to prejudice, but no scorn and no invective—simply a calm, direct, unanswerable appeal to the reason and the conscience. "If slavery is right," he said, "there is nothing that the South asks of us which we ought not to grant. If slavery is wrong we have no right to permit its establishment in territories under our control."

That is the sum and substance of his speech as it remains in my mind to-day, sixty-one years after it was delivered. And I went out, as did hundreds of others, that night from that meeting an enthusiastic disciple and follower of Abraham Lincoln. The faith in him then inspired never weakened in the darkest days of the Civil War. I sometimes doubted what the issue of that war would be, but never for a moment doubted that it was a righteous war. There were pacifists then as there have been more recently; but the lesson I then learned I never forgot. It is eternally true that there is something better than Peace:—Justice.

In this sketch I had written thus far in my bedroom in the early morning, rising before light in an endeavour to preserve the picture as it came to me in the night, before the life of the day had obscured it. Since then I have compared my recollection of the speech with the official report in the volumes of Abraham Lincoln's speeches and letters, and have found that I have stated, almost in the words of the great American prophet, the conclusions to which in that ever-memorable address he sought to lead his audience.

After his election preparations for secession were carried on by the aggressive and determined advocates of a new Southern empire founded on slavery as its corner stone. Some men were cajoled by an elusive dream of political ambition; some were coerced by fear of a civil war. Before Mr. Lincoln's inauguration seven Southern states had formally adopted ordinances of secession. In the North lovers of the Union, lovers of peace, yes, and lovers of liberty, fearing that a dissolution of the Union would be the death knell of liberty throughout the world, united in an endeavour to find some compromise between right and wrong. Political enemies assailed, political friends besought; but Mr. Lincoln never hesitated, never wavered, never said a word nor did an act incongruous with that simple and fundamental declaration: If slavery is right let us concede everything; if slavery is wrong there is nothing we can concede.

His first inaugural included a pathetic appeal to his dissatisfied fellow-countrymen: "You have no oath registered in heaven to destroy the government, while I shall have the most solemn one to 'preserve, protect and defend it.'" When the war broke upon the country he met it with the same faith in righteousness and a God of righteousness. When General David Hunter attempted to abolish slavery in a state occupied by his troops, Mr. Lincoln reversed the General's action. When it became clear to him and he could make it clear to the nation that slavery was aiding the assailants of the nation and that its abolition would weaken them, he proclaimed emancipation as a war measure. When, as the war drew toward its close, semi-official propositions for peace were made to him he replied that "The war will cease on the part of the Government whenever it shall have ceased on the part of those who began it"; and he repeated and re-repeated that three things were indispensable to peace: the restoration of the national authority throughout all the States, the acceptance of the Emancipation Proclamation, and the disbanding of all forces hostile to the Government. When after more than three years of war had passed and discouraged Democrats were beginning to affirm that it was a failure, and discouraged Republicans were looking about for new issues and a new leader, Lincoln met growing discontent by the affirmation "While I remain in my present position I shall not attempt to retract or modify the Emancipation Proclamation, nor shall I return to slavery any person who is free by the terms of that proclamation, nor by any of the acts of Congress. If the people should, by whatever mode or means, make it an executive duty to re-enslave such persons, another, and not I, must be their instrument to perform it." And when he was reëlected by an overwhelming majority his second inaugural repeated with a saddened but unwavering heart the principles of his pre-election speech: "With malice toward none; with charity for all; with firmness in the right, as God gives us to see the right, let us strive on to finish the work we are in; to bind up the nation's wounds; to care for him who shall have borne the battle, and for his widow, and his orphan—to do all which may achieve and cherish a just and lasting peace among ourselves, and with all nations."

Throughout the Civil War Mr. Lincoln was subject to violent criticism, sometimes honest, sometimes unscrupulous from two opposite quarters. The radical anti-slavery men of the East, especially of New England, criticized him for not initiating at once a policy of emancipation. Conservatives in the great commercial cities and in the Middle West criticized him for the policy of emancipation and for refusing proposals for compromise. Mr. Lincoln disregarded both groups of critics and seldom replied to either group. They both wanted him to govern; he believed and consistently acted on the belief that the people were to govern and that he was elected to carry out their will. The party which had elected him was pledged to maintain the Union and neither to interfere with slavery in the States nor to allow it in the Territories, and to carry out that policy they had elected a man who had declared in no uncertain terms his hostility to slavery as essentially and absolutely wrong. From the fulfilment of that pledge Mr. Lincoln never varied; for the method of its fulfilment he waited until he could lead the will of the people to the measure which he saw to be necessary.

During the Civil War I was pastor of a Congregational church in Terre Haute, Indiana, and, born and brought up in the East, could understand the public sentiment both of the Eastern and the Mid-Western states. There was probably no Northern state in which there was less anti-slavery sentiment and more anti-abolition sentiment than in Indiana. I believed then, as I believe now, that the President was right in waiting until he could educate a national sentiment which would justify emancipation. When the Emancipation Proclamation was issued, it was the act of the American people, though President Lincoln held the pen with which it was signed. It was this fact which gave to that Proclamation its efficiency.

In May, 1860, the Congregational Association of Indiana passed resolutions urging the better observance of the Sabbath and protesting against its too-prevalent desecration, but saying nothing concerning slavery. A year later they passed resolutions condemning slavery as antagonistic to humanity, to the Gospel, "and to those principles of liberty which underlie our nation." Three years later, when the proposals for peace founded upon compromise with the South were about to be passed upon by the nation, the same Association condemned compromise and approved immediate universal and irrevocable emancipation and the employment of coloured troops in the army and navy as national soldiers. The difference between these three sets of resolutions affords a fair indication of the progress of public sentiment in the nation under Abraham Lincoln's leadership toward the principles affirmed by him in his Cooper-Union speech.

That I can remember after sixty years and restate with almost verbal accuracy the fundamental principles of Mr. Lincoln's Cooper-Union speech; that the only references to slavery in the resolutions of the Congregational Association of Indiana in 1861 were introduced by me as amendments to the resolutions formulated by the Committee on Resolutions; and that, accepting Mr. Lincoln's fundamental belief that slavery was only a part of the labour question when slavery was abolished, I devoted myself, in the pulpit, on the platform, and in the press to the propagation of his principles of Industrial Democracy, are indications of the influence which he had upon the mind and the conscience of one of his fellow-citizens.

We may be sure that the same faith in right-eousness and a God of righteousness would in-spire Abraham Lincoln in his counsels to the nation in its present perplexity. There may be some doubt what policy he would advise concern-ing our international problems, but it is certain that he would not put "safety first," and that he would advise both against our assuming re-sponsibilities for the government of the Euro-pean States and against evasion of responsibilities which the God of history has, by the course of events, laid upon us.

And we can be in no doubt as to what would be his position on the labour question. For the principles which ought to guide our action have been very explicitly though briefly indicated in his speeches and by his acts.

To report at length his utterance directly or by necessary implication bearing on the labour problem of to-day would take me far beyond the limits of this brief sketch. It must suffice here to point out briefly the direction in which his principles and his spirit make for the solution of what is perhaps now the most perplexing and difficult problem for the human race to solve. But that the slavery question was one phase of the labour question, Mr. Lincoln declared in explicit terms. "The existing rebellion," he wrote to a committee from the Working Men's Association of New York, "is, in fact, a war upon the rights of all working people." And in describing his own experience he identified himself with working men and made that experience illustrate and enforce the lesson which he wished to impress upon them.   He said:

"I am not ashamed to confess that twenty-five years ago I was a hired labourer mending rails, at work on a flatboat—just what might happen to a poor man's son.   I want every man to have the chance—and I believe a black man is entitled to it—in which he can better his condition, when he may look forward and hope to be a hired labourer this year and the next, work for himself afterward, and finally hire men to work for him. That is the true system. . . . Then you can better your condition, and so it may go on and on in one ceaseless round so long as man exists on the face of the earth."

We may be sure that he who never denounced the slaveholder, who never did anything to intensify the prejudice of the South against the North or the North against the South, would enter into no class war, would never denounce the rich to the poor or the poor to the rich.

He who told the farmers of Wisconsin that the reason why there were more attempts to flatter them than any other class was because they could cast more votes, but that to his thinking they were neither better nor worse than other people, would never flatter the mechanic class to win for himself or his party a labour vote.

He who in 1864 held with working men that "the strongest bond of human sympathy outside of the family relation should be one uniting all working people of all nations and tongues and kindreds" would not condemn labour unions.

He who at the same time said to them, "Let not him who is houseless pull down the house of another, but let him work diligently and build one for himself," would condemn all lawless acts of violence whether against the employer of labour or against the non-union labourer who is employed.

He who thanked God that we have a system of labour where there can be a strike—a point where the working man may stop working—would not deny this right to the working man of to-day.

He who said in 1860, "I don't believe in a law to prevent a man from getting rich, and I do believe in allowing the humblest man an equal chance to get rich with any one else," would have found, not in war upon the wealthy, but in equal opportunity for all, the remedy for social and industrial inequalities.

He who condemned the mudsill theory, the theory that labour and education are incompatible and that "a blind horse upon a treadmill is a perfect illustration of what a labourer should be, all the better for being blind so that he could not kick understandingly," would be the earnest advocate of child labour laws and industrial education.

He who argued that "As the Author of man makes every individual with one head and one pair of hands it was probably intended that heads and hands should coöperate as friends, and that that particular head should direct and control that pair of hands," would believe in coöperation between Labour and Capital, leading on to the time when labourers should become capitalists and capitalists should become labourers.

He who held in 1854 that "The legitimate object of government is to do for the people what needs to be done, but which they cannot by individual effort do at all or do so well for themselves," would neither believe in the night-watchman theory of government which allows it to do nothing but police duty, nor in the socialistic theory of government which leaves nothing for individual effort to do for itself.

Two systems of industry are to-day proposed to the American people for adoption.

One proposes to destroy capitalism by substituting for the despotism of capital the despo-

tism of the proletariat. It has been recently
stated by Lenin in the following paragraph:

Any leader of Marx who fails to understand that so long
as Capitalist society exists every serious conflict between
the classes will eventuate either in an exclusive dictatorship of the Bourgeoisie or an exclusive dictatorship of a
proletariat, shows his incapacity to understand either the
economic or the political reasoning of our great leader.

The other plan proposes to destroy capitalism
by making it possible for every intelligent, industrious, able-bodied citizen to become a capitalist. It was defined by Abraham Lincoln with
great clearness in his first Annual Message and
to that statement he attached such importance
that he repeated it two years and a half later in
his letter to the Working Men's Association of
New York:

Labour is prior to, and independent of, capital. Capital
is only the fruit of labour, and could never have existed if
labour had not first existed. Labour is the superior of
capital, and deserves much the higher consideration.
Capital has its rights, which are as worthy of protection as
any other rights. Nor is it denied that there is, and probably always will be, a relation between labour and capital
producing mutual benefits. The error is in assuming that
the whole labour of the community exists within that relation. . . . There is not, of necessity, any such thing
as the free hired labourer being fixed to that condition for
life. Many independent men everywhere in these States

308

a few years back in their lives were hired labourers. The prudent, penniless beginner in the world labours for wages awhile, saves a surplus with which to buy tools and land for himself, then labours on his own account another while, and at length hires another new beginner to help him. This is the just and generous and prosperous system which opens the way to all—gives hope to all, and consequent energy and progress and improvement of condition to all.

What is the choice of the American people? Do they prefer Communism or Industrial Democracy? The life and teaching of Abraham Lincoln make perfectly clear his answer to that question, and they point out the successive steps which labour leaders and captains of industry must take to reach the goal which he commends to them. For this reason I count Abraham Lincoln America's greatest Labour Leader.

THEODORE ROOSEVELT, PREACHER OF RIGHTEOUSNESS

PRESIDENT ROOSEVELT was reading a part of one of his messages to a group of his friends whose advice he desired. Suddenly he stopped at the conclusion of a paragraph with the self-criticism: "I suppose my critics will call that preaching. But I have got such a bully pulpit." Yes! He did have a great pulpit, and he was a great preacher.

His greatest service to the world was not his initiation of a policy of National Conservation, nor the Russo-Japanese Peace, nor the Panama Canal—great as were these services. He did more than any other public man in our history, more even than Abraham Lincoln or Grover Cleveland, to transform politics from a corrupt traffic to a public service. He habitually acted on Grover Cleveland's motto: "A public office is a public trust." And he inspired the younger men of his generation with the faith of Rutherford B. Hayes that he serves his party best who best serves his country. The professional politicians of the Reconstruction Period had brought politics into disrepute. In my early manhood

310

to take any active part in political life was to
invite suspicion; the affirmation: "I take no interest in politics" was a common boast. One
of the popular arguments against suffrage for
women was that to take part in political activity
would degrade them. The day of Webster and
Clay had passed, the day of Blaine and Conkling
and Platt had come. President Hayes had secured in his cabinet men equally eminent for
their integrity and their ability, and had maintained civil-service reform in his administration
in spite of the efforts of Blaine and Conkling;
but he could not be re-nominated. That to-day
American political life appeals to young men
as a career worthy of their ambition is largely
due to two men—Grover Cleveland and Theodore Roosevelt.

Mr. Roosevelt's most striking *intellectual* characteristics were clearness of vision and energy in
action. His critics thought him to be impulsive.
If impulsiveness means acting first and thinking
afterwards, Mr. Roosevelt was not impulsive. He
never leaped before he looked; but it did not
take him long to look. His was the most alert
nature I have ever known. He was quick to
perceive, quick to decide, quick to act. Having
his coöperation in the *Outlook* for five years and
meeting him in editorial conference almost every
week when he was at home, I had some oppor-

tunity of becoming acquainted with his methods and habits. He always listened with respect to the opinions of the youngest of our staff. He was always ready to give the reason for his own opinion. And he was always ready to reconsider that opinion if any one had new light to throw upon the question. But I never knew him to take counsel of his prejudices, his passions, or his self-interest. He was a member of our staff during the Progressive Campaign, when he was a Presidential candidate in perhaps the most heated political campaign of our country subsequent to the Civil War. Never once did he even remotely suggest the question, what effect might any proposed utterance of the *Outlook* have upon his political fortunes; I do not think he ever once suggested the question, what effect might it have on the fortunes of the Progressive party. The three questions which apparently controlled him were: What is truth? How much of that truth can we get across to the readers of the *Outlook?* How can that best be done?

There were two reasons for the widespread impression that Mr. Roosevelt acted impulsively.

I frequently play solitaire as a brain rest, and I recommend the game to the brain-weary. In playing I have to study the relation of each card on the table to the other cards and take time to determine what my play shall be. Similarly, if a complicated question is put before me, I must take time to consider the relations of its various elements before coming to a decision. I should be ill fitted to be the editor of a daily paper. Mr. Roosevelt saw at a glance all the cards on the table, all the elements of any complicated problem put before him. Was it a national problem? What would be the effect of the proposed legislation on the working classes, on the employing classes, on the shippers, on the middlemen, on the purchasing classes, on Congress and on the party whose support was necessary to secure the legislation? Was it an international problem? What would be the effect of the proposed policy on our friendly relations with other nations?—On England? On France? On Italy? On Japan? To me the various elements of such a complicated problem are often like the dissevered portions of a picture puzzle: it takes me some time to see their relations to each other. Mr. Roosevelt generally seemed to see them instantly in their real relations; to see at once the completed picture. And all the resources of his past experiences and his various reading—and he was a rapid and omnivorous reader—were all pigeon-holed and indexed in a well-ordered mind; and memory, like a well-trained private secretary, was ready to hand out to him whatever fact he needed.

The other characteristic was his habitual
reference of special questions to certain fixed
principles by which he had previously determined to be governed. To illustrate: If he
had occasion to deal with a great organization
he would deal with whatever representative
that organization had selected. If as President,
he had to deal with England, he would deal with
the English Ambassador; if with Germany,
with the German Ambassador. That he had no
liking for the ambassador, or even no faith in
him, made no difference. So if he had to deal
with Pennsylvania or with New York, he dealt
with Mr. Quay or with Mr. Platt. Whether he
liked them or disliked them, whether he had
faith in them or distrusted them, made to him no
difference. Acting upon the same principle, if
he had to deal with the Republican party, he
dealt with the leaders of that party and appealed
from the leaders to the rank and file only as a
last resort. Following his election as governor
I was invited to the Executive Mansion at
Albany to spend the night. He had invited
some of the younger members of the newly
elected Assembly to meet him in the evening.
At the beginning of the conference, he said to
them something like this: "If you have come
to Albany to represent the interests of your
district, I shall always be glad to see you and

consult with you; if any of you have come here
to do the bidding of your boss I care no more to
consult with you than with any other kind of
cattle. I prefer to consult directly with your
boss."

I am not here considering whether Mr.
Roosevelt's principle was right or wrong, though,
personally, I think it right. I am only trying
here to point out to my readers one of the reasons
why he was able to decide many questions so
promptly. He had practically decided them
beforehand by his adoption of a general principle to which all questions of a certain class
could be instantly referred.

I have sometimes dissented from Mr. Roosevelt's quick decision of a question and been sometimes inclined to criticize what at first seemed
to me his impulsive action. But when I have
given to the problem the deliberate study which
my temper requires, I have come either to the
conclusion that Mr. Roosevelt was correct or else
that the difference between us was less than I
had thought it to be. When he ordered the
discharge of the Brownsville soldiers, some of
them for riotous conduct, others for sympathy
with it, I thought he had acted rashly. I went
to the Law Library, spent a morning in investigation of the authorities, and came to the
conclusion that he had acted fully within his

constitutional and legal powers and was fully sustained by military precedents. Later, taking up the official reports, I could come to no other conclusion than that he was equally sustained by the facts; and this was the result, as the reader will remember, reached by the United States Senate after three or four official investigations. He opposed the Arbitration Treaty negotiated by the Taft Administration. I supported that treaty. His views and mine were both given to the readers of the *Outlook* in its pages. But when our views were compared, we found the difference amounted simply to this: We both agreed that the new treaty could accomplish nothing more for peace than the treaty which it supplanted. He was opposed to it because it assumed to do what it could not do. I should have opposed negotiating it; but, as it had been negotiated, I thought its adoption could do no harm and might do a little good, and that its rejection could do no good and might do a little harm. I do not recall a single important instance in which my slowly formed opinion has differed from his almost instantaneous decision more widely than in the case of the Arbitration Treaty.

The charge was made against Mr. Roosevelt in 1912 by so wise a man as Mr. Eliot, President Emeritus of Harvard University, that: "The candidate of the Progressive party has shown himself capable while in power of taking grave public action—which, of course, seemed to him wise and right—in disregard of constitutional and legal limitations." This charge has been often made, and the friends of Mr. Roosevelt have often called for specifications of it; but the specifications have never been given. We have never been told what specific clause of the Constitution or what specific provision of law he ever disregarded by any act. In fact, during his long executive life as Governor of New York State and President of the United States, no act of Mr. Roosevelt's and no legislation which he has recommended has ever been declared unconstitutional by the courts, and I do not think that any administrative act of his as Civil Service Commissioner, Police Commissioner, and Assistant Secretary of the Navy was ever set aside by his superior officers because by it he transcended the limits of his legal authority. So much as to his supposed impulsiveness.

The most striking *moral* characteristic of Mr. Roosevelt was his passion for righteousness.

The occasions which excite a man's anger afford an excellent indication of his character. He may be slow to express his admiration, but in anger expression is apt to come before re-

flection. As from the heat of water bubbling
to the surface in a spring one perceives the
underground heat, so from the fire that flashes
from the eye or the hot words that leap from the
lips one perceives the passion beneath the surface. One need not look at the catalogue for
the title of Hogarth's famous picture "The
Distressed Musician": the angry face which looks
out upon the babel of sounds that issue from
the London street is unmistakably that of one
keenly sensitive to discord.

Theodore Roosevelt was extraordinarily patient—except with injustice. That he never
could endure. Whether the injustice was against
himself or against others made no difference.
Whether the evil it inflicted was little or great,
whether it was perpetrated by an individual, a
group, or a nation, made little difference. It was
the wrong, not the consequences of the wrong,
which inflamed his resentment. It might be a
cowboy in his employ putting the Roosevelt
brand on a calf that had strayed from its owner's
herd; it might be Colombia which endeavoured
by one and the same transaction to cheat France
and blackmail America—his wrath was irrepressible and its expression in action instantaneous
and efficient. The cowboy could not comprehend
the reason for his instant discharge; and there
were statesmen and editors who could not under-

stand the instant recognition of Panama's independence. Both the cowboy and the critics were insensitive to injustice if it promised to succeed.

To those who cannot understand the divine command, "Abhor that which is evil," the statement that Mr. Roosevelt's passionate resentment of injustice was the secret of his poise will seem incomprehensible. Nevertheless, the statement is true. He was equally indignant at the mob which hanged a defenseless Negro without giving him a trial and at the Negro troop which ran amuck through a peaceful Southern town; equally indignant at the denial of the right of every man to life, liberty, and the pursuit of happiness, whether the denial came from a labour union or from a modern feudal overlord. If he were living with us now, he would be equally ready to condemn Bolshevism and to condemn the autocracy which has by its oppression cultivated Bolshevism in Russia and sown the seeds of the same horrible harvest in the United States; equally ready to condemn the men who are attacking the moral foundations of civilized society and to condemn the men who would take advantage of this attack to reëstablish and reinforce the wrongs which made that attack possible.

Mr. Roosevelt was "fighting honest." He abhorred that which is evil. He hated, as

David did the enemies of Jehovah, with a perfect hatred, impurities, meannesses, falsehoods, shams, dishonesties of every description. Easygoing good nature is a natural American defect, and Mr. Roosevelt's hearty and, in the main, healthy hatred of wrong doing made him both the most loved and probably the most hated of American public men of his time.

It is true that his very virtues have sometimes led him into unjust judgments. His own understanding was so quick that he sometimes failed to appreciate the extraordinary inability of many men correctly to understand others or to interpret correctly themselves. This inability of apparently intelligent men to understand others is illustrated by a little incident in my own experience. Once, in the *Outlook*, I said that Jesus was the most selfless man that ever lived; the next week I got an indignant letter from a reader asking me what I meant by charging that Jesus was the most selfish man that ever lived. Men sometimes misunderstood Mr. Roosevelt and men sometimes misunderstood and misinterpreted themselves. As a result he received into what the press called his Ananias Club some men who should not have been admitted to it.

Nevertheless, his judgment against wrong, whoever committed it, was generally well balanced and essentially just; and it found frequent expression in private conversation and private correspondence no less than in public utterance and public acts. Two sentences from one of his personal letters to me, written in 1916, at the time when a national railroad strike was threatened in order to coerce Congress, may serve here as a striking illustration of his universal habit of mind: "I think it is as foolish and as wicked to back any labour union which is wrong as to back any great corporation which is wrong. It makes no difference to the state whether we suffer from a White Terror or a Red Terror; whether the tyranny is that of the Ministers of Louis XV or that of Robespierre, Danton, and Marat." And he coupled this statement with one defining what his policy would have been had he been president when that strike was threatened and Congress and the President yielded to it. "I should tell the railroad owners and the heads of the Brotherhood that I would appoint a commission which would have included men like Raymond Robins and Patrick Morrissey, and that every question, including the eight-hour-law question, without any reservation, would be put before that commission, and that I would tolerate no action by Congress in advance of the report of that commission, and that I would tolerate no tie-up of the transportation systems of the country, and that I would use the entire armed forces of the country, if necessary, to run the railroads pending the decision of the Commission. I would have also stated that I would see that the commission had the power to interpret and enforce its decrees, so that the men need have no fear that the railroad managers and owners would twist that arbitration so as to bear against them." In a matter of less importance he acted in this spirit in dealing with a strike during his own administration. In 1903 a man was discharged from the Government Printing Office, not because he did anything wrong, but because the Labour Union disciplined him and demanded that he should, therefore, be discharged, and enforced the demand by the threat of a strike. The President promptly reinstated Miller (the man who had been discharged) and to a correspondent who protested wrote as follows:

I have notified Palmer that he must reinstate Miller at once and then I will have an investigation made and see whether or not he has done anything which warrants his discharge, and notify all those under him that while there is no objection to the employees of the printing office forming a union or belonging to a union, yet that on the other hand I will not tolerate discrimination against a man because he does *not* belong to the union any more than against him because he *does* belong to it. In other words,

THEODORE ROOSEVELT

I will proceed upon the only plan possible for a self-respecting American president, and treat each man on his merits as a man. The labour unions shall have a square deal and the corporation shall have a square deal, and in addition all private citizens shall have a square deal.

This spirit of even-handed justice was perhaps the most distinguishing moral characteristic of Mr. Roosevelt's administration from his first entrance into politics in 1882 until his death. When he was nominated for the Assembly by the Republicans in 1881, in the twenty-third year of his age, his political sponsor took him to canvass the district, introduced him to a saloon keeper of importance in the district who thought the liquor licences were too high, and who said that he counted on Mr. Roosevelt, if elected, to use his influence for their reduction. The young candidate replied that he did not think them high enough and should probably use his influence to make them higher. This ended his canvass in the saloons, but he was, nevertheless, elected for three successive terms. Appointed on the Civil Service Commission he defined Civil Service Reform as "designed primarily to give the average American citizen a fair chance in politics," and in conducting an arduous campaign against the Spoils System was equally ready to antagonize influential Republicans and to coöperate with influential Democrats.

323

Thoughout his political career in maintaining Civil Service Reform he fought Senator Quay and Senator Hanna when they represented the Spoils System and coöperated with them when Quay maintained the rights of the Indians and Hanna was seeking to promote social justice. As Police Commissioner in New York City, at the time of strikes he protected the right of the working people to employ peaceable picketing and resolutely stopped every attempt of violence by or on behalf of strikers; in dealing with disorderly houses, he subjected men found in them to the same treatment to which women were subjected and regarded the men as truly fallen as the women; asked to prevent an anti-Jewish agitator from speaking, he refused to interfere with freedom of speech, but appointed Jewish policemen to furnish the speaker protection and so demonstrated the loyalty of the Jews as a class to the cause of law and order; and in his appointments and promotions in the police force neither politics nor personal favouritism had any place. "I never," he says, "coddled these men. I punish them severely whenever I think their conduct requires it. All I did was to try to be just; to reward them when they did well; in short, to act squarely by them." When he was elected Governor of the State of New York after the Spanish-American War, his spirit in dealing with the young men of the Assembly I have already indicated; his reform of a corrupt canal administration; his successful extension of civil service reform; his pushing through, in spite of great obstacles, a just tax on corporations that had theretofore been exempt, his too-little-known influence in preventing the scheme for handing over the proposed subways in the city of New York to private ownership, and the part he took in securing their permanent ownership by the city united against him influential leaders in his party and powerful financial interests, irrespective of party. Unable to defeat his recommendation they hoped to shelve him by making him Vice-President, a position, usually of more honour than influence. Made President by the death of Mr. McKinley, in his first annual message he indicated clearly his position respecting the still-perplexing problem of monopoly. He condemned the theories of the anarchists, declaring that anarchistic speeches, writings, and meetings are essentially seditious and treasonable, but he denied that as the rich have grown richer the poor have grown poorer; affirmed that, "on the contrary, never before has the average man, the wage worker, the farmer, the small trader been so well off as in this country"; and he recognized that it was necessary to use extreme care in dealing with corporate wealth. But he also affirmed that there were real and grave evils which must be studied and overcome; that combination and concentration "should be not prohibited, but supervised and within reasonable limits controlled"; and that this regulation and supervision of corporations should not be left to the individual state, but should be exercised by the Federal power over all corporations doing interstate business. This principle he carried out consistently, and with both vigour and patience throughout his two Presidential terms. The course which, as I have above indicated, he thought ought to have been pursued at the time the Adamson Bill was forced through Congress by a threatened strike, he had himself pursued when the nation was threatened with a coal famine by an industrial war between the coal owners and the coal workers. He obtained the consent of a commission of eminent citizens, with Grover Cleveland at its head, to serve in deciding the merits of the controversy and in recommending an adjustment fair to both parties and to the public, and then arranged for the United States army to run the mines if there proved to be any delay in accepting the arbitration. "In such cases," he wrote in a letter to me, "the three parties in interest are: 1—the property owners; 2—the labourers; 3—the public; and the President should act primarily as the representative of the public, that is, the people of this Nation as a whole; for this is a National question." For his interference in this case, Mr. Roosevelt has been sometimes sharply criticized. A sufficient answer to that criticism for the purposes of this paper is furnished by the general approval of the country as expressed by ex-President Cleveland in the sentences: "I do not think that any president ever acted more wisely, courageously, or promptly in a national crisis. Mr. Roosevelt deserves unstinted praise for what he did."

I shall not in this paper reopen the questions hotly debated during the Progressive campaign of 1912, but I may without impropriety give to my readers my conviction respecting the motives which inspired Mr. Roosevelt in his course at that time. I saw letters that he wrote; I consulted with him on actions that he took; I was present in conferences that he held with leading public men from various parts of the country. I say with confident assurance that he did not desire to enter again into political campaigning. He had no political ambition to assume the duties of the Presidency. He wished to avoid these duties if he could do so with honour. His answer in letters and conferences, reiterated in literally hundreds of cases, was always the same:

"I do not wish to be a candidate." So long as there was any prospect that Mr. La Follette could and would be accepted as a leader of the Progressive party movement Mr. Roosevelt abstained from political activity. Not until Mr. La Follette had broken down nervously in his Philadelphia speech, and his own friends had counselled him to withdraw, and it had become apparent to those who were interested in the Progressive principles and the Progressive movement that the movement was in danger of utter failure for want of a national leader, did Mr. Roosevelt reluctantly consent to accept the leadership which was urged upon him. His inmost feeling on the subject was revealed with characteristic frankness to his associates. To one of them he wrote in December, 1911, "I most emphatically do not wish the nomination. Personally, I should regard it as a calamity to be nominated. In the first place, I might very possibly be beaten, and in the next place, even if elected, I should be confronted with almost impossible conditions out of which to make good results."

I recall, as I write these lines, the day when that decision was apparently finally reached. It was about the time when seven governors presented to Mr. Roosevelt their united request that he become a candidate. He submitted to us, his associates on the *Outlook* staff, the question, Could he with honour decline? Each member of the staff was asked by him to give his opinion on that question. One of our number recalled the pledge that Mr. Roosevelt had given to the American people when he landed at the Battery, New York City, on his return from Europe: "I am ready and eager to do my part, so far as I am able, in helping solve problems which must be solved if we of this, the greatest democratic Republic upon which the sun has ever shone, are to see its destinies rise to the limit of our hopes and its opportunities." We all believed in the Progressive principles, and we all thought that the campaign for them at that time would be a forlorn hope. We all believed that could Mr. Roosevelt remain in retirement for four years, in 1916 Progressive principles would be certain of victory, but we all agreed that he had no option but to accede to the apparently unanimous request of those who had faith in Progressive principles and accept their proffered leadership, whatever the immediate political results might be. He himself summed up in a graphic figure our unanimous conditions: "I am not going to get those good fellows out on the end of a limb and then saw off the limb." He entered on the primary campaign in February, 1912, at the call of honour, when ambition, ease, and personal inclinations all combined in urging him to resist that call.

When at the close of his Presidency Mr. Roosevelt became a member of the editorial staff of the *Outlook*, it was clearly understood that he was at perfect liberty to utter through our columns whatever opinions he wished to communicate to the public and that we should be at perfect liberty to express our dissent. It was a rather fortunate circumstance that a few weeks before this arrangement could properly be announced to the public he wrote an article on Tolstoy and I accompanied it with another, the two articles differing in some important respects in their estimate of that enigmatical character. In the five years during which Mr. Roosevelt was thus associated with us nothing ever occurred to impair our mutual friendship; by his courtesy and consideration he won from the first the devotion of all members of what we are accustomed to call "the *Outlook* Family"; and when, after five years of coöperation in dealing with exciting political topics, he withdrew from the *Outlook*, it was with his regret and with ours. He continued to the end of his life to be an occasional contributor to our columns and to possess the confidence, esteem, and affection of all the men and women on the *Outlook*, from the errand boy to the editor-in-chief.

THEODORE ROOSEVELT

This sketch is neither a life of Theodore Roosevelt nor an impartial analysis of his character. I knew him well; I esteemed him as a genius; I honoured him as a patriot; I loved him as a friend; and I have never regarded the vivisection of my friends as either a public duty or an agreeable recreation. Mr. Roosevelt's faults were on the surface; his virtues were in his fibre. We are a young nation. The American people, like college boys, discern the virtues beneath the faults and give to him their honour, their esteem, their affection. He was a courageous fighter, a loyal friend, and always a hater of injustice and a lover of righteousness. He was a shrewd politician and a great statesman; a leader of the people but too good a democrat to be their ruler. Future history will honour him as one of the greatest citizens of a nation which has been prolific in great citizens. Of all the services he has rendered to his age, I count this the greatest: that by his words, his deeds, and his character he was always a preacher of righteousness.

JACOB ABBOTT, FRIEND OF CHILDREN

MY FIRST recollection of my father is an incident which, though slight, is very significant of his spirit in dealing with children. Recovery from scarlet fever had left me subject to gatherings in the ear which produced very severe ear-aches. Surgical operations for such trouble were then unknown. The only relief obtainable was soaking cotton-wool in laudanum and putting it in the ear to deaden the pain. My father was living in the part of New York City now called Greenwich Village, and, with his brothers, was carrying on a school for girls in the city. It was quite essential for his work that he should get his night's rest. He made a bargain with me: he would tell me a story for fifteen minutes, then I was to let him sleep for fifteen minutes, and so we would go through the night together. Whether this was done for only one night or many nights, I do not now recall. By this bargain he and I became partners; he carried my burden, but I also did something to carry his burden. He would help me bear my pain, but he trusted me to help him get ready for his morrow's work.

This confidence in children and coöperation with children was one of his distinguishing characteristics. I have known men as fond of children as my father, but I have never known a man who had for them such respect. In a true sense, it might be said that he treated children as his equals, not through any device or from any scheme, but spontaneously and naturally. He trusted the judgment of children, took counsel with them, and in all the matters which concerned them and their world was greatly influenced by their judgments. He threw responsibility upon them, great responsibility, and they realized it.

This respect which he showed to children inspired them with respect for themselves and for one another. It gave dignity to the children who came under his influence. That influence was a masterful one. I should misrepresent him if I gave the impression that he exercised no authority. On the contrary, his authority was supreme and final. He gave few commands, but he required prompt, implicit, and unquestioning obedience to those which he did give. I have known children to disobey him, but I never knew one to rebel against him. I do not know what would have happened in case of a rebellion. I think no child ever thought of it as possible. I never knew him to strike a blow. I do not recall that he ever sent a child to his room, or supperless to bed, or set him to write in his copy book, or to learn tasks, or resorted to any other of the similar expedients, necessary perhaps in school, and frequent in most families. In general, he simply administered natural penalties. If a child lied or broke his promises, he was distrusted. If he was careless or negligent, the things that were given to other children to play with were withheld from him. If he quarrelled, he was taken away from his playmates, but made as happy as he could be made in solitude.

This spirit of respect which my father had for children interprets his literary method. He never condescended to children, never talked down to them or wrote down to them. He believed they could understand large truths if they were simply and clearly stated. So in "Science for the Young" he dealt with some of the most interesting scientific phenomena; in his "Red Histories" he used biography to make clear the great historical epochs; in his Young Christian Series he interpreted some of the profoundest phases of spiritual experience. This spirit of confidence determined his style. He never sought for short and easy words, but selected what he thought the best word to express his meaning. The child, he said, will get the meaning of the word from the context, or if he does not, he will ask his mother what the word means, and so he will be learning language. He did not write books about children for grown people to read. He wrote books for children because he shared their life with them. Perhaps it is a son's prejudice, but his books still seem to me to be among the best of true children's books.

I have been often asked which one of his four sons was Rollo. The answer is: none of them. So far as I know, my father never painted a portrait, never took a single child out of real life and set him in a story; never made a character to represent a type; never undertook to work out through fiction the development of a character first philosophically conceived. He wrote his stories as he might have told them. If shorthand had been in vogue in his time, and one could have taken down any story of my father's as he might have told it to a group of children gathered about his chair, it would have been essentially the story as it is published from his pen. He did not form a plot beforehand. Each incident led on to the next incident; it might almost be said that each paragraph led on to the next paragraph; and when the allotted number of pages was finished, the story came to its end, much as the story-telling would come to an end when the clock struck nine and it was time for the children to go to bed. This method accounts for the artlessness of his narratives. They are natural portrayals of child life to children. The only approximation to portrait painting is in "Jonas," "Beechnut," and "Rainbow." These characters in his stories used the devices, employed the methods, manifested the spirit which were characteristic of his dealing with children. To this extent and to this only can they be called portraits, for in every other respect they are unlike one another and quite unlike him.

Let me go back a little and tell how he came to enter upon his life work—the writing of children's books.

My grandfather gave his five boys a college and a theological education and then left them to employ that education as they thought best. One of them continued a preacher throughout his life, combining authorship with his pastoral duties. The others became teachers. My father accepted a tutorship at Amherst College almost immediately after his graduation from Andover Theological Seminary and at the age of twenty-two was made full professor of mathematics and natural philosophy. In a journal that he kept during his college days I find indications of a growing ambition toward authorship. Among these is a plan for an undenominational religious journal of a high character, though even then his habitual financial caution shows itself in the question whether such a journal could be made self-supporting.

Four years later he accepted an invitation to go to Boston and there organize and carry on a school for the broader and better education of girls, one among the first in that movement for woman's education out of which have grown the girls' high schools and colleges. He had already in Amherst College tried successfully, though in a small way, the experiment of self-government; had organized out of the students a "Fraternity of the Chapel Entry"; put into their hands the task of seeing that this entry was kept in order and provided with light and heat; and had so far enrolled himself as a member of the Fraternity as to be liable with the others to assessment for taxes and subject to the rules which the Fraternity might adopt. This principle of self-government he carried out to a much greater extent in the Mt. Vernon school, in Boston, where he left the girls to study by themselves in a common schoolroom without teacher or monitor, and appointed one of the girls to manage a simple but ingenious mechanism which he devised for letting the students know when the time for recess had come.

Into this school he carried his ministerial ambitions and gave on Saturday mornings a series of religious lectures which led afterward to the publication of the Young Christian Series.*

To prepare these lectures, or to write them in book form for the press, he rose very early in the morning, and wrote for a couple of hours or so before his breakfast. His ambition proved too great for his physique. He resigned and moved his family to his father's home in Farmington, Maine. He purchased a wild place just across the road from his father's house, half sandhill, half marsh, with just room enough between the sandhill and the road for a little cottage. Here he wrote the Rollo Books in the mornings, and worked on hill and marsh in the afternoons. He gradually converted the marsh into a pond; he opened the sand-bank to the public, and the public carted so much away that, in time, the grounds about the house became adequate if not ample; one hill grew into a grassy slope, the other, turfed and covered with trees, gave the place its name of "Little Blue," derived from a mountain twenty miles away known as "Old Blue." He redeemed wildness in boy and land by the same process, working with Nature, and waiting long and patiently for Nature to do her work. In later life he found equal pleasure in

---

*"The Young Christian," "The Corner Stone," "The Way to Do Good," "Hoaryhead and McDonner."

labouring upon the grounds of the two of his
sons who had country homes; and the recreation
of his declining years was simple but artistic
landscape gardening at Fewacres, the old home-
stead. It was not enough for him to direct;
he always wished to labour with his own hands.
How often have I heard him say, when compelled
by fatigue to relinquish the spade or pick, "I
wish I could hire someone else's muscles and
use them myself."

The account which Samuel Butler has given of
his own childhood in that tragic story "The Way
of All Flesh" is perhaps an exaggerated account
of an exceptionally unhappy childhood. Yet it
is true that in the first half of the nineteenth
century the more or less deliberate purpose of
religious parents in Puritan households was the
government of the children by fear of a tyranny
which could not be resisted and the suppression
by that government of the natural instincts of
childhood. This purpose found expression in
two popular mottoes: "Children should be
seen and not heard" and "Spare the rod and
spoil the child." Each of these mottoes was
the outward expression of a deep-rooted Puritan
philosophy, which might be expressed thus:
From Adam all his descendants have inherited a
depraved nature. That nature must be eradi-
cated; the child's will broken; his evil tendencies

subdued. Only thus can he become a child of God. Jesus Christ had said: "Except ye become as little children, ye cannot enter the Kingdom of Heaven." Puritan theology had substituted: "Except ye become as grown-ups, ye cannot enter the Kingdom." The stories of childish saints is pathetic; the stories of the painstaking endeavour by pious parents to make childish saints is even more pathetic.

Some years ago I went on a boating expedition in Penobscot Bay. We went ashore to spend the night in a farmhouse which was hospitably open to "paying guests." On the parlour table I found a Sunday-school Story Book, dated about 1830. A new baby was to be christened. Her little sister, seven or eight years old, came aglow with eager expectation to the mother. "How are you going to dress the baby?" she asked. "My child," said the pained but patient mother, "bring me the Prayer Book." It was brought. "Now read what the God-father says at the time of the Christening." The child read as follows:

"Dost thou, in the name of this child, renounce the devil and all his works, the vain pomp and glory of the world, with all covetous desires of the same, and the sinful desires of the flesh, so that thou wilt not follow, nor be led by them?

"Answer: I renounce them all; and, by God's help, will endeavour not to follow, nor be led by them."

"Do you see, my child," said the mother, "how wicked it is to be thinking of the baby's dress at such a time? Go to your room and ask your Heavenly Father to forgive your worldly and sinful spirit."

My father abhorred controversies of every description and never attacked the current theology of his time, but all his children's books were based upon a psychological conception radically different. Toward the close of his life he published a volume entitled, "Gentle Measures in the Training of the Young." In this volume he interprets in a very simple form and with many concrete illustrations the philosophical principles on which all his children's books were based. Whether in 1834, when the first of the Rollo Books was published, he had defined to himself those principles and wrote his books to illustrate and enforce them, or whether he wrote his books and carried on his teaching for nearly forty years and then from his studies of children and his experiments with them evolved these principles, I do not know. I think the latter is more probably the truth. If so, if these principles were deduced from a third of a century's study and experiment, they are for that reason all the more valuable to the fathers and mothers of the present time.

He neither assumed that the child is a little

cherub or a little devil. He assumed that "in respect of moral conduct as well as of mental attainments children know nothing when they come into the world, but have everything to learn either from the instructions or from the examples of those around them." Therefore, the child must be trained to perceive the difference between truth and falsehood, generosity and selfishness, honesty and dishonesty exactly as he must be trained to walk or to talk. "The first time that a child attempts to walk alone what a feeble, staggering, and awkward exhibition it makes. And yet its mother shows by the excitement of her countenance and the delight expressed by her exclamations how pleased she is with the performance." He who really comprehends this philosophy and accepts it will realize that to train a child to perceive the sacredness of truth or recognize the rights of property requires infinite patience, and that the first failures of the child's conscience are no more deserving of punishment in the strict sense of that term than failures in his first experiments in walking. "The mother is thus to understand that the principle of obedience is not to be expected to come by nature into the heart of her child, but to be implanted by education. She must understand this so fully as to feel that if she finds that her children are disobedient to her commands—

leaving out of view cases of peculiar and extraordinary temptation—it is *her* fault, not theirs."

Though training in this spirit rarely, if ever, calls for punishment, it calls continually for discipline. The difference between the two is not in the act of the judge, but in his purpose and his spirit. I must here condense into a very few words a distinction to which my father gives a chapter of his book.

Punishment may be regarded as a penalty demanded by the eternal principles of justice and the natural consequence of the sin of the transgressor, or it may be considered as a remedial measure adopted solely to deter from similar errors or sins in time to come. "According to the first view, punishment is a *penalty* which *justice* demands as a satisfaction for the past. According to the other it is a *remedy* which *goodness* devises for the benefit of the future." Without discussing the question which of these principles actuates God in his dealing with sin and the State in dealing with crime, my father contents himself with the declaration that "the punishment of a child by a parent, or of a pupil by a teacher, ought certainly, one would think, to exclude the element of vindictive retribution altogether, and to be employed solely with reference to the salutary influence that may be expected from it in time to come."

With this distinction between punishment demanded by justice and punishment devised by benevolence my father coupled another—the difference between instinct and capacities. "The dog has an instinct impelling him to attach himself to and follow his master; but he has no instinct leading him to draw his master's cart. He requires no teaching for the one. It comes, of course, from the connate impulses of his nature. For the other he requires a skilful and careful training. . . . So with the child. If he does not seem to know how to take his food, or shows no disposition to run to his mother when he is hurt or when he is frightened, we have reason to suspect something wrong, or, at least, something abnormal, in his mental or physical constitution. But if he does not obey his mother's commands—no matter how insubordinate or unmanageable he may be—the fault does not, certainly, indicate anything at all wrong in *him*. The fault is in his training. In witnessing his disobedience, our reflection should be, not 'What a bad boy!' but 'What an unfaithful or incompetent mother!'"

These two fundamental distinctions must be borne in mind by any reader who desires to understand the principles of family and school government which my father inculcated and illustrated by his books.

The first lesson a child must learn is obedience. He comes into a world of law. He neither knows what the laws are nor why he should obey them. To the father and the mother is entrusted the duty of teaching these first lessons of life.

There are inexorable laws of nature. He who does not know and obey these laws may easily kill himself by a single act of innocent because ignorant disobedience, and he will be certain to injure himself by repeated acts of disobedience. There are unwritten laws of society which will confront him in the family, in the playground, and later in social and commercial circles. If he ignores and disregards them he will soon find himself a social outcast. His companions will assume that he knows them and disregards them deliberately because either of malice or stupidity. There are laws of the State. If he habitually ignores or disregards these laws, he may speedily find himself in prison. Courts will not listen to his plea that he was ignorant of them. Ignorance is an excuse which the community does not accept. Nature is pitiless. Society, if not absolutely pitiless, is wholly unsympathetic. It is, therefore, the first and most fundamental duty of the parent to teach the child that he is not independent; that he cannot live his own life regardless of other lives; that he must learn to yield his will to the wills of others and to the One Supreme Will, if he would live a happy and a useful life.

But there are comparatively few families in which this necessity is understood and in which the children are taught to obey promptly and without question. In some obedience is not taught at all; in some it is taught only irregularly and fitfully; in some disobedience is inculcated by the constant issuing of commands which there is no purpose to enforce and the threatening of penalties which there is no purpose to inflict. In one of my father's stories he puts the secret of good government in family or school in four sentences, thus:

> When you consent, consent cordially.
> When you refuse, refuse finally.
> When you punish, punish good-naturedly.
> Commend often; never scold.

My father's stories for children are largely employed in illustrating and enforcing these four principles. I could wish that everyone who has to do with the government of children would commit them to memory and would, from time to time, by these rules test his administration of that government. But he will find impossible the last two rules unless he believes, with my father, in the truth that the child is not morally to blame for the failure to understand moral principles which have never been inculcated.

Josie comes to visit Phonny and Malleville. Phonny comes up into Beechnut's room, to which he is confined by a slight illness, and tells Beechnut that Josie is coming to make him a visit.

"Ah!" said Beechnut, "then I must get acquainted with her. And the first thing is to find out whether I have got to teach her to obey me, or whether she has learned to obey already."

"How do you think it is?" asked Phonny.

"I think she has *not* learned to obey," said Beechnut.

"Why not?" asked Phonny.

"Because she is a city girl," said Beechnut, "and city girls are very seldom taught to obey."

"Why not?" asked Phonny again.

"Oh, because," said Beechnut, "they are put away from their mother's care and into the care of nursery-maids so much. The nursery-maids coax them, and bribe them, and deceive them —and do everything to them except teach them simply to obey."

"And how are you going to find out," asked Phonny, "whether Josie has been taught to obey?"

"You will see," said Beechnut.

He finds out in a very simple manner. Josie starts to open the drawers of the little bureau, pays no attention to Beechnut's telling her not to do so and finds the drawers empty.

"Why, Beechnut," said Josie, "what did you say I must not open these drawers for? There is nothing in them."

"There is a knob," suggested Malleville.

"Yes; nothing but the knob," said Josie. "What was the reason?" repeated Josie.

"I *had* a reason," replied Beechnut.

"What was it?" persisted Josie.

"I know what it was," said Phonny.

"What?" asked Josie.

Phonny hesitated a moment, not being quite sure whether it would be polite for him to tell what he thought. At length he said, somewhat timidly:

"To see whether you would obey him or not."

"Was that the reason?" asked Josie.

"Yes," said Beechnut.

"Truly!" said Josie.

"Yes," said Beechnut, "really and truly."

Josephine looked a little ashamed and confused when she heard this, but presently recovering herself a little she asked Beechnut what made him wish to know particularly whether she would obey him.

"Because," said Beechnut, "I have got a

348

number of pictures, and picture-books, and
curiosities of various kinds up in my room,
which perhaps it would amuse you to see. I
let children go up and see them sometimes without me if I am only sure beforehand that they
will follow precisely the directions that I give
them."

Josie has thus had an opportunity to learn
her first lesson: obedience is not a door of admission into a prison, it is a door of exit into
liberty; it is an achievement by which one's
powers and privileges are increased. It is curious how slow even philosophy has been to learn
that all our powers over nature have been acquired by intelligent obedience of the laws of
nature, and how, similarly, freedom in the moral
realm is acquired only by voluntary obedience of
the moral laws written in the constitution of man
and of human society. "The first duty," says
my father, "which devolves upon the mother
in the training of her child is the establishment
of her *authority* over him." . . . "The first
essential condition required for the performance
of this duty is the fixing of the conviction in
her own mind that it *is* a duty."

The penalty need not be severe. It is not
by the severity but by the certainty of the penalty
that a habit of obedience is developed. But
whatever the penalty, it must not only always be

just, but if possible, such as will seem just to the child. For the object of the ruler should be not to suppress, but to develop the child. Not infrequently in his books my father illustrates methods by which the coöperation of the child can be secured in selecting and enforcing discipline. The penalty need not necessarily inflict any pain; since the object is not to deter by fear, but to secure the aid of the child in future endeavours to cure his fault, not infrequently the penalty is even amusing. Phonny in harnessing the horse which is to take them to ride has failed to follow Beechnut's directions. Beechnut at the time says nothing, but after they have started on their ride he suggests that Phonny would enjoy his ride more if he were first to be punished for his disobedience. He suggests that Phonny mount upon the horse with his face toward his tail and ride in that way for a quarter of a mile. Phonny accepts the punishment. Malleville and Phonny are both greatly amused during the operation, though Phonny's seat proved to be very uncomfortable.

Though discipline is not always terrifying and sometimes may even be amusing, it must always be sufficient at the time to secure obedience. Severity in punishment is rarely necessary, but certainty of some punishment is necessary. And no inconvenience that the enforcement of law may occasion to the parent or teacher furnishes any excuse for allowing disobedience to pass without such penalty as the circumstances may require.

Jonas, with three boys, is sailing on a pond to take some grain to the mill. Jonas is in command of the expedition. Josey, who has not yet learned to obey, disregards Jonas's directions, and undertakes to go forward to take a seat which Jonas has assigned to another boy. As he starts to go forward Jonas with his paddle brings the boat around. The boom comes thumping against Josey's head and shoulders and he sinks down into the bottom of the boat to get out of the way. "What was that for?" asks Josey. "I am going to put you ashore," replied Jonas. "Me ashore!" repeated Josey, more and more surprised. He looked forward, and saw that the boat was now pointed toward the shore, at a place on the back side of the point of land which they had just passed.

"Yes," said Jonas, "the only way, when we have an unmanageable passenger on board, is to put him ashore upon the nearest land." . . . "But what shall I do," said he, "if you put me ashore?"

"You can either walk home, or wait there till we come back from the mill. I'll call for you when I come back."

The other two boys finally interceded for Josey, and Jonas, with some hesitation, accedes to their request. But Josey had learned his lesson that "there is no getting along out at sea without obeying the commander."

The reader will observe another element in this incident: Jonas is sustained by the public opinion of the community, that is, by the other two boys. I am almost inclined to the opinion that all rebellion against government, whether in school, factory, or nation, is partly due to the fault of the governor. My father was professor in a college and three times principal in schools of considerable size, and so far as I know, never had the slightest difficulty in enforcing law and maintaining order. The reason, I think, was that he was always supported in his administration by the public opinion of the students. Government by force over an objecting population is always a despotism, though it may be a benevolent despotism. My father was constitutionally a democrat, that is, a believer in self-government, and it was because he believed in self-government that he laid stress upon the duty of the parent and the teacher, to maintain his authority by so exercising it as to develop self-control in his subjects.

The last ten years of his life my father spent quietly with his two sisters in what had been his father's home in Farmington, Maine. Here his children and grandchildren delighted to visit him; here he organized a school of a unique character composed of his grandchildren and some of their playmates. Admission to this school was by invitation. There were no fees and no entrance examinations, and attendance was voluntary. But if the child entered the school it was as a loyal subject of an educational commonwealth. He could not be sometimes a citizen and sometimes an alien. To be admitted to this school was accounted, by its pupils, a high privilege. One of these pupils has written for me, at my request, the following reminiscence which will give to the readers not only a graphic picture of the school, but an interesting illustration of my father's method.

"When I was a boy, ten or eleven years of age, I spent one winter and a part of two summers, I think, with my grandfather, Jacob Abbott, at his home in Farmington, Maine, carrying on my studies under his supervision.

"No elements of knowledge seemed to him too abstract or difficult to interest a child, and his methods of teaching were such that they did interest the children. I studied with him, for example, some of the simple problems of Euclidean geometry, and for many years kept the blank books in which I had drawn my diagrams and written my demonstrations. His method was to make every study apply in some way or other to the actual life round about us. Two instances illustrating this method of teaching have remained in my memory for fifty years. I was studying arithmetic and came to percentage. Now my experience with my own children is that percentage as ordinarily taught in the schools is a horrible bore. It means learning rules by rote with very little conception of the practical use and operation of percentage. My grandfather solved the difficulty in this way. When we came to percentage he entrusted me with the duty of making his deposits, cheques and cash, in the village bank, which was about half a mile away. I had to write out the deposit slips and take the pass book and have the proper entry made. He made a contract with me that I was to be paid for this work on a percentage basis. I do not remember what the rate was, but let us say it was a quarter of 1 per cent. or a tenth of 1 per cent. If the latter was the rate I therefore got ten cents for making a deposit of one hundred dollars, or a fraction of ten cents for a lesser sum. Both the purpose and operation of percentage were thus fixed in my mind and by a process which was the very reverse of boresome.

"In a garden adjoining the house there was a

martin box, that is to say a bird-house rather elaborately built on the top of a tall painted pole, to house the martins, a bird of the swallow family which frequents parts of New England and is welcomed by the householders both because it is picturesque in its swooping flight and because it clears the garden of insects and worms. One day a conversation like this took place between my grandfather and myself, my grandfather being at that time a man of about sixty-five years of age:

"*Grandfather.* L., how would you like to measure the height of a martin pole without getting within twenty-five feet of it?

"*L.* Pooh! It can't be done.

"*Grandfather.* Yes, I think you could do it if you are willing to take a little pains.

"*L.* Do you really think I could do it?

"*Grandfather.* Yes, I think you can if you are willing to take the pains that surveyors take when they build a railroad.

"*L.* Do they have to measure things without going near them?

"*Grandfather.* Yes, they have to measure the height of precipices, sometimes of mountains.

"*L.* (*His curiosity now somewhat excited*). How do they do that?

"*Grandfather.* By what is called triangulation

and by using some interesting tables of figures called logarithms.

"To make a long story short, I was enticed by this method into studying the very simple elements of surveying, and I did measure the height of a martin pole and used a logarithm table in the process. Instead of being a dry-as-dust study which I rebelled against, it was transformed into a game which I really enjoyed. In the same way my elemental French and elemental Latin were applied to the objects and the life round about us. My grandfather was, I think, one of the pioneers in this country in the application of this principle of interesting the child in its studies.

"Quarrels and controversies between the grandchildren or the village children who came to Fewacres to play were settled by the application of this principle. A court would be organized, one of the quarrellers would be the plaintiff, the other the defendant. Witnesses would be summoned; a small jury would be empanelled and my grandfather would be the judge. If the defendant was found guilty he usually was punished by a fine of some kind, perhaps suggested by the judge, but generally determined by the jury. If it was a quarrel over a swing, for example, and the defendant was found guilty he might be sentenced not to use the swing for an hour or for a day, as the case might be, and the police who were duly appointed among the children were expected to see that the sentence was carried out. The result was that Fewacres was not only the favourite resort of the grandchildren, but the favourite resort of many of the village children, who, I am sure, like myself, had impressed upon their minds, although wholly subconsciously, some of the elemental principles of science and government that were very useful to them in after life."

Another grandchild has told me that a bank was organized with a president, a board of directors, a cashier, and a teller, in which ivory counters served as coin. Bank bills were issued, promissory notes were discounted, and all the ordinary operations of banking were carried on in what was at once a game and a study. My father used a very simple method to teach the children the difference between labour and commodities, a difference which even to this day some larger employers of labour appear not to comprehend. "Grandfather," says my informant, "would send two of us into the village to make a purchase for him. Sometimes he would tell us that if we would get the needed article he would purchase it from us, in which case, we sold it to him at a small profit, but if we could not get the article at the stores, we got nothing for our errand. Sometimes he would employ us to do the errand and then we were paid whether we succeeded or failed."

My father accumulated few books and nothing that could be called a library, but his method of using books was of a great service to his neighbours. There is an excellent village library in Farmington and its catalogue shows large and constant contributions from Fewacres, which include many of which my father was the author. He also sent periodically to this library the weekly papers and monthly magazines after their immediate use by the Fewacres' household. He took no active part in church affairs, and I do not think ever attended the monthly meeting for the transaction of church business. But he habitually attended the church service on Sunday mornings, where his presence was an inspiration to the preacher. His pastor, the Reverend George N. Marden, subsequently a professor in Colorado College, in a manuscript account of his recollections of my father, says, "Before me, at this moment, lies a note from his hand, in which, with a modest apology, he refers to the sermon of the previous day as likely to call forth various opinions and states that he wishes to state his own decided approbation." In such simple and characteristic ways as this, he showed himself to be an appreciative rather than a critical hearer.

He did not take any active part in village politics and never, so far as I know, any other active part than that of a voter in the politics of either the state or the nation. But his view of what was due to the Government under which he lived is indicated by an incident which Mr. Marden relates: "Mr. Abbott's sterling integrity as a citizen was illustrated when having changed his legal residence from New York to Farmington he stated the amount of his taxable property. The astonished assessor exclaimed, 'Why, Mr. Abbott, if you are assessed on this entire sum you will pay a larger tax than any man in Farmington, you will pay more than your share.' Mr. Abbott quietly replied, 'I know but one way of stating the amount of my taxable property and that is to state it *just as it is.*'"

Thus my father spent his last years peacefully and quietly in his old home, honoured by his fellow-citizens, adored by the children. He died in 1879 in the seventy-sixth year of his age. His youngest son and I were with him at the time of his death. My brother, who was stronger than I, lifted my father up during a paroxysm of pain and then laid him down again upon the pillow, saying to him, "Are you more comfortable now, Father?" and received the whispered answer, "Too comfortable. I hoped that I was going." These were, I think, his last words.

In his preface to the Franconia Stories my father states the principle by which he has been guided in all his story-writing for children: "The development of the moral sentiments in the human heart, in early life—and everything, in fact, which relates to the formation of character—is determined in a far greater degree by sympathy, and by the influence of example, than by formal precepts and didactic instruction." . . . "It is in accordance with this philosophy that these stories, though written mainly with a view to their moral influence on the hearts and dispositions of the readers, contain very little formal exhortation and instruction."

Therefore, in his stories for children, my father's religious teaching was implied, rather than directly expressed; but it was not less effective for that reason. To his Christian faith he has given expression in the Young Christian Series, though even in those volumes it is expressed, never in the abstract terms of scholastic theology, but in dramatic forms and by simple illustrations taken from our common life. Faith in a Heavenly Father as a friend and companion made known to us by the human

life of Jesus of Nazareth, and a supreme desire
to know his will, deserve his confidence, and
coöperate with him in his work, were the secrets
of my father's religious experience, the foundation of his theological philosophy, and the inspiration of his life-long industry. This simple
creed I have inherited from him. It has been
the substance and the inspiration of my teaching for over three quarters of a century, and for
it I am indebted to lessons received and spirit
imbibed from the author of the Rollo Books, the
Franconia Stories, and the Young Christian
Series.

THE END

THE COUNTRY LIFE PRESS
GARDEN CITY, N. Y.